MULTILING

MW01610242

Throughout its history, America has been the scene of multiple encounters between communities speaking different languages. Literature has long sought to represent these encounters in various ways, from James Fenimore Cooper's frontier fictions to the Jewish-American writers who popularized Yiddish as a highly influential modern vernacular. While other studies have concentrated on isolated parts of this history, Lawrence Rosenwald's book is the first to consider the whole story of linguistic representation in American literature, and to consider how multilingual fictions can be translated and incorporated into a national literary history. He uses case studies to analyze the most important kinds of linguistic encounters, such as those between Europeans and Native Americans, those between slaveholders and African slaves, and those between immigrants and American citizens. This ambitious, engaging book is an important contribution to the study of American literature, history, and culture.

LAWRENCE ALAN ROSENWALD is Anne Pierce Rogers Professor of American Literature at Wellesley College.

MULTILINGUAL AMERICA

Language and the Making of American Literature

LAWRENCE ALAN ROSENWALD

CAMBRIDGE
UNIVERSITY PRESS

CAMBRIDGE UNIVERSITY PRESS
Cambridge, New York, Melbourne, Madrid, Cape Town, Singapore, São Paulo, Delhi

Cambridge University Press
The Edinburgh Building, Cambridge CB2 8RU, UK

Published in the United States of America by Cambridge University Press, New York

www.cambridge.org
Information on this title: www.cambridge.org/9780521721615

First published 2008

Printed in the United Kingdom at the University Press, Cambridge

A catalog record for this publication is available from the British Library

Library of Congress Cataloging-in-Publication data

Rosenwald, Lawrence Alan, 1948–
Multilingual America: language and the making of American literature / Lawrence Alan Rosenwald.
p.   cm. – (Cambridge studies in American literature and culture; 157)
Includes bibliographical references and index.
ISBN 978-0-521-89686-3 (alk. paper)
1. American literature – History and criticism.   2. Multilingualism and literature – United States.
I. Title.   II. Series.
PS169.M85R67   2008
810.9′34 – dc22   2008015445

ISBN 978-0-521-89686-3 hardback
ISBN 978-0-521-72161-5 paperback

For Sacvan Bercovitch
Teacher and Friend

Contents

Preface

I

This book is about how writers of American literature, both in English and in other languages, have represented encounters in America between communities speaking different languages, in particular those between Europeans and Native Americans, those between slaveholders and African slaves, and those between immigrants and Americans.

Most definitions, even the simplest, have hidden complexities and polemical points to make; mine has three. The first concerns the word "American." It is an imprecise term; as used above, it implies wrongly that America is co-extensive with the United States. But "United States" is also an imprecise term, especially when it is used to refer to events in parts of North America that became part of the United States only later. There is no perfect term here; I use the imperfect ones as seems appropriate, and "American" more often.

The second concerns the word "encounters." A fair amount of recent sociolinguistic work argues against using that term (or terms similar to it, e.g., "contacts"), and in favor of using the term "conflict." "The debate," writes Henri Boyer, "between the advocates of a sociolinguistics that *describes language contacts* and those of a sociolinguistics that *investigates language conflicts*, whether latent or declared, is still alive."[1] Those who prefer "conflicts" have much going for them; too often terms like "encounter" or "contact" have been used to obscure invasion, oppression, slavery, all the horrific instances of what Louis-Jean Calvet has called "glottophagie," the eating up of languages.[2] But to use "conflicts" to replace "encounters" altogether is to deny in advance the possibility of happily productive relations between languages – for example, the interinanimation of Yiddish and English that

---

[1] Henri Boyer (ed.), *Plurilinguisme: "contact" ou "conflit" de langues?* (Paris: L'Harmattan, 1997), p. 7. This translation, and all translations not otherwise attributed, are my own.

[2] See Louis-Jean Calvet, *Linguistique et colonialisme: petit traité de glottophagie* (Paris: Payot, 1974).

produced, among other great texts, Jacob Glatshteyn's "If Joyce had Written Yiddish." Many of the language encounters this book investigates are full of conflict; but I retain the term "encounters" so as not to determine the outcome of the investigations in advance.

The third concerns the word "communities," which I use to imply a defining exclusion: the wide range of distinguished American memoirs about the complexly multilingual lives of individuals – for example, in alphabetical order, Theresa Hak-Kyung Cha's *Dictée*, Eva Hoffman's *Lost in Translation*, Alice Kaplan's *French Lessons*, Vladimir Nabokov's *Speak, Memory*, and Charles Simic's *A Fly in the Soup*. I admire them all. But this book is not focused on their vivid, individual cosmopolitanism. Rather it is focused on literature that seeks to represent *collective* encounters.

So defined and circumscribed, the topic of this book matters in two ways: as bearing on some crucial patterns in American history, and as bearing on how literature works and is judged.

Developing the first point means, to begin with, establishing the importance of the subject matter. That is easy. Colonization, slavery, immigration have shaped and are shaping American life. They need to be understood in all their aspects, linguistic aspects included.

Linguistic aspects in particular, in fact. The historical record consistently dramatizes what we know from our own daily experience: the intimate, frequent, almost universal relations between language[3] and individual and collective identity, between language and communication. Christopher Columbus's journal of his first landing in the Caribbean (which did not as yet have that name): "I have caused six of [the inhabitants] to be taken on board and sent to your Majesties, that they may learn to speak."[4] Olaudah Equiano, a newly arrived slave in mid-eighteenth-century Virginia: "I was now exceedingly miserable, and thought myself worse off than any of the rest of my companions; for they could talk to each other, but I had no person to speak to that I could understand."[5] Theodore Roosevelt in 1917, a high point of immigration to the United States: "We must have but one flag. We must also have but one language . . . We cannot tolerate

---

[3] More than once, in working on this project, I have wished English had the distinction French has, between *langue* and *langage*, *langue* being used to refer to such things as French, English, and German, *langage* to refer to our particular mode of using whatever *langue* we're speaking. I have tried to make that distinction explicit, but the ambiguity in the English word is hard to resist.

[4] Oliver Dunn and James E. Kelley, Jr. (eds. and trans.), *The Diario of Christopher Columbus's First Voyage to America, 1492–1493, Abstracted by Fray Bartolomé de las Casas* (Norman: University of Oklahoma Press, 1989), p. 68.

[5] Olaudah Equiano, "The Life of Olaudah Equiano, or Gustavus Vassa, the African, Written by Himself," in Arna Bontemps (ed.), *Great Slave Narratives* (Boston: Beacon Press, 1969), p. 34.

any attempt to oppose or supplant the language and culture that has [sic] come down to us from the builders of this Republic with the language and culture of any European country."[6]

To understand these large dramas in American linguistic history we need to read linguistics, and this book draws on a fair amount of writing by linguists then and now. But we also need to read literature. For one thing, literature plays a primary role in the reception and interpretation of linguistic history. James Fenimore Cooper's novels of the frontier, Kate Chopin's stories of Louisiana, Anzia Yezierska's *Bread-Givers* have done more to shape a shared sense of the language encounters they depict than have Ives Goddard's expert accounts of Delaware and Delaware Pidgin, Albert Valdman's dictionary of Louisiana French Creole, or Max Weinreich's "Vegn englishe elementn in undzer kulturshprakh" ("On English Elements in Our Culture-Language").

We also need to read literature to understand linguistic history itself; we need the artistic imagination if we are to integrate linguistic fact into a portrait of individual and social experience. It is that imagination which seeks to figure out, say, what it felt like to be made a slave, stripped of one's language, obliged to create language anew; what the relation was between that linguistic trauma and the physical burdens of slavery, its daily oppression, the slaves' hidden moments of solidarity, their sly or open rebellions, the coded language in which these rebellions were plotted or announced; the slaves' search to build new families, knit together by a new language, the experience of having those families torn apart, the language for lamenting that sundering. Makers of imaginative literature may not succeed in so ambitious an enterprise; but even their failures are instructive, and their successes are revelatory.

So literature can teach us something about linguistic history. The reverse is true as well, indeed is true in consequence. If, that is, we argue that literature has something to teach us about linguistic history, then we have to consider the quality of its teaching, its intelligence about these matters, as an element of its aesthetic success or failure. We cannot, to put it over-schematically, think of literature as a mode of truth-telling and then not require it to tell the truth – about language and language encounters no less than about, say, the experience of working women and slaves and union organizers, the details of meat processing in Chicago or migrant labor in California, Nat Turner's Rebellion or the American Revolution. There

---

[6] James Crawford (ed.), *Language Loyalties: A Source Book on the Official English Controversy* (Chicago: University of Chicago Press, 1992), p. 85.

are facts of the matter here, and literature needs to be judged at least in part on its representation of them.[7] Much of Cooper's *Last of the Mohicans* represents Native American languages as non-linguistic: as gesture, as music, as grunt and exclamation. Most of Chopin's stories represent Louisiana French Creole as a quaint shade of local color. Much of Yezierska's *Bread-Givers* represents Yiddish simply as a series of curses, and in a crucial scene the narrator refers to the Yiddish influence on Jewish immigrant English as "murdering the language." These are all falsifications, however influential then or now, and it is important to expose them.

It is also important to praise what is praiseworthy, and censoriousness makes that possible; condemning literary failure enables us to admire literary success. A few passages of Cooper's novel anticipate by over a century the fine insights into Native American poetry of such twentieth-century anthropologist-translators as Dell Hymes and Dennis Tedlock. A few passages of Yezierska's, not crucial passages, seeming almost casual, suggest in their rhythm and syntax something of the wonderfully fruitful influences English and Yiddish were to exercise on each other across the twentieth century and beyond. Chopin's "La Belle Zoraïde," or rather a single moment of that deeply ambivalent story, lets us see Louisiana French Creole as a real language, one that we do not know but which is full of expressive power. These representations convey surprising truths and deserve celebration.

II

The book consists of seven sections. The first two, consisting of this preface and a methodological introduction, are an orientation. They are followed by three lengthy case studies, each commenting on both a particular language encounter and a particular text representing it. In the first case study, the language encounter is that between Native Americans and Europeans, and the text is Cooper's *The Last of the Mohicans*. In the second, the language encounter is that among English, French, and Louisiana French Creole, and the texts are George Washington Cable's *The Grandissimes* and Alfred Mercier's *L'Habitation Saint-Ybars* ("The Saint-Ybars Plantation"). In the third, the language encounter is that between Yiddish and English, and the text is Sholem Aleichem's *Motl Peyse dem khazns* ("Motl the Cantor Peyse's Son"). The last two chapters of the book, one on translating multilingual literature and one on how to write the history of American literature in

---

[7] See on this Christopher Ricks's wonderful "Literature and the Matter of Fact," in *Essays in Appreciation* (New York: Clarendon Press, 1996).

all its languages, explore how the great American language fictions can be integrated into our sense of American literature.

The methodological introduction is necessary for a high reason and a low one. The high reason is that assessing literary works as language fictions requires figuring out some difficult questions of poetics, of literature's means of mimesis. The introduction is intended to contribute to that large task. The low reason is that much assessment of language fictions has been done very badly. It has too often depended on sloppy description, on unexamined assumptions about what is and is not possible in literature, on confusions between dialect and language, on being insufficiently attentive to the constraints and possibilities of particular genres, on unwarranted indifference to linguistic fact. The introduction is also intended to expose and get rid of some of these hindering practices.

I have written about what I could read and what interested me. But I have also chosen texts and encounters in relation to my sense of American linguistic history. I have come to see language encounters in America as falling into three large categories: between invaders and locals, between immigrants and locals, and between slaves and slaveholders. Believing that a book intended to offer a broad view of this subject should consider all three, I have devoted one case study to each.

There are leaks in these categories, of course, and cases right at the boundaries between one category and another. But the categories are both typological and historical; each corresponds to a kind of relationship between two language groups encountering each other, but each real encounter happens in a particular time and place. Classifying encounters is therefore less tricky than it might seem; it depends not only on the languages in question but on the historical situation in which they meet. In the sixteenth century, in Mexico, Spanish-speakers were invaders in relation to Nahuatl-speaking locals. In the twenty-first century, in New York, Spanish-speakers are for the most part immigrants in relation to English-speaking locals. In the sixteenth century, in much of North America, both English and French were invaders' languages in relation to Native American languages. After the Civil War, in Louisiana, English was the invaders' language, French that of the locals.

The first category is best exemplified by encounters between Europeans (and later European Americans) and Native Americans. Europeans came to the world they called new, sought to take control of the land, sought variously to conquer, dispossess, exploit, convert, study, remake, and unmake its inhabitants. Native Americans sought for the most part to resist these undertakings, though also to engage the invaders to their own benefit. The linguistic aspects of these encounters include, on the European side, study and classification and evaluation and suppression of Native American languages, contrastive evaluation of European ones; on the Native American side, surely a reciprocal study and classification and evaluation of European languages (though much less abundantly documented than on the European side), imposition of Native American languages on European ones, resistance in diverse forms to having Native American languages suppressed and supplanted.

These encounters began with Columbus's 1492 arrival at Guanahanì, which he renamed San Salvador, and a good many of them had taken place before 1826, when Cooper published *The Last of the Mohicans*. But Cooper was the first great American writer to make these language encounters a central artistic subject. Nor was he simply looking backward at that subject. Rather his complex and influential novel, tenaciously attentive to the representation of language and languages, was written during a grimly important episode in American intercultural history, namely that of the United States' project of Indian Removal, intended to expel eastern Native Americans from their lands, and thereby to make those lands available for European American use. In life, Cooper supported that project and the linguistic ideas that rationalized it, but he also read and admired the work of his contemporaries John Heckewelder and Peter Duponceau, meticulous students and admirers of Native American languages, whose sense of those languages was sharply at odds with the arguments by which Removal was defended. Cooper's novel both undergirds and undermines the project of Removal that was its most pertinent environment.

The second category, encounters between immigrants and locals, is the reverse of the first. Again, groups choose to come to North America from other parts of the world. But now they seek not to conquer but almost to be conquered: to be assimilated, to become citizens of the local state. Here too the linguistic story is complicated. On the immigrant side, it includes learning and judging the new language, sometimes abandoning the old and sometimes stubbornly holding on to it, incorporating elements of the new into the old, having arguments about such incorporation. On the local side, the issues are similar: judging the immigrant language, teaching the local language, incorporating elements of the former into the latter, arguing about the propriety of doing that.

The peak year of American immigration is 1907, the peak period between 1880 and 1924. Of the immigrant literatures I know from that tumultuous period, the richest in texts dealing with language encounters is that of the Eastern European Jews who came to the United States towards the end of the nineteenth century and the beginning of the twentieth. They spoke and wrote Yiddish (among other languages) in Eastern Europe, and they often held fast to Yiddish when they came to the United States, stubbornly choosing to write in it long after they had mastered English, making it the vehicle of their perceptively ambivalent accounts of two languages and civilizations in contact. The fictions of Joseph Opatoshu, the poems of Anna Margolin and Moyshe-Leyb Halpern, the sketches of Moshe Nadir all bear witness to that encounter. But no work in the repertory is more dazzlingly, playfully perceptive than Sholem Aleichem's *Motl the Cantor's Son*, one of the great American language fictions, and the most cheerful.

The third category consists of encounters between slaves and those who enslave and then exploit them. Here the linguistic story involves not only relations between pre-existing languages, but also the creation of new ones, which most linguists call creoles. The process is both common and almost miraculous. First, contact languages – jargons, pidgins – are improvised for communication between slaves on the one hand, slave-traders and slave-holders on the other, and among slaves not having another language in common. (Usually the slave-traders' language becomes what linguists call the lexifier, i.e., the principal though not exclusive source of vocabulary.) But then, and most often when slaves' access to the lexifier is sharply restricted, contact languages become nativized – that is, become the native languages, often the only native languages, among slaves' children; and in becoming nativized they acquire the full range of expression, suppleness, and complexity that all languages have that are someone's native language. In slavery, despite slavery, slaves create and develop new languages.

In the United States, creoles are rare. Jean Bernabé, Patrick Chamoiseau, and Raphaël Confiant argue in *Éloge de la créolité* that this has to do with an American habit of mind:

The sociohistorical processes that produced Americanization are not of the same sort as those at work in producing Creolization. Americanization, and thus the feeling of Americanness that emerges from it, is a term describing the gradual adaptation of western peoples to the realities of the world they called new . . . Americanness is thus in large measure an emigrant culture in splendid isolation.[8]

But the better and simpler explanation is demographic. Many linguists argue that for a creole to develop, one needs a slave:slaveholder ratio of at least 4:1; otherwise access to the lexifier isn't hard enough to get. In most parts of America where slaves were held, the ratio was lower. The two

---

[8] Jean Bernabé, Patrick Chamoiseau, and Raphaël Confiant, *Éloge de la créolité* (Paris: Gallimard, 1993), pp. 29–30 (my translation).

creoles documented in North America, English-based Gullah and French-based Louisiana Creole, confirm these principles of explanation. Gullah speakers were cut off geographically from access to the English lexifier; Louisiana Creole did not originate in Louisiana, but came there by way of the Caribbean, its place of origin, where the slave:slaveholder ratio was 4:1 and higher.[9]

Of the two creoles we have, Louisiana Creole has the advantage, for a critic looking for complex language encounters, of being situated in an already polyglot context; French and English had already begun their long conflict in Louisiana when Creole arrived there, with Spanish also playing a significant role. Creole is also the more richly documented of the two languages, the more vigorously disputed, and the more ambitiously and exactly depicted.

It is not, as it happens, documented by any distinguished literary artist at the moment of its forming, in the early eighteenth century; as with the encounter between Native American languages and European ones, the encounters between Louisiana Creole and the languages interacting with it become a literary subject only sometime after the encounters have begun. The two great accounts of that subject date from the late nineteenth century: George Washington Cable's *The Grandissimes* and Alfred Mercier's *L'Habitation Saint-Ybars*, published respectively in 1880 and 1881, differing sharply in mode of representation, similar in seriousness of purpose and closeness of attention.

For distinguished American non-anglophone language fictions to matter, two things have to happen. First, we have to figure out how to translate them into English; otherwise they won't be read. Second, we have to figure out how to write the history of a national literature in multiple languages; otherwise these fictions can't be integrated into our national story.

Chapters 4 and 5, the last two chapters of the book, are devoted to these two tasks. Chapter 4 concerns translation, exploring how, as a matter of the translator's art, the task of translation can be accomplished. Translating works that seriously seek to represent language encounters raises tricky questions for translation theory generally, which for the most part rests on an unstated assumption that both source work and target work are

---

[9] Some linguists regard Black English as a creole; see, e.g., J. L. Dillard, *Black English* (New York: Vintage, 1973). I don't find their arguments convincing; in all the documents we have, Black English seems to me a variety of English, not a language distinct from English in the way that Haitian Creole is distinct from French. On creoles generally, see Chapter 2. My thanks to John McWhorter for help in understanding these issues.

unilingual. So does translating such works when, as often happens, a single language, in this case English, is both one of the languages represented by the work and the target language of the translation.

The chapter begins with some general reflections on the translation of multilingual texts, then presents brief case studies of five texts, two previously discussed and three new ones: Mercier's *L'Habitation Saint-Ybars*; Sholem Aleichem's *Motl*; Jeannette Lander's 1971 German-language American novel, *Ein Sommer in der Woche der Itke K.* ("A Summer in the Week of Itke K."); the Puerto Rican writer Ana Lydia Vega's 1981 story, "Pollito: Chicken"; and the Chicano writer Rolando Hinojosa's 1981 novel, *Mi querido Rafa*, and his 1985 translation of it, *Dear Rafe*.

Chapter 5 concerns the writing of literary history. No comprehensive history of American literature even comes close to representing the multilingual literatures of America, and though some of the deficiencies result from ordinary laziness and shortsightedness, some result from stubborn problems of theory. The chapter begins with some reflections on the definition of American literature; it then examines how our comprehensive literary histories, above all Sacvan Bercovitch's ambitious and often wonderful *Cambridge History of American Literature*, have dealt with non-anglophone American literatures, assesses their successes and failures, and offers suggestions about how to do better.

III

Some of the best work on this subject in its broadest sense has focused on the literary representation of dialect. I have read some of that work and learned much from it. But dialect encounters are significantly different from language encounters; so are texts representing the former from texts representing the latter; so are critical studies of the one sort of text from critical studies of the other.[10]

Of the work that does focus specifically on the literary representation of language encounters, some is hampered by the critic's decision to look at that topic in isolation from whatever can be known about the languages and language encounters themselves. Thus Andrew Newman's thoughtful essay, "Sublime Translation in the Novels of James Fenimore Cooper and Walter Scott," which quotes Flora's remark in *Waverley* that Gaelic is an "uncommonly vocalic" language but does not investigate whether that claim is true, is practicing another kind of criticism than the sort I have in

---

[10] See below, pp. 5–11, for an extended technical account of the distinction.

mind here,[11] which is distinguished by its insistence both on knowing the linguistic facts and on judging literature in relation to them.

Other work, notably that of the fine critic Doris Sommer, is hampered by its own passionate advocacy; her enterprise might be summed up as a case for polyglot cosmopolitanism. Sommer describes her *Bilingual Aesthetics* as "a range of friendly provocations about the benefits of bilingualism."[12] "Come play bilingual games with me," she says to her readers. "Maybe you already play them . . . In that case, the invitation is to think together about why the games are good for you and good for the country" (xi). Or, more exaggeratedly: "only on the multilinguistic borders, where Rabelais wrote, are reason, humor, and wisdom available" (50).

There is great value, in this often rigidly unilingual country, in celebrating complexly multilingual identities and their multilingual literary expressions. But such celebration can become melodrama, featuring multilingual heroes and unilingual villains. It assumes we have already assigned positive values to hybridity, multilingualism, and *mestizaje*, negative ones to parochialism and homogeneity. That assumption is a limitation; the values of these qualities need to be investigated, and respectful attention paid to works that portray, say, the unilingual as the servant of her endangered culture, the multilingual as the rootless cosmopolitan, the polyglot as the traitor from within. As a matter of personal choice, I side with the cosmopolitan. But the goal of this book is investigation.[13]

That leaves a small body of fine work on the topic as I define it, investigating it by what seem to me the necessary methods. Of that work I would single out Meir Sternberg's fundamental theoretical investigations; the wide-ranging explorations, both critical and anthological, of Jonathan Arac, Eric Cheyfitz, Gavin Jones, Marc Shell, and Werner Sollors; and particular studies of Cooper and his context by Helen Carr, Cheyfitz, and David Simpson, of the multilingual literature of Louisiana by Jones, and of literature representing the encounter between English and Yiddish by Sollors, Aviva Taubenfeld, Hana Wirth-Nesher, and Kenneth Wishnia.[14]

---

[11] Andrew Newman, "Sublime Translation in the Novels of James Fenimore Cooper and Walter Scott," *Nineteenth-Century Literature* 59: 1 (2004), p. 14.

[12] Doris Sommer, *Bilingual Aesthetics: A New Sentimental Education* (Durham, NC: Duke University Press, 2004), p. viii. Page numbers for subsequent quotations from this work will be given in the text.

[13] Not always, but often, critics like Sommer focus not on the social fictions that are my central texts here, but on the brilliant personal memoirs I have chosen not to consider. That focus is in accord with the aim of such criticism, i.e., to celebrate cosmopolitan individuals.

[14] For Sternberg's work see the Introduction. For the other scholars cited: Jonathan Arac, "Babel and Vernacular in a Postcolonial Empire of Immigrants: Howells and the Languages of American Fiction," *Boundary 2* 34:2 (Summer 2007), pp. 1–20, and "Global and Babel: Two Perspectives

It's a tricky balancing act, on the one hand acknowledging the work of other scholars, on the other defining one's own new contribution. I owe the scholars just cited a great debt of gratitude, impersonal in some cases, happily personal in most; their work has enabled me to take some new steps in our collective investigation, in particular to bring together aspects of that investigation that have mostly been carried out in isolation from one another. This is, to my knowledge, the only book on our shared subject that begins by sketching a technical method of analysis, proceeds to consider all the chief kinds of language encounter, and before concluding explores how the literature of American multilingualism can be brought into our readerly consciousness and our national narrative. It offers, that is, a first synthesis, tentative and no doubt impermanent, but useful.

IV

One Saturday morning in the summer of 2005, traveling from South Station in Boston to Davis Square in Somerville on the way to shabbat services at Havurat Shalom, I noted in my commonplace book all the languages I encountered along the way, plus a number of other evocations of American multilingualism. The first part of the trip was in a subway car; there I noted the familiar English/Spanish bilingualism of the transit authority notices – for example, "Passenger emergency intercom unit at end of car/ Sistema de intercomunicación para pasajeros en caso de emergencia situado al extremo del tren"; an advertisement for "guaranteed Swahili"; a similar

on Language in American Literature," *ESQ* 50:1–3 (2004), pp. 95–119; Eric Cheyfitz, *The Poetics of Imperialism: Translation and Colonization from* The Tempest *to* Tarzan (New York: Oxford University Press, 1991); Gavin Jones, *Strange Talk: The Politics of Dialect Literature in Gilded Age America* (Berkeley: University of California Press, 1999), above all the chapter called "White Writers, Creole Languages"; Marc Shell, "Babel in America: Or, The Politics of Language Diversity in the United States," *Critical Inquiry* 20:1 (Autumn 1993), pp. 103–27, and Shell (ed.), *American Babel: Literatures of the United States from Abnaki to Zuni* (Cambridge, MA: Harvard University Press, 2002); Werner Sollors (ed.), *Multilingual America: Transnationalism, Ethnicity and the Languages of American Literature* (New York: New York University Press, 1998); Shell and Sollors (eds.), *The Multilingual Anthology of American Literature* (New York: New York University Press, 2000); Helen Carr, *Inventing the American Primitive: Politics, Gender and the Reception of Native American Literature, 1790–1936* (Cork: Cork University Press, 1996); Cheyfitz, "Literally White, Figuratively Red: The Frontier of Translation in *The Pioneers*," in Robert Clark (ed.), *James Fenimore Cooper: New Critical Essays* (London: Vision and Barnes & Noble, 1985); David Simpson, *The Politics of American English, 1776–1850* (New York: Oxford University Press, 1986); Aviva Taubenfeld, "'Only an L': Linguistic Borders and the Immigrant Author in Abraham Cahan's *Yekl* and *Yankel der Yankee*," in Sollors (ed.), *Multilingual America*; Hana Wirth-Nesher (ed.), *New Essays on* Call It Sleep (Cambridge and New York: Cambridge University Press, 1996), which includes fine essays both by Sollors and by Wirth-Nesher herself; Wirth-Nesher, *Call It English: The Languages of Jewish American Literature* (Princeton: Princeton University Press, 2006); and Kenneth Wishnia, "'A Different Kind of Hell': Orality, Multilingualism, and American Yiddish in the Translation of Sholem Aleichem's *Mister Boym in Klozet*," *AJS Review* 20:2 (1993), pp. 333–58.

advertisement for TOEFL courses; a man to my left reading a newspaper in a language that looked to me like Chinese; two men across from me conducting a conversation in Amharic (not a language I recognize, but as one of them left the car I asked him, in English, what language he had been speaking). I was making my own contribution to this multilingual scene, too, in that when I wasn't looking around or writing something down I was reading Goethe's *Die Wahlverwandtschaften*.

Then, walking on College Avenue from Davis Square to Havurat Shalom, I passed the Église Baptiste de la Bible, a Haitian church with a Haitian-speaking congregation but a French name and two French Bible verses posted outside: "Levons-nous et Bâtissons," "Voici la porte de l'éternel; c'est par elle qu'entrent les justes." The latter verse was especially resonant for me; I had seen it, or rather its Hebrew original (*zeh ha-she'ar hashem, tsaddikim yavo'u vo*), on the shadowed front door of a synagogue in Ahmad-abad, in India, and I have often sung it in its Hebrew form, since it is part of the Jewish liturgy on most holidays. When I reached Havurat Shalom, I encountered the last two languages of my unspectacular morning journey: the Hebrew of the liturgy, which this morning did not include the Haitian church's Bible verse, and the Russian spoken by two members of my congregation (one Russian, one American) to each other and to their infant daughter.

It is exhilarating to imagine a novelist, one with a Dickens-like alertness to the ways in which apparently sundered lives intersect one another, who could make these diverse phenomena into a single story. It would be a story of modes of immigration, of individual and collective choices to assimilate or to refuse assimilation, of religious communities linked by common texts but understanding and using those texts in deeply opposed ways, of the local rootedness of congregations and communities juxtaposed to the cheerful globalism of "guaranteed Swahili," of the simple, solid, official bilingualism of the subway car juxtaposed to the dazzling multilingualism of the car's transient passengers, of the relation in language use between collective and individual identity.

Such a novel would have to be a multilingual one, one that found ways of doing justice to the linguistic diversity of its characters and scenes. Neither American literature nor any other literature I know has many such novels, and that fact seems to me to mark a failure of response and ambition. A final aim of this book is to help create a climate in which gifted writers might dream of such a novel as a legitimate artistic goal, publishers assess such a novel as an enterprise worth supporting, and readers and critics feel that such a novel should command their attention.

Acknowledgments

In writing this book I have been more than usually dependent on the generosity of other scholars, and am deeply grateful to those who have helped me.

I shall group most of these generous colleagues in relation to the chapters on which I consulted them. For the Introduction, Meir Sternberg. For Chapter 1, Gregory Dowd, Jan Terje Faarlund, Ives Goddard, Victor Golla, Steven Hackel, Kenneth Lincoln, Peter Nabokov, Andrew Newman, Barry O'Connell, Vicki Patterson, Blair Rudes, Peter Wogan, and above all Edward Gray and Laura Murray, who have been supporters and wise counselors for this part of my project for a good many years. For Chapter 2, Yvonne Hajda, Gavin Jones, Dana Kress, Andrea Levitt, Ingrid Neumann-Holzschuh, David Sutcliffe, and Henry Zenk, with special thanks to a small group of creolists whose generosity was not only admirable but also indispensable: Michel DeGraff, Marie-Christine Hazaël-Massieux, Tom Klingler, Mikael Parkvall, and John McWhorter. (As anyone who knows the creolist world will know, these scholars have their disagreements, but they share a willingness to help educate a curious outsider.) For Chapter 3, Gershon Freidlin, Stephen Jones, Michael Kramer, Eliezer Niborski, Joel Ratner, Karen Rosenberg, and Margaret Winters; special thanks to Hana Wirth-Nesher, and thanks above all to David Roskies, without whom – I mean this literally – my life and work would never have been such that I could write the chapter at all. For Chapter 4, Mona Baker, Dolores Prida, Raul Rubio, Judith Weiss, and especially my patient and generous Wellesley colleague Nancy Hall.

Some colleagues are harder to categorize, their contributions going beyond the scope of any single chapter. My thanks to Ray Ryan and Ross Posnock, for being willing to have a look at this idiosyncratic book, and to my Cambridge University Press readers, both for their support and for their criticism. Alison Thomas, the book's Argus-eyed copy-editor, read the manuscript with great care and improved it in numerous ways. My research assistant, Julie Camarda, did an astonishingly meticulous review of the footnotes and bibliography. Great gratitude to Jonathan Arac, who by some marvelous synchronicity would send me his illuminating essays just as I'd reached the point in my work where their illuminations were most needed. And I owe more than I can say to Marc Shell and Werner Sollors, who in this scholarly project we are all engaged in have been patrons, critics, models, inspirations, and friends.

I owe a special debt to three Wellesley English Department colleagues: Bill Cain, Lisa Rodensky, and Margery Sabin. All read many of the chapters, all improved whatever they read, all supported the project as a whole, Bill put me in touch with Cambridge University Press, Margery vigorously supported the project even at moments when I was ready to give up on it. Lisa and I were on leave together when I was writing the book, and she read, scrutinized, and improved each chapter and each argument.

My wife, Cynthia Schwan, is my most rigorous and supportive reader; she demands that I make sense and not be pompous.

Two chapters draw significantly on earlier work of mine on this subject. Chapter 2 draws on "*The Last of the Mohicans* and the Languages of America," *College English* 60:1 (January 1998), pp. 9–30; Chapter 3 draws on "Alfred Mercier's Polyglot Plantation Novel," in Marc Shell (ed.), *American Babel: Literatures of the United States from Abnaki to Zuni* (Cambridge, MA: Harvard University Press, 2002), and on "Sur quelques aspects de la traduction de textes créoles louisianais du xixème siècle" ("On the translation of Nineteenth-Century Louisiana Creole Texts"), *Études Créoles* 25:2 (2002), pp. 153–71.

We read in *Pirkei Avot, aseh lecha rav, ukeney lecha chaver,* "get yourself a teacher, find yourself a friend." Saki Bercovitch has been both teacher and friend to me since we first met, in 1970, and it gives me great, heartfelt pleasure to honor his teaching and friendship by dedicating this book to him.

Introduction: techniques, methods, theses

TERMS AND CATEGORIES

The Israeli critic Meir Sternberg is not very well known among Americanists, or for that matter among American literary critics generally, but his theoretical work on the representation of what he calls "polylingual discourse"[1] is the best account of it available. So there's no better way to begin investigating the technical aspects of that subject than by setting out some of Sternberg's terms and categories and formulations – beginning with his formulation of the basic issue here, which is that "literary art . . . finds itself confronted by a formidable mimetic challenge: how to represent the reality of polylingual discourse through a communicative medium which is normally unilingual" (222).

Sternberg first identifies three ways of "circumventing" (223) the challenge. The first, "referential restriction," involves confining one's literary attention "to the limits of a single, linguistically uniform community whose speech-patterns correspond to those of the implied audience"; Sternberg cites as an example the novels of Jane Austen. The second, "vehicular matching . . . suits the variation in the representational medium to the variation

---

[1] Meir Sternberg, "Polylingualism as Reality and Translation as Mimesis," *Poetics Today* 2:4 (1981), p. 222. Page numbers for subsequent quotations from this work will be given in the text.

Sternberg "deliberately avoid[s] the sociolinguistic terms 'multilingual' and 'monolingual,' which are (and should be) used to characterize the linguistic range of a single speaker or community. In contrast, a work may be said to represent a polylingual reality of discourse even though each individual speaker or milieu is strictly monolingual, and to represent a unilingual reality of discourse even though each speaker is potentially multilingual. The terms are thus complementary" (222n). Useful distinctions of category, but not, in my judgment, easy to maintain by these distinctions of term; I've sought to observe the latter but not the former.

"Polylingualism as Reality and Translation as Mimesis" is Sternberg's most important essay on this subject, but see also "Proteus in Quotation-Land: Mimesis and the Forms of Reported Discourse," *Poetics Today* 3:2 (1982), pp. 107–56; "Point of View and the Indirections of Direct Speech," *Language and Style* 15 (1982), pp. 67–117; and *Hebrews between Cultures: Group Portraits and National Literature* (Bloomington: Indiana University Press, 1998). My thanks to Professor Sternberg for his encouragement, and for guiding me to the latter three of these four works.

in the represented object" – that is, whatever languages characters are imagined or identified as speaking are the languages they actually are made to
speak. Sternberg's examples, one film and one play, are Jean Renoir's *La
Grande Illusion* and Shaw's *Pygmalion*. The third, "homogenizing convention," is in play when an author, having decided to represent a multilingual
community, "dismisses the resultant variations in the language presumably
spoken by the characters as an irrelevant, if not distracting, representational
factor" (224). Thus Carroll's White Rabbit and Shakespeare's Romans and
Italians speak English, Homer's Trojans speak Greek, Vergil's Greeks speak
Latin.

As noted, these are for Sternberg ways of "circumventing" the challenge.
He reports on them fairly, and the terms he devises for them have the
technical specificity of good legal jargon, but in his view their "extremity . . . frequently disqualifies them from serving as viable artistic strategies"
(225). He argues in particular against vehicular matching, on the ground
that it is "too inconsistent with the normal conditions and prerequisites of
communication in art as well as in life."[2]

What he favors more is what he calls "translational mimesis," or "mimetic
compromise" (225). Here too he has devised apt terms, four in particular.
(1) "Selective reproduction" – that is, "intermittent quotation of the original heterolingual[3] discourse as uttered by the speaker(s), or in literature,
as supposed to have been uttered by the fictive speaker(s)" (225). A characteristic example (mine, not Sternberg's) is in Henry Roth's *Call It Sleep*:
the conversation in the first chapter between Albert Schearl and his wife
Genya. It's identified as taking place in Yiddish, but almost all the quoted
speeches are in English. Then, at the very end, we get two speeches in
Yiddish: "Gehen vir voinen du? In Nev York? . . . Nein. Bronzeville. Ich
hud dir schoin geschriben" ("Will we live there? In New York? . . . No.
Bronzeville. I already wrote you").[4] (2) "Verbal transposition" – that is, "the
poetic or communicative twist given to what sociolinguists call bilingual
interference" (227). Examples are: "the literally rendered Spanish idioms
in Hemingway's *For Whom the Bell Tolls*" (228), or every time an English
"thou" is used to express a putative original *tu* or *du* in French or German or
Yiddish.[5] (3) "Conceptual reflection" – that is, a strategy aimed at rendering

[2] Sternberg, "Point of View," p. 88.
[3] Sternberg uses "heterolingual" (sometimes "heterophone") to "denote a foreign language (or dialect) –
usually a language other than that of the reporting speech-event" (222n). I too use that term.
[4] Henry Roth, *Call It Sleep* (New York: Noonday Press, 1991), p. 16. Page numbers for subsequent
quotations from this work will be given in the text.
[5] Sternberg rightly distinguishes between this strategy and what happens when an author is simply
reproducing the linguistic-interference-affected speech of a character, e.g., the wonderful scene in

"not so much the verbal forms of the foreign code as the underlying socio-cultural norms" (230). Sternberg gives a striking example, from the Second Book of Samuel. In Hebrew, *elohim*, "God," is plural in form but treated as singular. When the Philistines use it, though, they treat it as a plural, reflecting the biblical author's sense of their more polytheistic theology: "these [are] the gods [*elohim*] who smote the Egyptians," they say. Much representation of Native American speech is similar in this regard; it is filled with metaphors drawn from nature, and seeks to represent, not the grammatical structure of Native American languages, but a nature-centered worldview being attributed to the Native American mind. (4) "Explicit attribution" – that is, "a direct statement on the reporter's (or even the reportee's) part concerning the language (or some aspect of the language) in which the reported speech was originally made" (231). A simple example, from the passage in *Call It Sleep* cited previously: "'And this is the Golden Land.' She spoke in Yiddish" (11). Presumably Sternberg would also want to include here not only statements naming languages, but also statements characterizing them – for example, in Kate Chopin's "La Belle Zoraïde," "she told [the story] to her mistress in the soft Creole patois, whose music and charm no English words can convey"[6] – though he gives no examples of this latter sort of comment.

Having set out these terms, Sternberg makes some shrewd remarks about how critics should use them. He notes that one might be tempted to rank the strategies in "degree of quotational interference" (232), from smallest degree to greatest, from most faithful to least: vehicular matching, selective reproduction, verbal transposition, conceptual reflection, explicit attribution, and homogenizing convention. But he argues, justly, that doing so would be wrong, for two reasons. First, such a scale "classifies types or aspects of translational mimesis rather than texts or textual segments" – an error because each mode "may variously coexist and interact with the others within a given textual framework." Second, such a scale suffers from "the failure to distinguish formal mode and functional system" (233); "in different contexts," he notes, "the same translational form may serve different functions and the same function may be served by different forms," and he stresses the importance of passing "from the typology to the functionality of translational mimesis" – that is, what is the author seeking to *do*?

Casablanca where two prospective emigrants to America sit in Rick's cafe and practice their English: "What watch? Six watch," they say, badly translating *Wieviel Uhr? Sechs Uhr*.

[6] Kate Chopin, *The Awakening and Selected Stories* (New York: Penguin, 1984), p. 196.

THE LIMITS OF WHAT'S POSSIBLE

Sternberg is a good enough critic that even when he's wrong, it is illuminating to work out one's own view in relation to his always exact and forthright account of his. As, for instance, his view – which reflects an unspoken and unexamined consensus among literary critics generally – of "vehicular matching." Its "extremity," he says, "frequently disqualifies [it] from serving as [a] viable artistic strateg[y]," in "a communicative medium which is normally unilingual."

But "normally" is not an argument; creative writers are always doing things that aren't "normal." And like vehicular matching, some of those things make reading difficult – for example, Joyce's wonderful rendering of the stream of consciousness in *Ulysses*, or Gertrude Stein's of the repetitions of human speech in "Melanctha." We shouldn't make a cult of such difficulty. But we should approach the question of what is "viable," even if difficult, with an open mind.

The following texts, among others, are pertinent to answering that question, because all of them go further in vehicular matching than Sternberg's work would make one think possible, and all are works of accepted distinction.[7] (1) Charlotte Brontë's *Villette*, full of passages in French, both in conversation and in the narrative, dispersed throughout the novel. (2) H. Rider Haggard's *She*, the chapter called "The Sherd of Amenartas," filled with pages and pages of Greek and Latin and Old English texts. (3) Thomas Mann's *The Magic Mountain*, with the extended French-language conversation presented by its German narrative in the chapter called, appropriately enough, "Walpurgisnacht." (4) Helen Lowe-Porter's translation of the same novel, which retains the French material as is. Translations even more than original works are "normally" unilingual, but Lowe-Porter's noble choice to flout that norm did not keep her translation from being widely read, or from contributing to Mann's international reputation. (5) Jeannette Lander's *Ein Sommer in der Woche der Itke K.*, a German novel filled with dialogue in transliterated Yiddish. (6) Theresa Hak-Kyung Cha's *Dictée*, in English but interspersed with passages of French (some translated, some not) and photographs of Korean. (7) Dolores Prida's play *Coser y cantar*, about half Spanish and half English, neither translated for a reader knowing only one, with its magnificent stage direction, "this play

---

[7] It is important that all these works are narratives or theater pieces. We accept multilingualism more readily in poetry than we do in fiction or drama; in film, subtitling makes vehicular matching easy. Fiction and drama are the crucial cases here. For further remarks on genre and the representation of multilingualism, see below, pp. 11–13.

must NEVER be performed in just one language."[8] (8) Tony Kushner's play *Homebody/ Kabul*, a patchwork quilt of English, Dari, Pashtun, Arabic, Russian, French, German, and Esperanto.

None of these is as challenging to read as would be, say, the unedited transcript of a good many conversations going on in subway cars in cosmopolitan cities. Each, except maybe Prida's play, has a single dominant language. But each is capaciously open to at least one other language, and each has a history of critical and readerly success. Taken together, they imply that vehicular matching is a more useful artistic strategy than we often presume it to be; our standards of critical judgment should take account of that.

DIALECT AND LANGUAGE

For Sternberg, the literary representation of the multilingual world and that of the multidialectal world are essentially similar; *La Grande Illusion* (French and German) is one example of vehicular matching, *Pygmalion* (Cockney and Standard British English) is another, with no consideration being given to the difference between them. Sternberg's view of this matter is widely shared. William Stanley Braithwaite, for example, bases his argument for an exact literary representation of African-American English on Frédéric Mistral's exact literary representation of Provençal.[9] Gloria Anzaldúa, rightly claiming that accepting her own "legitimacy" means accepting as legitimate "all the . . . languages [she speaks]," lists among those "languages" such speech varieties as "Standard English," "working class and slang English," "Standard Spanish," "Standard Mexican Spanish," and "North Mexican Spanish dialect."[10]

The common view is wrong. But it is not implausible, because the differences between the two tasks of representation are complicated, and it is an important view to scrutinize, not only because it helps us get rid of a common misconception, but also because disentangling the two practices helps us understand more precisely what is actually involved in each of them.

First, though, a clarification. Too often colonizers have used "language" to refer to what they themselves speak, "dialect" to refer to what the colonized

---

[8] Dolores Prida, *Coser y cantar*, in *Beautiful Señoritas and Other Plays* (Houston: Arte Público Press, 1991), p. 49.

[9] Henry Louis Gates, "Dis and Dat: Dialect and the Descent," in *Figures in Black: Words, Signs, and the "Racial" Self* (New York: Oxford University Press, 1987), p. 181.

[10] Gloria Anzaldúa, *Borderlands/ La Frontera: The New Mestiza* (San Francisco: Spinsters/Aunt Lute, 1987), pp. 55, 59.

speak. That is nonsense and worse, and the best intellectual antidote to it is a celebrated remark attributed to the Yiddish linguist Max Weinreich: "a language is a dialect with an army and a navy." There is a useful distinction to be made between the two terms, as when we say that Yiddish is a language, then distinguish within that language its Litvish, Polish/Galician, and Ukrainian dialects. That is a distinction of kind, and worth making. There is no use in a distinction between the two terms that claims to be a distinction of value.

When I walk into a first class on *Huck Finn* and ask students for their initial reactions and questions, often a student will say that she had a hard time reading Jim's speeches. Then I suggest reading those speeches aloud, or describe Twain's technique for representing pronunciation, and after a while, the student usually finds the difficulty diminishing.

When I walk into a first class on *Angels in America*, on the other hand, and a student asks about Emily's bewildering speeches in Act III, Scene 2, asks what they mean or for that matter what language they're in, the only thing I can do to help her is to tell her the answers – that is, that Emily is speaking in Ashkenazic Hebrew, and that what she is saying is a prayer for the dead; there is no technique of skilled reading to employ here, nothing to say about Kushner's means of representing Ashkenazic Hebrew that will enable the student to read it. Reading other languages doesn't get easier unless readers actually go out and learn them; what readers are confronting here is not difficulty but impossibility.[11]

The representation of non-standard speech varieties in their own language invites readers to confront and interpret the diversity *within* that language, within that speech community – diversity of class, region, education, occupation, age. The representation of heterophone languages forces readers to confront and interpret the multiplicity of speech communities in the world, the impossibility of understanding the speech of communities other than their own, their own position in the labyrinth of languages.

Fictions representing multiple languages through vehicular matching are rare. Fictions representing multiple dialects by that means are common; for example, to cite only some noted American examples, much work by Washington Irving, James Fenimore Cooper, Harriet Beecher Stowe, Joel Chandler Harris, Mark Twain, George W. Cable, Henry Roth, Zora Neale Hurston, Eugene O'Neill, Alice Walker, and August Wilson. Writers seeking to represent multiple dialects seldom avail themselves of the indirect

---

[11] For some reason, students in my experience are *less* likely to ask questions about Emily's speeches than about Jim's.

strategies Sternberg identifies. "'I shall be there tomorrow morning,' he said in the diction and cadence of a Mississippi plantation-owner" is not a sort of sentence we often encounter; instead the writer seeks to reproduce that cadence and diction.

It is because this is the case, probably, that there are disputes among writers about whether and how to have characters speak in non-standard dialects, and none that I know of about whether and how to represent multiple languages. Since it's a real possibility, it's worth arguing about. Braithwaite argues for it:

[Dialect] may be employed as the langue d'oc of Frederic Mistral's Provençal poems, as a preserved tongue, the only adequate medium of rendering the psychology of character, and of describing the background of the people whose lives and experience are kept within the environment where the dialect survives as the universal speech; or it may be employed as a special mark of emphasis upon the peculiar characteristic and temperamental traits of a people whose action and experiences are given in contact and relationship with a dominant language, and are set in a literary fabric of which they are but one strand of man in the weaving.[12]

James Weldon Johnson argues against it, at least as regards African-American English, because of "the limitations on Negro dialect imposed by the fixing effects of long convention."[13] (Johnson is thinking of the "long convention" of the minstrel show, with its "unrealistic – indeed, insidious – archetypal portraiture of the black man as a head-scratching, foot-shuffling, happy-go-lucky fool.") Henry James argues against it more generally, denouncing "the riot of the vulgar tongue" across the board:

The thousands of celebrated productions raised their monument but to the bastard vernacular of communities disinherited of the felt difference between the speech of the soil and the speech of the newspaper, and capable thereby, accordingly, of taking slang for simplicity, the composite for the quaint and the vulgar for the natural . . . The monument was there, if one would, but was one to regret one's own failure to have contributed a stone? Perish, and all ignobly, the thought![14]

Pro or con, long-winded or concise, general or specific, these writers have something in common; as they work out their positions, dialect writing is in fashion, almost a norm. There has not yet been an influential fashion for language writing, and it has certainly never been a norm, so no one needs to take up its cause or fend it off.

---

[12] Quoted in Gates, "Dis and Dat," p. 181.
[13] Ibid., p. 179.
[14] Henry James, "Preface to *Daisy Miller*," in *The Art of the Novel: Critical Prefaces*, ed. R. P. Blackmur (New York: Scribner's, 1934), pp. 279–80.

No extant writing system is solely a means of representing pronunciation. That means that the representation of multiple dialects involves using a writing system in two different ways, or in a sense using two different systems.[15] The first is whatever is standard – for example, the way I am using the English writing system in this book, holding to its orthography and punctuation and capitalization rules, which do not vary from one writer to another according to dialect, do not reflect the difference between how I would read these words and how my Canadian neighbor would. The second is non-standard, has a less stylized, more mimetic relation to pronunciation, and does vary according to dialect. The two systems are not parallel; to use Marie-Christine Hazaël-Massieux's terms, one system is a writing system, the other a transcription system.[16] The former results from the long labor of a community, the latter from the ad hoc work of an individual.

The representation of multiple languages is different. It is most different when both or all of the languages represented have writing systems of their own, as in many of the multilingual fictions cited previously. In the German text of Mann's *The Magic Mountain*, for example, the French-language remarks of Hans Castorp and Claudia Chauchat are notated as they are not to represent either character's pronunciation, in particular Castorp's no doubt German-influenced one, but because that is how standard French orthography requires Mann to notate them. French and German are not being given equal time, or equal importance; but they are being represented by equal means.

Sometimes, though, the heterophone language does *not* have a writing system. Sometimes a heterophone language with a writing system is written with a different alphabet from that of the dominant language, with no established rules for representing it in that language, nothing like the YIVO rules for romanizing Yiddish or the pinyin rules for romanizing Chinese. In such cases – and such cases are prominent in this book – writers seeking to notate a heterophone language have to devise a transcription system for it, and in their texts that system will be juxtaposed to the dominant language's writing system. In such cases, the representation of multiple dialects and that of multiple languages are more alike.

---

[15] I speak only of alphabetical writing systems; I do not know how other writing systems, e.g., the one devised for Chinese, represent multiple dialects or second-language interference.

[16] Marie-Christine Hazaël-Massieux, *Écrire en créole: oralité et écriture aux Antilles* (Paris: L'Harmattan, 1994), pp. 11–38; see also Geoffrey Sampson, *Writing Systems* (Stanford: Stanford University Press, 1985), especially the chapter on English.

But still not identical. Notating a non-standard dialect means adjusting a writing system, pushing it in the direction of representing pronunciation, but not jettisoning the system altogether. And it is because one retains the basic system that its dialect-representing modification can be read with relative ease, at least after one has gotten used to it, and often with pleasure; William Dean Howells, for example, wrote to George Washington Cable after reading *The Grandissimes*:

Deuce take you, how could you do it so well? . . . My wife kept reading me that first call of Frowenfeld's on the Nancanou ladies till I was intoxicated with their delightfulness. Oh the charm of their English! We speak nothing else now but that dialect.[17]

Notating a heterophone language by means of a transcription system is often very unlike that. Consider one of Khwaja's Pashtun speeches in Tony Kushner's *Homebody/ Kabul*: "Dah bah ghalatah kar wee cheh dah khuzah woo wah hal shee. Hagha yaway milmana dah ow dah kho de mil mastiyah deh oosool puhrkhelahv yaway kar-wee" ("It would be wrong to beat her, she is a guest, our guest, it would be offensive to the laws of hospitality to – ").[18] How are we to read that? What kind of information can we get from it? Where words end, where sentences end, and something about pronunciation – but not very much, only coarse information, since we haven't been told how to read this system, and no information at all about stress, either within words or over the span of sentences. Compared with Mark Twain's portrait of Jim's speech in *Huck Finn*, this is a very blurry image.

Sometimes, of course, the heterophone language is a lot closer to the dominant one than Pashtun is to English. Consider the first creolophone utterance of Alfred Mercier's francophone novel, *L'Habitation Saint-Ybars*: "Vous pa oua don, Michié? . . . cé nég pou vende" ("You don't see, Sir? . . . they are Blacks to be sold").[19] The historical record suggests that a good many readers had trouble figuring out what such utterances

---

17 Quoted in Arlin Turner, *George W. Cable: A Biography* (Durham, NC: Duke University Press, 1956), p. 99. Note also Turner's remark that "like Mark Twain, William Dean Howells, and others afterwards, [Cable's friend and discoverer Edward King] spoke in Creole, he said, and he scattered Creole expressions through his letters" (54).

18 Tony Kushner, *Homebody/ Kabul* (New York: Theatre Communications Group, 2002), p. 48. The translation is given in Kushner's text.
   This is a play, of course, and in the theater the audience would hear the pronunciation as the actor had worked it up. But plays have a real existence as read texts, not just as performed ones, and it's as a read text that it's being considered here.

19 Alfred Mercier, *L'Habitation Saint-Ybars, ou, Maîtres et esclaves en Louisiane (Récit social)*, ed. Réginald Hamel (Montreal: Guérin, 1989), p. 79.

meant, nor can the francophone character to whom this particular speech is addressed understand it; but anyone who can read French can figure out what it sounds like. As can Germans reading the Yiddish parts of Jeannette Lander's *Itke K.* – for example, "Oi! Itkele, in der alten Heem is alles, alles, anderesch gewe'en" ("Oy, little Itke, in the old home [i.e., when we lived in Poland] everything, everything was different").[20]

But even here a distinction needs to be made. Dialect orthography renders, sometimes successfully, the pronunciation of particular groups of people and particular individuals. It can do that because readers who know how the writing system works normally can interpret it when it is working non-normally. With Mercier and Lander, though, we cannot tell whether what's being offered us is a standard orthography or an altered one, an image of what the heterophone language sounds like generally or what it sounds like when spoken by a particular character.

The underlying point, constant despite the surface variation, is that when an author represents the dominant language with a writing system and heterophone languages with transcription systems, a false impression is given, an impression of inequality. (This need not be, and often is not, the author's intention; it is simply a consequence of the situation.) German and French are equally languages in *Der Zauberberg*, English and Spanish equally languages in *Coser y cantar*. But though English and Pashtun are equally languages in the world, they are not equally languages in the text of *Homebody/Kabul*, because the systems used to represent them are not parallel; Pashtun – or any other heterophone language represented by a transcription system – *looks* like a dialect, whatever its actual linguistic status.

The distinction between multilingual fictions and multidialectal ones is best dramatized by Mark Twain, in a conversation in *Huck Finn* as good as almost anything in Plato:

"Why Huck, doan' de French people talk de same way we does?"
"*No*, Jim; you couldn't understand a word they said – not a single word."
"Well now, I be ding-busted! How do dat come?"
"*I* don't know; but it's so. I got some of their jabber out of a book. Spose a man was to come to you and say *Polly-voo-franzy*– what would you think?"
"I wouldn' think nuff'n; I'd take en bust him over de head. Dat is, if he warn't white. I wouldn't 'low no nigger to call me dat."

[20] Jeannette Lander, *Ein Sommer in der Woche der Itke K.* (Frankfurt am Main: Insel, 1971), p. 15. If one translates the sentence into German as a German might do on reading it, one can see, even without knowing German, how similar the two sentences are; the German would be, "Ach, Itkelein, in dem alten Heim ist alles, alles anders gewesen." Lander may in fact be pushing the Yiddish towards German; a more standard Yiddish would be, "in der alter heym iz alts, alts andersh geven."

"Shucks, it ain't calling you anything. It's only saying do you know how to talk French."

"Well, den, why couldn't he *say* it?"

"Why, he *is* a-saying it. That's a Frenchman's *way* of saying it."

"Well, it's a blame' ridicklous way, en I doan' want to hear no mo' bout it. Dey ain' no sense in it."[21]

Huck and Jim speak different dialects, "the ordinary 'Pike-County' dialect" and "the Missouri negro dialect" (2) respectively. To represent those dialects, Twain uses – virtuosically – only one strategy, namely, vehicular matching; Jim's speeches are in the dialect Jim speaks, Huck's narrative and speeches in the dialect Huck speaks.[22] To show us the difference between English and French, on the other hand, Twain uses all the other strategies Sternberg identifies: the two characters talk about French, speak and distort French, argue about French, translate French, imagine French. To represent the multidialectal world in literature is one thing, to represent the multilingual world in literature is another.

EPIC, LYRIC, DRAMATIC

Many critics of multilingual literature, Sternberg among them, lump together multilingual texts in different genres. There is much to be said for that unfussy eclecticism, and for the wonderfully surprising juxtapositions it makes possible. But there is also something to be said for setting out some of the ways in which epic, dramatic, and lyric genres differ in this respect.

Drama is transparent; we have for the most part only direct access to dramatic characters' language and languages. They speak, and we hear them, in whatever dialect and language the playwright and actor offer us. The playwright cannot write, "then Doña Ana said, in her elegant Castilian Spanish, 'how seldom do we confront the fact of our own mortality.'" The playwright can indicate accent – for example, Lillian Hellman's stage direction for *The Little Foxes*, "it is to be understood that the accents are southern."[23] But that's about it for indirect means of mimesis. *Characters* can tell stories, become the writers of narrative, make use of such indirect means. But playwrights can't.

[21] Mark Twain, *The Adventures of Huckleberry Finn*, ed. Sculley Bradley *et al.* (New York: Norton, 1977), pp. 66–67. Page numbers for subsequent quotations from this work will be given in the text.

[22] For a more detailed analysis, see my "Anglophone Literature and Multilingual America," in Werner Sollors (ed.), *Multilingual America: Transnationalism, Ethnicity, and the Languages of American Literature* (New York: New York University Press, 1998), pp. 338–41.

[23] Lillian Hellman, *The Little Foxes. Six Plays by Lillian Hellman* (New York: Vintage, 1979), p. 150.

This necessary directness or transparency is drama's challenge, strength, and limitation. "Challenge," because there's no way around the necessary work; playwrights can't fake it. "Strength," because with linguistically competent playwrights, or playwrights willing to ask for linguistic help, and with competent actors, theater can offer us a brilliantly exact and direct account of the multilingual world. And "limitation," because it means that a wide variety of strategies for representing the multilingual world can't be made use of – all the strategies, that is, by which writers of narrative *can* fake it, for better as well as for worse.

In narrative, especially in third-person narrative, languages can be spoken about as well as spoken. Fraud is possible, but so are reflection, commentary, annotation, significant and sometimes ironic juxtapositions between theory and practice. Caroline Link's beautiful film *Jenseits der Stille* ("Beyond Silence"), about the hearing child of deaf parents, directly presents both spoken German and sign language. The book made from the film cannot do that; but it can offer assertions and accounts that the film cannot – for example, that the sign language "enables people such as [the narrator's] deaf parents to express with their hands everything they think and feel,"[24] or that the sign language, though invented by the deaf, does not take place in silence: "sign language is very animated; one strikes one's breast, slaps one's hands together, rubs one's sleeve. [My parents] seldom argued, but when they did, I heard how forcefully their hands clapped at each other" (12–13). Kate Chopin can tell us that Louisiana French Creole has a "music and charm no English words can convey"; but then, as if challenging or complicating that assertion, she can offer a supposed translation of that "music and charm," by means of verbal transposition; and then she can undermine both assertion and translation by presenting, but not translating, a few crucial speeches in the language itself; and then we, as readers, can figure out how to put together the claims these diverse modes of representation advance.

Lyric is more like narrative here. There is no *formal* obstacle to a lyrical representation of the multilingual world; a first-person narrator can use most of the same mimetic strategies that a third-person narrator can. Nor is there any shortage of complexly multilingual lyric: poems by T. S. Eliot and Irena Klepfisz, memoirs and essays by Gloria Anzaldúa, Abraham Cahan, Elias Canetti, Eva Hoffmann, Alice Kaplan, Vladimir Nabokov, and Richard Rodriguez. In practice, though, these works are

---

[24] Caroline Link, *Jenseits der Stille* (Berlin: Aufbau, 1997), p. 11 (my translation). Page numbers for subsequent quotations from this work will be given in the text.

not doing what narrative has often done. That is partly because, again in practice, the focus is on the polyglot individual rather than the multilingual scene. The multilingualism being represented is the individual's cosmopolitan accomplishment, not the polyphony of the community.

There is a wonderful example of this, almost an allegory of the distinction, in the first volume of Canetti's memoir, *Die gerettete Zunge*, talking of his childhood in Rustchuk, in Bulgaria:

> Of the tales I heard, I remember only those about werewolves and vampires ... They are present to me in every detail, but not in the language in which I heard them. I heard them in Bulgarian, but know them in German; this mysterious transposition is perhaps the most remarkable thing I have to tell about my childhood ...
>
> My parents spoke German with each other, of which I was to understand nothing. To the children and to all relatives and friends they spoke Spanish ... The peasant girls in the house spoke only Bulgarian, and it was chiefly with them, probably, that I learned it. But since I never went to a Bulgarian school and left Rustchuk when I was six, I soon forgot it altogether. All the events of those first years took place in Spanish or Bulgarian. For the most part, they later translated themselves for me into German ... Everything Bulgarian in particular, e.g., the tales, I hold in my mind in German.
>
> How that happened, I cannot say ... Only one thing can I say with certainty: the events of those years are present to me in all their force and freshness – I have been nurtured by them for more than sixty years – but they are for the most part bound to words that at that time I did not know.[25]

As noted, a wonderful passage, rigorously setting out a perplexing and evocative experience. But the focus is not on the multilingual world Canetti grew up in; that world is only the background, the account of it is exact but not vivid, no one is quoted, we do not see the peasant girls speaking or moving. The focus is on Canetti, and in fact the focus is precisely on the way in which, in Canetti's mind, the multilingual diversity of his childhood has been absorbed into the beautiful, fluid German of his narrative – a figure, perhaps, for what often happens to the multilingual world in the best of multilingual lyric.

LITERATURE AND THE LINGUISTIC FACTS

How much does linguistic accuracy matter in the depiction of linguistic reality? For Sternberg, as for many other critics, not very much. Sternberg in particular forthrightly claims that "the realistic force of polylingual

---

[25] Elias Canetti, *Die gerettete Zunge: Geschichte einer Jugend* (Frankfurt am Main: Fischer, 1984), pp. 15–16 (my translation).

representation . . . is relatively independent of the objective (verbal and extraverbal) facts as viewed and established by scientific inquiry" (235). That amounts to saying that the artistic success of linguistic representation is independent of the "linguistic reality" being represented. For Sternberg, "linguistic reality" matters less than do "the model(s) of that reality" provided by the work, the work's literary tradition, and the work's readers reading within a given cultural framework.

This view seems to me wrong. It artificially limits our real power as readers, and it is sharply at odds with our ordinary experience of reading and judging. As we read, we continually ask, and should ask, whether a literary work justly represents whatever phenomena in the external world we have or can acquire an exact independent sense of, from Native American languages to the Triangle Shirtwaist Factory fire to the Goldberg Variations, and the answers we get to such questions affect, and should affect, our judgment of the work and the use we can make of it.[26]

With regard to linguistic facts in particular, there are two sorts of questions to ask. The first bears on how accurately a particular language is being represented; the answers to that question affect, both positively and negatively, our trust in a writer's expertise. For a positive example, consider some passages in W. G. Sebald's *Austerlitz*. The novel is filled with speeches made by Austerlitz to the narrator; they are identified as taking place in French and English, but are presented largely in German. Occasional phrases are presented in English, by the strategy Sternberg calls "selective reproduction." These phrases are of special importance, for example:

Vorderhand allerdings sei er verpflichtet, mir zu eröffnen, daß ich auf meine Examenspapiere nicht Dafydd Elias, sondern Jacques Austerlitz schreiben müsse. It appears, sagte Penrith-Smith, that this is your real name. ["First, however, he said he was obliged to reveal to me that I should write on my examination papers not Dafydd Elias, but Jacques Austerlitz. *It appears*, said Penrith-Smith, *that this is your real name*."][27]

The English is idiomatic and well-formed – not a surprise, given Sebald's long residence in England, but surely a pleasure, and a pleasure that increases our trust in Sebald as a guide to the world through which he is conducting us.

For a contrasting example, consider the good-hearted Socialist German character Von Baumser in Arthur Conan Doyle's rousing novel, *The Firm*

---

[26] See on this Christopher Ricks, "Literature and the Matter of Fact," in *Essays in Appreciation* (New York: Clarendon Press, 1996).

[27] W. G. Sebald, *Austerlitz* (Frankfurt am Main: Fischer, 2003), p. 101 (my translation).

of Girdlestone. His English is comically imperfect, and from time to time Doyle has him speak German – for example, when his friend and roommate Major Clutterbuck brings home some unexpected (and ill-gotten) cash:

"Mein Gott!" he exclaimed. "Gnâdinger Vater! Ach Himmel! Was fur [*sic*] eine Schatze! Donnerwetter!" and a thousand other cacophonous expressions of satisfaction and amazement.[28]

"Cacophonous" they may be, but they're not good German, or for that matter possible German. "Mein Gott," "Ach Himmel," and "Donnerwetter" are fine. "Gnâdinger Vater" should be "Gnädiger Vater," and "Was fur eine Schatze" should be "Was für ein Schatz." Nor, for that matter, is "Von Baumser" a plausible German name; a Google search for it turns up only sites having to do with the novel, none connected with actual Germans. These small inaccuracies don't keep Doyle's novel from engaging us as readers, but they do undercut the narrator's assumed cosmopolitanism; and in a novel that depends for its effect on our belief that the author is a man of the world, a man who understands rugby and the markets and the diamond trade, that undercutting has real consequences.

In such cases, writers are laying their cards on the table. In other cases, their strategy is less transparent, and our scrutiny has to be more elaborate. Consider this passage from Dan Jacobson's *The Beginners*: "Finally Meyer said impatiently, in Yiddish, 'It's time to go. Come, Benny. Goodbye, father.' "[29] Perfectly ordinary, but if we pause and ask what's happening, it becomes complicated. Taken literally, in relation to the convention according to which quotation marks enclose an utterance the character is identified as actually speaking, the passage is nonsense; what's between the quotation marks is in English, not in Yiddish. To make sense of this, we have to presume one of two longer explanations. The first would be something like this: "Meyer spoke impatiently in Yiddish, and this is a translation into English of what he said." In that case, we're being asked to accept Jacobson as a Yiddish-speaker and translator, imagining his characters speaking particular Yiddish sentences, knowing enough Yiddish to imagine these sentences idiomatically, knowing enough English to translate them. Or maybe the explanation we're being asked to accept is something like this: "Given who Meyer, Avrom, and Benny were, I know they would be speaking Yiddish to each other. I do not know enough Yiddish to hear or imagine what they would have said, to put idiomatic Yiddish phrases in their mouths. I do, though, have a feeling for the content of what they

[28] Arthur Conan Doyle, *Works* (New York: Walter J. Black, n.d.), p. 784.
[29] Dan Jacobson, *The Beginners* (London: House of Stratus, 2001), p. 4.

would have said in that language, and I am unwilling to renounce my imaginative intuitions simply because I cannot speak the language they would surely have spoken. Accordingly, I ask you to believe that an apt translation of the sense of what they really would have said is, 'It's time to go. Come, Benny. Goodbye, father.'"

There are good reasons why so few authors make use of either of these formulae!³⁰ But one formula or the other is often true to what's happening in this sort of literary situation; and both reveal the extent to which, when an author depicts a heterolingual conversation by means other than vehicular matching, we are being asked as readers to take something on faith.

If we are critical readers, we are not altogether willing to do that; we cannot help wondering whether we're being had. We look at whatever passages are "selectively reproduced" to see whether they're idiomatic or improbably flawed; we look at what is "translated," that is, presented in English, to see whether the translation strengthens or weakens our faith in the author's expertise.

The Jacobson passage leaves one uncertain; nothing there suggests any of the characteristics of Yiddish, but not much is at odds with them either. A small, not very pronounced example of the latter: "Goodbye" comes from "God be with you." Yiddish ordinarily makes use of different wishes for leave-taking: *a gutn tog, a gut yor, zay(t) gezunt* ("a good day," "a good year," "be well"). It also has *adye*, a Yiddishization of *adieu*, but nothing about Jacobson's characters suggests they would be making use of that unusual expression. Maybe Jacobson knows all this, maybe he doesn't; there's not enough evidence, so we remain skeptical.

Henry Roth's "translation" of putatively Yiddish speeches wins our trust more decisively. We note his evocation of Genya's distrustful use of the formal rather than the familiar with her boarder Mr. Luter, for example:

She laughed. "Don't be foolish, Mr. Luter!"
"Mr. Luter!" He looked annoyed for a moment, then shrugged and smiled. "Now that you know me so well, why use the formal still?"(44)³¹

---

³⁰ Some do, actually; Cooper in *The Last of the Mohicans* (New York: Penguin, 1986) presents Natty Bumppo's first speech as being "in the tongue which was known to all the natives who formerly inhabited the country between the Hudson and the Potomack," then adds, "we shall a give a free translation [of it] for the benefit of the readers; endeavouring, at the same time, to preserve some of the peculiarities, both of the individual and of the language" (30). A painstakingly self-conscious account – though a fraudulent one, given Cooper's entire ignorance of Delaware. Page numbers for subsequent quotations from this work will be given in the text.

³¹ Like French and German, Yiddish has both familiar and formal pronouns, *du* and *ir*, and verb endings associated with them. Roth evokes Genya's use of *ir* by having her say "Mr. Luter," though probably in the Yiddish speech Roth is imagining, Genya just uses *zayt*, the formal form of the imperative of the verb *zayn*, "to be," instead of *zay*, the familiar form.

Or even smaller things – for example, "peasant" used to mean "Gentile peasant" (or sometimes simply "Gentile"), just as *poyersh* is almost always used in Yiddish; or the foreign feel of Genya's explanation to her son David of why gypsies "roam" – "it pleases them," which in comparison with the more ordinary "they like to" feels stilted, but also evokes the Yiddish construction, *es gefelt zey*. Small matters in a big book, to be sure. But the accumulation of them strengthens our trust in the author.

The second sort of scrutiny bears on evaluative comparisons *between* languages. It affects our judgment, not of the writer's expertise, but of his or her imaginative generosity.

For contemporary linguists, all languages are in an important sense equal. So David Crystal, for example, in the *Cambridge Encyclopedia of Language*:

all languages are arguably equal in the sense that there is nothing intrinsically limiting, demeaning, or handicapping about any of them. All languages meet the social and psychological needs of their speakers.[32]

Elsewhere, though, all languages are *not* equal. Many people have believed them to be, and still believe them to be, essentially different in value. Yiddish, for example, had for a long time an almost sub-linguistic status within the Jewish community; one of its own names for itself was *zhargon*, "jargon," its fitness for literary use was disputed, and it was a point of pride for some Jews to be ignorant of it.[33] Another example: in 1868, a report issued by the so-called "Peace Commission" said of Native Americans that "their barbarous dialects should be blotted out, and the English language substituted."[34] A third: the noted linguist Leonard Bloomfield wrote in 1933 that "the creolized language has the status of an inferior dialect of the masters' speech. It is subject to constant leveling-out and improvement in the direction of the latter."[35]

---

[32] David Crystal, *Cambridge Encyclopedia of Language* (Cambridge: Cambridge University Press, 1997), p. 6.

[33] On this, see Sander Gilman, *Jewish Self-Hatred: Anti-Semitism and the Hidden Language of the Jews* (Baltimore: Johns Hopkins University Press, 1986).

[34] James Crawford (ed.), *Language Loyalties* (Chicago: University of Chicago Press, 1992), p. 48. L.-J. Calvet notes how often languages are called "dialects" by people who wish to lower their linguistic status; see his *Linguistique et colonialisme: petit traité de glottophagie* (Paris: Payot, 1974), pp. 40–54.

[35] Quoted in Michel DeGraff, "Against Creole Exceptionalism," *Language* 79:2 (2003), p. 394; note also the remark, also quoted by DeGraff, of the eminent French linguist Antoine Meillet: "'Creole' modes of speaking – Spanish Creole or French Creole – ... constitute varieties of Spanish or French that are deprived of almost all their grammar, weakened in their pronunciation, reduced to a small lexicon" (394). My thanks to Professor DeGraff for sending me this excellent essay.

Languages do differ from one another, of course, and figuring out these differences is an important enterprise for linguists and writers alike. But creating a value-hierarchy of languages is an error, as is denying that a particular language is a language at all. Uncritically dramatizing these errors in literature is the linguistic form of racism; it denies full humanity to particular characters on the basis of the language they speak, and is at odds with literature's noble ambition to see each character through his or her own eyes, to hear each character in his or her own language.

That ambition can be thwarted in numerous ways. One is referring to a language by some term other than "language" – for example, early in the film *Lost Horizon*, when British diplomat Robert Conway, played by Ronald Colman, is listening to some angry Asian locals outside the airplane he's in – there are disturbances, and he's fleeing – and says, "I can't get their dialect." How would our response change if he said, "I can't understand their language"? Alternatively, languages other than the dominant one can be represented as restricted to a small range, whether emotional or referential – by having their speakers tell stories but not make arguments, say, curse but not bless, make jokes but not mourn (or the reverse). (Not every language has a technical vocabulary for classifying ice or parts of speech, of course. The error is in presenting languages as lacking capacities that *every* language has.) Or authors may compare other languages than the dominant one to such non-linguistic semiotic systems as animal noises[36] or music or gesture, even (or especially) when those comparisons seem flattering – for example, when Cooper writes, of a conversation in Delaware between Chingachgook and his son Uncas, "It is impossible to describe the music of their language, while thus engaged in laughter and endearments, in such a way as to render it intelligible to those whose ears have never listened to its melody. The compass of their voices, particularly that of the youth, was wonderful; extending from the deepest bass, to tones that were even feminine in softness" (200). Lovely – but surely what's being said has meaning as well as music, and the meaning has gotten lost.[37]

---

[36] Frantz Fanon, *Les damnés de la terre* (Paris: Gallimard, 1991, first published 1961): "the colonist's language, when he speaks of the colonized, is the language of zoology. Reference is made to the Yellow man's slithering movements, to the smells of the indigenous city, to hordes, stink, pullulation, swarming, gesturing" (73, my translation).

[37] This is not to deny the special associations between particular languages and particular musics, e.g., what Wai Chee Dimock calls "a synthesis of the verbal and the nonverbal . . . central to African-American poetics in general, and to Caribbean poetics in particular," in *Through Other Continents: American Literature Across Deep Time* (Princeton: Princeton University Press, 2006), p. 156. All

That ambition can also be accomplished in numerous ways. The works cited above as examples of "vehicular matching" make good use of one of them, and it is certainly part of my purpose here to make a case for that strategy. But it is not the only strategy that works. Consider again Roth's *Call It Sleep*. It depicts the Yiddish/Hebrew world of the Jewish Lower East Side. Yiddish almost never appears on the page. But Roth's scheme of linguistic representation makes it appear vividly in the mind. Conversation in English is presented in English, with exact orthographic fidelity to each speaker's mode of speech. Hebrew – which we encounter only as a read language, never as a spoken one – is presented in transliteration. Conversation and meditation in Yiddish are represented through English, but a quite different English than that used to transcribe anglophone conversation. It is orthographically standard, for one thing. It is rich and often formal, and as noted is often an English verbally transposed to evoke Yiddish structures and idioms. Yiddish as Roth represents it is both standard and exotic, both native and foreign; English is its means of representation, but the vivid distinction between English and Yiddish in the world the book depicts is brilliantly clear – a compromise that is, almost miraculously, not compromising.

A BRIEF CONCLUSION

For a chapter like this one, more a tool chest than a single sustained argument, what is needed in a conclusion is an inventory of the tools the chapter contains. Those are: some terms for describing the ways authors seek to represent the multilingual world in literature; some challenges to received opinion about how that work of representation should be done; some distinctions between representing the multilingual world and representing the multidialectal one; some reflections on how strategies of representation are likely to vary with literary genre; and some standards for assessing the correspondence between literary representation and the real linguistic world. A miscellaneous group of ideas, surely, a mix of screwdrivers and hammers and tape measures and nails; but these are the ideas I have found myself most in need of in doing this work, and the ones by which the remainder of this book is made possible.

---

languages have their music, and comparing those musics makes sense. What does not make sense is to treat one language as having a music, another as having none. See the whole of Dimock's excellent and learned account of Black English, and also Paul Gilroy, *Black Atlantic: Modernity and Double Consciousness* (Cambridge, MA: Harvard University Press, 1993).

CHAPTER I

Cooper's The Last of the Mohicans *and the* languages of America

Translation was, and still is, the central act of European colonization and imperialism in the Americas.

– Eric Cheyfitz, *The Poetics of Imperialism*

We shall give a free translation [of the speech] for the benefit of the readers; endeavouring, at the same time, to preserve some of the peculiarities, both of the individual and of the language.

– James Fenimore Cooper, *The Last of the Mohicans*

In Chapter X of Cooper's *The Last of the Mohicans*, the villain Magua, a Huron, makes a sharp, unflattering comparison between Native American languages and European ones: "the pale faces are prattling women! They have two words for each thing, while a red skin will make the sound of his voice speak for him."[1] A haunting remark, because it represents a mode of thought unattested in the documentary record. There is nothing in that record, that is, to tell us how Native Americans experienced European languages.[2]

---

[1] James Fenimore Cooper, *The Last of the Mohicans* (New York: Penguin, 1986), p. 91. Page numbers for subsequent quotations from this book will be given in the text.

[2] See on this, among other studies: Emmanuel Drechsel, "'Ha, Now Me Stomany that': A Summary of Pidginization and Creolization of North American Indian Languages," *International Journal of the Sociology of Language* 7 (1976), pp. 63–68; Edward Gray and Norman Fiering (eds.), *The Language Encounter in the Americas 1492–1800* (New York: Berghahn, 2000); Frances Karttunen, *Between Worlds* (New Brunswick: Rutgers University Press, 1994); Laura Murray, "Vocabularies of Native American Languages: A Historical and Literary Investigation of an Elusive Genre," *American Quarterly* 53:4 (2001), pp. 590–623; Peter Nabokov, *Native American Testimony: A Chronicle of Indian-White Relations from Prophecy to the Present* (New York: Penguin, 1991); Nancy Shoemaker, *A Strange Likeness: Becoming Red and White in Eighteenth-Century North America* (New York: Oxford University Press, 2004); Michael Silverstein, "Dynamics of Linguistic Contact," in Ives Goddard (ed.), *Handbook of North American Indians* 17: *Languages* (Washington, DC: Smithsonian Institution, 1996), pp. 117–36, and "Encountering Language and the Languages of Encounter," *Journal of Linguistic Anthropology* 6 (1996), pp. 126–44; and Peter Wogan, "Perceptions of European Literacy in Early Contact Situations," *Ethnohistory* 41 (1994), pp. 407–29.

My thanks to Ives Goddard, Victor Golla, Edward Gray, Steven Hackel, Frances Karttunen, Lucy Maddox, Laura Murray, Peter Nabokov, Barry O'Connell, and Peter Wogan for generous and helpful responses to queries I sent them on this matter.

There are, to be fair, some data about Native American responses to the *writtenness* of European languages, some anecdotes and some studies of those anecdotes. The anecdotes often tell of wonder. Grigorii Shelikhov, writing in the 1780s, reports sending Kodiak Island Eskimos with letters to his workmen; the Eskimos, he wrote, then

fell into the utmost astonishment, that they [the workmen] should send me back exactly what they knew I wanted from what I had said to them a day or two before, though they had not spoke a word of it. I sent one of them . . . with a letter to one of my under-traffickers, desiring him to send me some plums and other dried fruits. My messenger, unable to resist the temptation, ate up half of them by the way, as I found by comparing the quantity he brought me with that mentioned in the letter. For this, I chid [sic] him . . . On this he expressed the most extreme surprise, persuaded as he was that the letter had seen him eat [the fruit].[3]

The studies critique the anecdotes, suggesting that the wonder they tell of may not be genuine, that the Europeans who recorded the anecdotes had something invested in regarding writing as a superior technology, that Native Americans themselves had a more ambivalent view of it and for that matter had their own graphic systems for recording traditions and treaties.[4]

With that exception, though, there is no record of an early Native American view of European languages, and nothing even remotely comparable to the thick European discourse regarding the languages of America: no handbooks, no instructive dialogues, no phrase books, no anecdotes, no critiques, no grammars, no classification systems or hierarchies, no literary representation. One reason for that, probably, is that Native American languages at this time were almost all languages without writing systems.[5] It may also be the case that European linguistic discourse is a specifically European artifact, a specifically European mode of making sense of a language encounter, and that Native American ways of performing that task didn't produce that sort of artifact. Whatever the reasons, the facts are what they are.

And those facts put limits on the following account. Cooper is working hard in his novel to dramatize the language encounters between Native Americans and European Americans. Understanding and assessing what

[3] Gray and Fiering (eds.), *Language Encounter*, p. 6.
[4] See on this James Axtell, "Babel of Tongues: Communicating with the Indians in Eastern North America," in Gray and Fiering (eds.), *Language Encounter*, pp. 15–60; the chapter called "Writing" in Shoemaker's *Strange Likeness*; and Wogan's "Perceptions of European Literacy."
[5] See on this Willard B. Walker, "Native Writing Systems," in Goddard (ed.), *Languages*, pp. 158–84. The most notable exception to the generalization is the Cherokee syllabary, invented by Sequoya in 1819.

he is doing, learning and critiquing what he has to teach, requires us to set his account in relation to what actually happened in those encounters, how they were experienced and understood by all those who took a role in them or had a view of them. But we can't do that. We can set his account in its abundant and diverse European American contexts, and in doing so see more clearly something of what Cooper was up to. But that's as far as we can go. In his capacity as language theorist, Cooper's imagined Magua has no historical counterparts.

There are two relevant, available local contexts for thinking about Cooper's novel as a language fiction. The intellectual context is the European American discourse about Native American cultures. The political context is Indian Removal.

European American ideas about Native American cultures were centered around the idea of savagism. That idea consisted of several propositions: that Europeans were civilized and that Native Americans were not, were "savages"; that savagism was an early stage of human progress, civilization a late one; that savagism must therefore inevitably lead to civilization, and inevitably be supplanted by it; and that, in Lucy Maddox's pointed summary, "there were only two options for the Indians: to become *civilized*, or to become *extinct*."[6] European Americans who favored or foresaw civilization disagreed with European Americans who favored or foresaw extinction; European Americans who thought the clearest marker of civilization was Christianity disagreed with European Americans who thought it was agriculture; European Americans like Cooper, who sometimes portrayed Native Americans as noble savages, differed from European Americans like Francis Parkman, who thought they were all degraded wretches. But almost all European Americans believed that civilization and extinction were the only two possible futures for the native peoples of the continent, and virtually no European Americans could let themselves see that Native Americans were civilized already, equally but differently.

---

[6] Lucy Maddox, *Removals: Nineteenth-Century American Literature and the Politics of Indian Affairs* (New York: Oxford University Press, 1991), p. 24. Page numbers for subsequent quotations from this work will be given in the text.

   Of the general studies of Native American–European relations I'm familiar with, Maddox's fine book is one of the two most attentive to linguistic questions, the other being Helen Carr's interesting *Inventing the American Primitive* (Cork: Cork University Press, 1996; page numbers for subsequent quotations from this work will be given in the text). Roy Harvey Pearce's classic *The Savages of America* devotes one page to ideas about Native American languages; Robert Berkhofer's likely classic *The White Man's Indian*, which Carr rightly compares with Edward Said's *Orientalism* (10), has even less; Louise Barnett's *The Ignoble Savage*, a study of "American literary racism," and Richard Drinnon's *Facing West*, a study of Indian-hating, both pretty much ignore the matter.

Now for most European Americans, Native American languages were a further proof of Native American savagism; as Maddox writes:

white observers consistently concluded that because of the limitations of his or her language, the most complex intellectual maneuver any Indian (of whatever language group) could manage was the construction of a simple metaphor, or occasionally an analogy; the Indian could not speculate about things that have no visible form, nor comprehend notional ideas. (24)

Amos Stoddard, later to be Governor of Louisiana, wrote in 1805 that Native American language was "barren"; Lewis Cass, then Governor of the Michigan Territory, wrote in 1826 that Huron was "harsh, guttural, and undistinguishable; filled with intonations, that seem to start from the speaker with great pain and effort." European American writers on these subjects had European authorities to back them, for example, Monboddo; but they gave the European prejudices new energy and specificity.[7]

But some European Americans had other views. Among them was the Moravian missionary John Heckewelder, whom Cooper read and admired. Heckewelder's *History, Manners, and Customs of the Indian Nations Who Once Inhabited Pennsylvania and the Neighbouring States* includes a remarkable eighty-page correspondence on Native American languages between Heckewelder and Peter Duponceau, one of the great pioneers in the study and description of these languages. Both writers present the languages as complex social constructs. Both contrast the complexity they see with the idea of savagism that is everywhere received as truth. Heckewelder specifically states it as his goal

to satisfy the world that the languages of the Indians are not so poor, so devoid of variety of expression, so inadequate to the communication even of abstract ideas, or in a word so *barbarous*, as has been generally imagined.[8]

---

[7] Stoddard's remark is quoted in Bernard W. Sheehan, *Seeds of Extinction: Jeffersonian Philanthropy and the American Indian* (Chapel Hill: University of North Carolina Press for the Institute of Early American History and Culture at Williamsburg, Virginia, 1973), p. 108; Cass's is quoted in Julie Tetel Andresen, *Linguistics in America 1769–1924: A Critical History* (London and New York: Routledge, 1990), p. 86. On Monboddo and the European background see Rüdiger Schreyer, "Deaf Mutes, Feral Children and Savages: Of Analogical Evidence in Eighteenth Century Theoretical History of Language," in Günther Blaicher and Brigitte Glaser (eds.), *Anglistentag 1993 Eichstätt* (Tübingen: Niemeyer, 1994), pp. 70–86.

[8] John Heckewelder, *History, Manners, and Customs of the Indian Nations Who Once Inhabited Pennsylvania and the Neighbouring States* (Philadelphia: Historical Society of Pennsylvania, 1876, repr. 1990), p. 125. Page numbers for subsequent quotations from this book will be given in the text.

And Duponceau makes good on Heckewelder's claim by his comments on particular words:

Wulamalessohalian! THOU WHO MAKEST ME HAPPY!
... How delighted would be Moore, the poet of the loves and graces, if his language, instead of five or six tedious words slowly following in the rear of each other, had furnished him with an expression like this, in which the lover, the object beloved, and the delicious sentiment which their mutual passion inspires, are blended, are fused together in one comprehensive appellative term? And it is in the languages of savages that these beautiful forms are found! What a subject for reflection, and how little do we know, as yet, of the astonishing things that the world contains. (405)

We can't not notice that Duponceau retains the term "savages" here, with all the ideological connotations of that word. Neither he nor Heckewelder is a cultural relativist. But no one who reads their work can casually dismiss Native American languages as primitive, and the humility of Duponceau's last sentence puts all ideologies at risk.

The political context of Cooper's work was Indian Removal. The goal of that federal project was to expel eastern Native Americans from their lands, and thereby to make those lands available for European American use. The project is usually associated with Andrew Jackson, and in fact the Indian Removal Act was passed in 1830, two years after Jackson was elected President. But the development and realization of the project dominated the whole second quarter of the century – Edward Everett persuasively called the Indian Removal Act, which allotted funds to carry out the project, "the greatest question that ever came before Congress, short of the question of peace and war"[9] – and it was already an important and controversial subject in 1826, when Cooper published *The Last of the Mohicans*.

This means that in Cooper's political world, speculative ideas about Native American culture and language were charged with the possibility of becoming practical arguments for and against Indian Removal. Georgia Congressman Richard Wilde, for example, claimed that "we should take direct control of Indian land." Against those who complained that such a course might lead to extinction of the dispossessed tribes, he made an argument about culture and language:

When gentleman talk of preserving the Indians, what is it that they mean to preserve? Is it their mode of life? No. You intend to convert them from hunters to agriculturalists or herdsmen . . . Their language? No. You intend to supersede

---

[9] Michael Rogin, *Fathers and Children: Andrew Jackson and the Subjugation of the American Indian* (New Brunswick: Transaction, 1991), p. 206. Page numbers for subsequent quotations from this work will be given in the text.

their imperfect jargon by teaching them your own rich, copious, energetic tongue. (Rogin, *Fathers and Children* 210–11)

In the context of Indian Removal, European American ideas about Native American languages were matters of life and death.

Reading Cooper in these contexts reveals a writer who can do what Fitzgerald said artists must do, namely, maintain two contradictory ideas without going crazy. The first idea, prominent for most of the novel, is that Native American languages are inferior to European languages, indeed are not really languages at all. The second idea, prominent towards the novel's end, is that Native American languages are indeed languages, different from European languages but not inferior to them, equal to them in complexity and mystery.[10]

Consider as an example of the former idea the passage discussed previously, in which the Huron villain Magua is trying to learn from the British officer Duncan Heyward what has become of the Mohican warrior Uncas, also called *Le Cerf Agile*.

"'Le Cerf Agile' is not here?"

"I know not whom you call the 'nimble deer,'" said Duncan, gladly profiting by any excuse to create delay.

"Uncas," returned Magua, pronouncing the Delaware name with even greater difficulty than he spoke his English words. "'Bounding elk' is what the white man says when he calls to the young Mohican."

"Here is some confusion in names between us, le Renard," said Duncan, hoping to provoke a discussion. "Daim is the French for deer, and cerf for stag; élan is the true term, when one would speak of an elk."

---

[10] Among other studies of these themes in the novel, see Dennis W. Allen, "'By All the Truth of Signs': James Fenimore Cooper's *The Last of the Mohicans*," *Studies in American Fiction* 9:2 (1981), pp. 159–79; Steven Blakemore, "Strange Tongues: Cooper's Fiction of Language in *The Last of the Mohicans*," *Early American Literature* 19 (1984), pp. 21–41; François Brunet, "'Linguisters on the prairie': formes et enjeux littéraires de la polémique herméneutique dans *The Prairie*," *Revue française d'études américaines* 37 (July 1988), pp. 238–66; Eric Fassin, "Théorie du langage et idéologie dans *La Prairie* de James Fenimore Cooper," *Revue française d'études américaines* 37 (July 1988), pp. 267–82; and Andrew Newman, "Sublime Translation in the Novels of James Fenimore Cooper and Walter Scott," *Nineteenth-Century Literature* 59:1 (2004), pp. 1–26.

Most of these, even Newman's learned and thoughtful essay, aren't usable for my purposes, because they don't test Cooper's novel against the linguistic facts, and because they don't situate Cooper's representation of language in its pertinent political contexts, and thus cannot ask what the patterns they discern could possibly have *meant* in Cooper's time. Steven Blakemore's essay, which does ask that question, seems to me wrong in many of its individual readings.

More useful than any of these, though not concerned specifically with *The Last of the Mohicans*, are Eric Cheyfitz's "Literally White, Figuratively Red: The Frontier of Translation in *The Pioneers*," in Robert Clark (ed.), *James Fenimore Cooper: New Critical Essays* (London: Vision and Barnes & Noble, 1985), pp. 55–95, and David Simpson's *The Politics of American English, 1776–1850* (New York: Oxford University Press, 1986).

"Yes," muttered the Indian, in his native tongue; "the pale faces are prattling women!¹¹ they have two words for each thing, while a red skin will make the sound of his voice speak for him." Then changing his language, he continued, adhering to the imperfect nomenclature of his provincial instructers [sic], "The deer is swift, but weak; the elk is swift, but strong; and the son of 'le serpent' is 'le cerf agile.' Has he leaped the river to the woods?" (91)

Magua accurately states Uncas's epithets in French and English. Duncan argues that the English and French epithets for Uncas do not mean the same thing, and attributes the disparity to a "confusion." Magua objects not to Duncan's pedantry but to the nature of white languages; white languages, he says, "have two words for each thing."

We might at this point expect Magua to celebrate Native American languages for having only one word for each thing. We might read that celebration as Cooper's covert attack on what Tocqueville was to call the "unsettled condition" of words in a democracy.¹² But Magua does something different; he makes Native American languages non-linguistic. He draws a contrast, that is, not between two names and one, but between names and sounds: "a red skin will make the *sound of his voice* speak for him" (my emphasis). He thus implies that a Native speaker can do all the ordinary work of language by sound alone, without the distinctions. The conventional idiom "red skin" for Native American intensifies the physicality of this idea of Native American communication: being is replaced by skin as words are replaced by sound. How fitting that the one Native American word appearing in the speeches of Cooper's Native American characters is the "never-failing" exclamation "Hugh!" (262), which seems, from the variety of circumstances in which it is used, to be able to mean almost anything.

How fitting also that in several moving scenes Cooper portrays Native American language as a mode of music:

It is impossible to describe the music of their language [i.e., of the conversation between Chingachgook and Uncas], while thus engaged in laughter and endearments, in such a way as to render it intelligible to those whose ears have never listened to its melody. The compass of their voices, particularly that of the youth, was wonderful; extending from the deepest bass, to tones that were even feminine in softness. The eyes of the father followed the plastic and ingenious movements

¹¹ Carr, *Inventing the Primitive*, discusses "the linkage between the Indian and the feminine" (90). Magua's utterance, of course, links the European and the feminine. In both cases, what is seen as other by race is also seen as other by gender, both by European American males and by Native American ones.

¹² Alexis de Tocqueville, *Democracy in America*, trans. Henry Reeve, rev. Francis Bowen, ed. Phillips Bradley, 2 vols. (New York: Vintage, 1990, copyright Knopf 1945), vol. II, p. 67.

of the son with open delight, and he never failed to smile in reply to the other's contagious, but low laughter. (200)

We know from this passage that father and son are "engaged in laughter and endearments," that "the compass of their voices" is wide, that the father watches the son, that the father smiles in reply to the son's laughter. But what on earth are they saying? Cooper so emphasizes the melody of the conversation as to suggest that the language in which it is conducted has no words.

What it has, and has in abundance, is gesture. Consider a passage from Chapter XIX, a debate between the hero Hawk-eye and his two Mohican companions, Chingachgook and Uncas. The debate is conducted in Delaware, and its subject is whether the three men and their party should continue their journey by land or by water. Hawk-eye argues for the latter, the others for the former. At the beginning of the debate, Hawk-eye is losing, because, Cooper tells us, "he rather affected the cold and inartificial [sic] manner, which characterizes all classes of Anglo-Americans, when unexcited" (199). To win the debate, he has to change his manner. He becomes more animated, adopts "all the arts of native eloquence" (199), and persuades his companions to follow his advice.

European American admiration for "native eloquence" was nothing new; Thomas Jefferson, for example, writing early in the 1780s, had challenged "the whole orations of Demosthenes and Cicero . . . to produce a single passage, superior to the speech of Logan, a Mingo chief."[13] But what Jefferson admired was Logan's power over words. In Cooper, "the arts of native eloquence" turn out to be principally the arts of gesture. The debate is conducted in Delaware, which the listening Heyward does not know; but "the language of the Mohicans," Cooper writes, "was accompanied by gestures so direct and natural, that Heyward had but little difficulty in following the thread of their argument" (198–99). Hawk-eye, on the other hand, is "obscure" (199); that is, he does not make many gestures, so Heyward cannot understand him. When he adopts "the arts of native eloquence," though, his meaning becomes miraculously clear:

Elevating an arm, he pointed out the track of the sun, repeating the gesture for every day that was necessary to accomplish their object. Then he delineated a long and painful path, amid rocks and water courses. The age and weakness of the slumbering and unconscious Munro, were indicated by signs too palpable to

[13] Thomas Jefferson, *Notes on the State of Virginia* (New York: Penguin, 1999), p. 67; see on the case Edward Gray's excellent "The Making of Logan, the Mingo Orator," in Gray and Fiering (eds.), *Language Encounter*.

be mistaken. Duncan perceived that even his own powers were spoken lightly of, as the scout extended his palm, and mentioned him by the appellation of the "open hand;" [sic] a name his liberality had purchased of all the friendly tribes. Then came the representation of the light and graceful movements of a canoe, set in forcible contrast to the tottering steps of one enfeebled and tired. He concluded by pointing to the scalp of the Oneida, and apparently urging the necessity of their departing speedily, and in a manner that should leave no trail.

The Mohicans listened gravely, and with countenances that reflected the sentiments of the speaker. (199)

This is preposterous. It is, for one thing, preposterous to suggest that Native American speakers characteristically accompany speech with gesture – Cooper writes in another place of "those significant gestures with which an Indian *always* illustrates his eloquence" (106; emphasis added) – and that European American speakers characteristically do not. We know perfectly well that all speech is accompanied by gesture. Cooper's sources know this too. Heckewelder makes the point clearly:

It has been asserted by many persons that the languages of the Indians are deficient in words, and that, in order to make themselves understood, they are obliged to resort to motions and signs with their hands. This is entirely a mistake. I do not know a nation of whom foreigners do not say the same things. (128)

Lewis Cass criticized both Heckewelder and Cooper for what he regarded as their too flattering portraits of Indians; but even he knows that Cooper's distinction here is false:

"They number," says one of the speakers in [Cooper's 1827 novel] *The Prairie*, "as many as the fingers of my hand." No Indian from Patagonia to Hudson's Bay ever used this periphrastic expression for the simple word *ten*. It is rather difficult to believe the author can be serious. An Indian will hold up his fingers if apprehensive he cannot be understood, and appeal by significant gestures to the eye; but to those who understand him he will use the proper numeral.[14]

Cooper's distinction between a speech always accompanied by gesture and a speech always devoid of it is his own reductive invention.

Nor in Cooper is Native American speech merely "accompanied" or "illustrated" by gesture; in the passage quoted, and in several others, Native American speech is in fact entirely doubled by gesture, translated by gesture, almost rendered unnecessary by gesture, and Heyward, who understands no Delaware, understands the whole of Hawk-eye's Delaware argument simply by watching the movements of his body. This too is preposterous. What gestures could Hawk-eye possibly be making to "delineate a long and

---

[14] Lewis Cass, "Structure of Indian Languages," *North American Review* 26 (April 1828), pp. 374–75.

painful path, amid rocks and water courses"? What is he doing to represent "the light and graceful movements of a canoe"? He is not Marcel Marceau; he is making the gestures used to accompany speech, not those that mimes use to replace it.

Some comparisons will sharpen the point here. The French language theorist Condillac – Cooper probably had not read him, but his influence was widely diffused – talks at some length about a universal language of gesture. But as Hans Aarsleff points out, the gestures Condillac has in mind, though they "constitute a rudimentary mode of expression and communication . . . do not constitute the language peculiar to man";[15] they can express pain or pleasure, but not, say, "the light and graceful movements of a canoe, set in forcible contrast to the tottering steps of one enfeebled and tired." What is distinctive about Cooper's universal language of gesture is that it is sufficient by itself.

Or compare Cooper's novel with Catharine Sedgwick's *Hope Leslie*, published only a year after it. In Sedgwick's novel too, meaning is sometimes communicated by gesture; when the Native American Magawisca intercedes with her father for her friend Everell Fletcher's life, we read that "Everell had observed, and understood her intercession, for, though her words were uttered in her own tongue, there was no mistaking her significant manner."[16] But what Everell understands is the overall fact of the intercession, not the twists and turns of Magawisca's argument. In Cooper, he would have understood every clause.

Here again Cooper presents Native American languages as something less than European languages, but here what he denies them is not meaning but difficulty, the difficulty inseparable from the study of language. Consider again the Heckewelder–Duponceau correspondence. In that correspondence Duponceau is a student – a gifted polyglot, but ignorant of Delaware. He poses queries to Heckewelder as his teacher:

I find in Zeisberger's Grammar something that I cannot well comprehend. It is the verb "*n'dellauchsi*" which he translates "I live, move about," or "I so live that I move about." Pray, is this the only verb in Delaware language, which signifies "*to live*," and have the Indians no idea of "life," but when connected with "*locomotion*"? (380)

Heckewelder answers, mildly reproving the overquick generalizations of his precocious student:

Surely they have; and I do not see that the contrary follows from Mr. Zeisberger's having chosen this particular verb as an example of the first conjugation. I perceive

[15] Hans Aarsleff, *From Locke to Saussure* (Minneapolis: University of Minnesota Press, 1982), pp. 108–9.
[16] Catharine Maria Sedgwick, *Hope Leslie; Or, Early Times in the Massachusetts*, ed. Mary Kelley (New Brunswick: Rutgers University Press, 1987), p. 75.

you have not yet an adequate idea of the copiousness of the Indian languages, which possess an immense number of comprehensive words, expressive of almost every possible combination of ideas. (383)

The correspondence dramatizes the difficulty of learning a Native American language. In Cooper's scenes of magical translation, learning the language is unnecessary; the language presents no resistance to gestural translation, the gestural translation presents no difficulty to the learner. It is, as Cooper says, "natural," and what that means in practice is that it is not "cultural," and need not be learned.

Cooper's representation of French is quite different. For one thing, it includes an extended *presentation* of French: the French-Canadian names of various characters, but also several conversations in French, for which Cooper provides no translation. These conversations will bewilder unilingual anglophone readers; this reminds us that bewilderment, not magical understanding, is the normal condition of those who listen to a language they do not know. Some of the conversations also dramatize the acquired power to understand and imitate a foreign language that is the mirror image of such bewilderment. The first of them takes place, appropriately enough, in a dense fog, outside Fort William Henry. Hawk-eye and Heyward are trying to guide Colonel Munro's daughters Cora and Alice to their father in the fort, but the fort is surrounded by French troops. One French soldier calls out "Qui vive?" (136). Hawk-eye does not understand, and knows it: "'What says it?' whispered the scout; 'it speaks neither Indian nor English!'" But Heyward speaks fluent French, and successfully presents himself to the French soldier as a French officer who has taken the Munro daughters captive. In a later conversation, still closer to the fort, Heyward tries again to impersonate "un ami de la France" (144); this time he fails, and the party barely escapes. Later Heyward serves as interpreter in a conversation between Munro and the French commander Montcalm. Montcalm flatters Heyward's French and his soldierly character; later, though, Montcalm responds directly to an untranslated remark of Munro's, and we realize that Montcalm's flattery of Heyward's French was intended to conceal his own knowledge of English, which has enabled him to understand supposedly confidential dealings between the two British soldiers. The real use of a language in a multilingual environment entails bewilderment based on ignorance, impersonation based on study. That Cooper knows this in relation to French shows how hard he is working not to know it in relation to Delaware – how hard, that is, he is working to represent as transparent a language that must in fact be opaque.

In this context, a strange fact about Cooper's strategy of representation takes on a preciser meaning. Characters in the novel are described as speaking languages imperfectly; never, though, are they *shown* speaking languages imperfectly. Cooper says of Magua that he pronounced "the Delaware name [Uncas] with even greater difficulty than he spoke his English words." A non-native speaker of both English and Delaware, then. But these are the non-native speaker's ensuing English speeches: "'Bounding elk' is what the white man says when he calls to the young Mohican . . . The deer is swift, but weak; the elk is swift, but strong; and the son of 'le serpent' is 'le cerf agile.' Has he leaped the river to the woods?" (91) No mistakes of diction, idiom, subject–verb agreement, here or anywhere else. Why not?

One might argue that Cooper's reasons are practical: the writer's difficulty in rendering Huron-influenced English, the reader's in making sense of it. Certainly such difficulties would have presented themselves. But Cooper would have tried to overcome them if he had thought them important. In his great multidialectal novel *The Pioneers*, we notice the stiff bookishness of much of what is presented as oral, but we also notice the scrupulous, stubborn care with which Cooper differentiates one character's dialect from another's. John Cage told a wonderful story about a conversation with Arnold Schoenberg:

After I had been studying with him for two years, Schoenberg said, "In order to write music, you must have a feeling for harmony." I explained to him that I had no feeling for harmony. He then said that I would always encounter an obstacle, that it would be as though I came to a wall through which I could not pass. I said, "In that case I shall devote my life to beating my head against that wall."[17]

Cooper was like Cage. So when he decides not to confront a difficulty, we should try to imagine other reasons for his choice than the difficulty itself.

The imperfect speaking of any one language implies the existence of two: the one that's being spoken imperfectly, and the one that's causing the imperfections to take place, and in which the speaker would be competent. George Washington Cable renders the French-influenced English of a New Orleans Creole aristocrat as follows: "Didn' I had to run," asks one such aristocrat in Cable's *The Grandissimes*, "from Bras Coupé in de haidge of de swamp be'ine de 'abitation of my cousin Honoré, one time? You can hask 'oo you like!"[18] "'Abitation" is unidiomatic and non-standardly pronounced; the word the speaker wants but can't find, for translating the

---

[17] John Cage, "Indeterminacy," in *Silence: Lectures and Writings* (Middletown: Wesleyan University Press, 1961), p. 261.
[18] George Washington Cable, *The Grandissimes* (New York: Hill and Wang, 1957), p. 10.

French *habitation*, is "plantation." But getting it wrong in English implies getting it right in French. So does dropping the initial *h*, which is non-standard in English but standard in French. The bad English mirrors good French. That no one in Cooper's novel is shown speaking any language imperfectly means that we're not made in reading it to feel the irreducible fact of a multiplicity of jostling languages in contact, each exerting an influence on the other; and absent that pressure, it is easier to accept the trick by which Cooper so often makes Native American languages disappear.

Cooper's trick here draws on the oldest European tradition for making sense of Native American languages. Christopher Columbus was a polyglot; he knew Italian, Latin, Spanish, and Portuguese. His interpreter Luis de Torres knew Hebrew and Arabic, and by some accounts Chaldaean. None of these languages helped at all in the first encounter with the radically alien languages of the New World. Eric Cheyfitz argues suggestively that this impasse, this irremediable bewilderment, may well have "challenged . . . Columbus's European paradigm of what a language was."[19] In his diary, though, Columbus owns no such anxiety. He concludes his account of the first landing as follows: "I have caused six of [the inhabitants] to be taken on board and sent to your Majesties, that they may learn to speak." Editors and translators have sometimes wrongly amended this to, "that they may learn to speak Spanish." But the Spanish text is clear: *para que deprendan fablar.*[20] To judge from what he writes, Columbus seems not to have thought that the Indians' language was a language at all; depressingly often, Cooper's novel is in accord with him.

Cooper is a novelist as well as an ideologue, and in the end he has to have his Native American characters do something that can count for readers as speaking in Native American languages. So he presents himself as a translator. He introduces Hawk-eye's first speech as being "in the tongue which was known to all the natives who formerly inhabited the country between the Hudson and the Potomack" – that is, Delaware – then adds,

[19] Eric Cheyfitz, *The Poetics of Imperialism: Translation and Colonization from* The Tempest *to* Tarzan (New York: Oxford University Press, 1991), p. 110. Page numbers for subsequent quotations from this work will be given in the text. The passage is worth quoting at length: "Perhaps what is troubling Columbus throughout his journal is not the question of whether the Indians possess a language, but the question of whether he possesses one, that is, the question of what a language is. For having voyaged from a place of comfortably recognizable languages to a place of radically unrecognizable ones, which, yet, no matter how far-fetched in appearance were still recognizable as language, Columbus's European paradigm of what a language was, and hence of what a human was, must have been challenged."

[20] Oliver Dunn and James E. Kelley, Jr. (eds. and trans.), *The* Diario *of Christopher Columbus's First Voyage to America, 1492–1493, Abstracted by Fray Bartolomé de las Casas* (Norman: University of Oklahoma Press, 1989), p. 68.

"we shall a give a free translation [of it] for the benefit of the readers; endeavouring, at the same time, to preserve some of the peculiarities, both of the individual and of the language" (30). Critics sometimes point out how fraudulent this claim is, given Cooper's ignorance of the "tongue" in question. It is indeed fraudulent. But it is also highly significant.

The novel provides three kinds of quoted speech: that identified as being spoken in a Native American language, that spoken by Native Americans in an English said to be affected by their native language, and that spoken in "foreigner talk," the mode of speech used by native speakers of English when they try, in speaking with a Native American, to adapt their English to the presumptive character of Delaware and Huron.

Most of the traits of this corpus are conventional, observable not only in Cooper but also in his novelist contemporaries, in his novelist successors, in twentieth-century films and comic books. Native American language by these conventions is relatively simple in syntax. It consists mostly of independent declarative clauses and questions. Hypotaxis is less common than parataxis. The most common rhetorical figures are those of repetition and parallelism. Diction is concrete. Abstract and technical terms are rare. Metaphors are abundant, and most of them refer to nature; "the Indian," as Cooper tells us in the Introduction he added to the novel in 1831, "draws his metaphors from the clouds, the seasons, the birds, the beasts, and the vegetable world" (5).

As is no doubt clear by now, these traits have nothing to do with actual Delaware or Huron, and Cooper knew that or easily could have. Sometimes Cooper makes linguistic traits up from scratch, for example, syntactic simplicity. (The Heckewelder–Duponceau correspondence does not provide an extended corpus of Delaware speech, so we cannot really know from it what sorts of sentences Delaware speakers prefer, or for that matter whether they prefer any one sort to another, or vary in this regard much as speakers of English do.) Sometimes Cooper simply dismisses what is not in accord with his views, for example, the range of actual vocabulary. Zeisberger's *Indian Dictionary*, for example, which was one of Heckewelder's sources, juxtaposes concrete terms like "snake" and "snow" with abstract ones like "society, company" and "soft" and "triangular."[21] Cooper also dismisses the morphological complexity Heckewelder and Duponceau celebrate – for example, "in the verb '*to see*,' the same distinction is made between things animate and inanimate. *Newau*, 'I see,'

---

[21] David Zeisberger, *Zeisberger's Indian Dictionary: English, German, Iroquois – the Onondaga and Algonquin – the Delaware* (Cambridge, MA: John Wilson & Son University Press, 1887), pp. 177 and 204.

applies only to the former, and *nemen* to the latter" (423). And of course he excludes from consideration the suggestions of complexity conveyed by the language as transcribed – for example, "Ki Wetóchemelenk talli épian Awosságame" (424; "Thou/our-Father/there/dwelling/beyond-the-clouds," Heckewelder's translation of the beginning of the Lord's Prayer).[22]

That said – and it's important to have it said, and to keep reminding oneself of its truth, of the fact that Cooper's "verbal transposition" of English to make it, he says, resemble Delaware has nothing, absolutely nothing, to do with Delaware as spoken – what Cooper is doing is of great interest, and the traits of his invented Delaware have important meanings. They allow two readings. In one, they distinguish a natural and poetic language from languages seen as decadent and artificial. Thus Hugh Blair, whose lectures on rhetoric were, as Helen Carr writes, "the single most popular work of literary criticism in the States from the time of their publication until the mid-nineteenth century" (64), writes that

the character of the American and Indian languages [is] bold, picturesque, and metaphorical; full of strong allusions to sensible qualities, and to such objects as struck them most in their wild and solitary life. An Indian chief makes an harangue to his tribe, in a style full of stronger metaphors than an European would use in an epic poem. (Carr, *Inventing the Primitive* 63)

Dennis W. Allen, arguing that "Indian language [in Cooper] is closer to nature than white speech, and its proximity to the incarnation of value renders it purer than white language," and Steven Blakemore, calling that language "a natural language, in organic contact with the images of nature," are simply echoing Blair's point.[23]

But this reading ignores politics. In Cooper's political context, the meaning of these linguistic traits is that Native American languages are primitive, bearing the same relation to European languages that savagism does to civilization. European American writers on Native American metaphor, for example, understand it in two ways. Sometimes they attribute it to barbaric bad taste. Heckewelder in one of his more conventional moments treats it as analogous to the taste for baubles: "[metaphors] are to [Delawares'] discourse what feathers and beads are to their persons, a gaudy but tasteless ornament" (137). He admits that "even in enlightened Europe, many centuries have not elapsed since the best and most celebrated writers employed this figure in a profuse manner," and cites as an example "the immortal Shakspeare" (137). In doing that, he places metaphor at a safe distance, far

---

[22] Heckewelder does speak of a Delaware fondness for metaphor; see below, pp. 34–35.
[23] Allen, "'By All the Truth of Signs,'" p. 174; Blakemore, "Strange Tongues," p. 27.

from the good taste of the cultured present moment; but at least he makes it a trait of culture rather than nature, and finds analogies to it in European practice.

The other and commoner notion attributes Native American metaphor to linguistic impoverishment. Blair himself writes that "all Languages are most figurative in their early state . . . Language is then most barren; the stock of proper names which have been invented for things is small." Amos Stoddard writes in 1805 that "[Native American] language is barren; and hence they are obliged to resort to metaphor, or to use much circumlocution in the expression of their sentiments." In one view, Native American languages are flawed by excess, in the other by deficiency; in both, these languages are conceived as immature forms of the European languages they must inevitably develop into.[24]

All these traits are conventional. Less so is Cooper's suppression of the first and second grammatical persons, his tendency, in constructing Native American speech, to put personal names and epithets and third-person pronouns where we would expect first- and second-person pronouns and possessive adjectives, and his corresponding tendency to put third-person verbs where we would expect first- and second-person ones.

"Uncas is here!" said another voice, in the same soft, guttural tones, near [Hawk-eye's] elbow; "who speaks to Uncas?" (33)

The "other voice" is the voice of Uncas himself, twice referring to himself in the third person. Over the course of the novel we see this trait a lot, not only in the representation of Native American speech, but also in the representation of Native Americans speaking English and French, and sometimes in the representation of European Americans speaking English and French foreigner talk to Native Americans. Consider a characteristic conversation between Magua, also called le Renard Subtil, and Duncan Heyward. They are talking about Hawk-eye, whom Duncan and his party have recently encountered in the woods; Magua wants to know whether Hawk-eye is alone. At first, Heyward makes ordinary use of the first and second persons, while Magua restricts himself to the third.

"Alone!" hesitatingly answered Heyward, to whom deception was too new to be assumed without embarrassment. "Oh! not alone, surely, Magua, for *you* know that *we* are with him."

---

[24] Blair quoted in Carr, *Inventing the Primitive*, p. 63; Stoddard quoted in Sheehan, *Seeds of Extinction*, p. 108.

"Then *le Renard Subtil* will go," returned the runner, coolly raising his little wallet from the place where it had lain at his feet; "and *the pale faces* will see none but *their* own colour."

"Go! Whom call *you* le Renard?"

" 'Tis the name *his* Canada fathers have given to *Magua*," returned the runner, with an air that manifested his pride at the distinction. "Night is the same as day to *le Subtil*, when Munro waits for *him*." (41; emphasis added)

But then Heyward gets used to Native American discourse, and begins to imitate Magua in this respect:

"And what account will *le Renard* give the chief of William Henry concerning his daughters? will *he* dare to tell the hot-blooded Scotsman that his children are left without a guide, though *Magua* promised to be one?"

"Though the gray head has a loud voice, and a long arm, *le Renard* will not hear him or feel him in the woods." (41–42; emphasis added)

The conversation concludes with a beautifully economical dramatization of the distinction:

"What say you, Renard?"

"*Le Subtil* says it is good." (42; emphasis added)

None of Cooper's predecessors or contemporaries has anything much like this. We find it neither in European theories of the beginnings of language, such as Rousseau's; nor in European dramatizations of Native American languages, such as Chateaubriand's; nor in representations of Gaelic speech in Ossian or Scott; nor in Heckewelder's occasional representations of Delaware speech; nor in nineteenth-century European American accounts of Native American languages.

We do find it occasionally in Lydia Maria Child's 1824 novel *Hobomok*, and Child's handling of the trait can sharpen our sense of Cooper's. We first see the Native American Hobomok in conversation with Mary Conant; he surprises her, she jumps, and he asks, "What for makes you afraid of Hobomok?" Explaining his presence, he says, "Hobomok much late has been out to watch the deer tracks"; at the end of the scene, performing a magical rite, he mutters, "three times much winnit Abbamocho [Child glosses this as "very good devil," i.e., successful prophet or priest] said; three times me do".[25] Child thus presents Hobomok as speaking a very limited English (at one point she shows him unable to remember the word "candle"); and because this is the case, we have to read his use of "Hobomok"

---

[25] Lydia Maria Child, *Hobomok and Other Writings on Indians*, ed. Carolyn L. Karcher (New Brunswick: Rutgers University Press, 1986), p. 14.

in place of "me" or "I" as reflecting his inability to use what linguists call shifters. Small children's language, and the language adults use to speak with small children, have this feature also – for example, "Daddy does not want Lili to throw her food on the floor."[26]

Now in Cooper, this avoidance of the first and second person is not associated with other flawed constructions. Moreover, as noted, it occurs even when the characters are said to be speaking Native American languages, as in the utterance of Uncas quoted above. So it cannot be read as reflecting an imperfect knowledge of English. What then does it mean?

The association with imperfectly spoken English and with children's language patterns has some effect on how we respond to the trait; we cannot help finding it childish. What probably has more effect is the deep nature of the pronouns that Magua is not using. The French linguist Émile Benveniste has shown that first- and second-person pronouns differ radically from third-person ones. Third-person pronouns are references to nouns. First- and second-person pronouns are markers of position in discourse. "I," for example, refers not to a particular entity but to the person who happens to be speaking or writing at the moment at which the word is used; "you" refers to the person that "I" happens to be addressing. "Moi," says Benveniste,

is the momentary proper name of any speaker, a self-reference in discourse, an antonym [i.e., etymologically, a name (*onymos*) in place of something (*anti*)]; *Pierre* is the permanent proper name of an individual, an objective reference in society, an anthroponym. [An utterance like "MOI, *Pierre*"] defines the subject simultaneously by its contingent situation of speaking and by its distinctive individuality in the community.[27]

For Benveniste, first- and second-person pronouns are inextricably linked to "discourse," to conversation; third-person pronouns are linked to history, to narration. Benveniste claims in fact that the possibility for subjectivity in language, the possibility of being a subject, is inextricable from the deictic gestures made by competent users of "I."

Consider in this connection the real people who talk like Magua. Mostly they are celebrity politicians or celebrity athletes, fixed in public positions and almost incapable of becoming private subjects. "Bill Clinton will keep

---

[26] For more on this see www.linguistlist.org/issues/8/8-209.html#1, a summary of responses from the LINGUIST list to a query I posed on the subject.

[27] Émile Benveniste, "L'Antonyme et le pronom en français moderne," in *Problèmes de linguistique générale*, 2 vols. (Paris: Gallimard, 1974), vol. II, p. 201 (my translation). See also his "La nature des pronoms" and "De la subjectivité dans le langage," in *Problèmes de linguistique générale*, 2 vols. (Paris: Gallimard, 1966), vol. I, pp. 251–57 and 258–66.

his campaign promises," Bill Clinton might say; but we would wonder what his private and subjective self was saying. "Michael Jordan will be playing to win today," Michael Jordan might say; but what is he feeling when he has to start a sentence with "I?" The morning after the New Hampshire Republican primary of 1996, the second-place finisher said something more complicated: "anyone who knows Bob Dole knows that I'm a fighter." When Dole referred to himself as "Bob Dole," he was referring to an object, an abstract and public character, an accumulation of visible history from which character emerges. But when he said, "I'm a fighter," he became a subject; he was saying something that no one else could have said for him.[28]

But we know that our celebrities have private selves; we know that this is one of their modes of speech rather than their only mode. We do not know this about Cooper's Native Americans. And given all the other ways in which the speech of Native Americans is truncated, there is no reason to presume that they have both a private and a public mode of speech, no reason to presume that Cooper's Native Americans add to their "distinctive individuality in the community" the variable and fluid identity that arises from the "contingent situation of speaking," and which is a necessary component of a complex identity. They are trapped in poses of public majesty. Magua wants Cora Munro for his wife, and there is much horror in the novel at this prospect. Most of it is connected with a horror of miscegenation, some of it with the fearful threats Magua makes to avenge on Cora's body the insults done to him by the British. But some of it may also have to do with the terrifying difficulty of imagining Magua in a private space, a man speaking and being spoken to by his family.

To sum up, then: most of the time, in this novel, Cooper associates Native American languages with vocal sound, with music, and with intricate yet universally comprehensible gesture. He makes them vigorous in diction, uncluttered in syntax, rich in metaphor, idiosyncratic in grammar, full of public majesty. He makes them fascinating; but he also makes them something less than European languages, and their speakers less than adult members of a complex culture. A diverse collection of traits, but all of them in accord with the idea of savagism and the project of Indian Removal.

We know how often writers write against their own intentions, but it is still surprising to see how brilliantly Cooper contradicts himself in two scenes towards the end of his novel. Both are centered on the doomed

---

[28] I have left the names unchanged from an earlier version of this essay; it would be easy enough to provide more up-to-date ones, things not having changed much in this regard.

Uncas, and in both Cooper represents Native American languages as verbally complex, culturally specific, and resistant to translation.

The first of them is the account of Uncas's "war-song," the chant he makes and performs to prepare himself for what will be his final battle. This is how Cooper presents it:

If it were possible to translate the comprehensive and melodious language in which he spoke, the ode might read something like the following:

> Manitto! Manitto! Manitto!
> Thou art great – thou art good – thou art wise –
> Manitto! Manitto!
> Thou art just!
>
> In the heavens, in the clouds, Oh! I see!
> Many spots – many dark – many red –
> In the heavens, Oh! I see!
> Many clouds.
>
> In the heavens, in the clouds, Oh! I see!
> The whoop, the long yell, and the cry –
> In the woods, Oh! I hear!
> The loud whoop!
>
> Manitto! Manitto! Manitto!
> I am weak – thou art strong – I am slow –
> Manitto! Manitto!
> Give me aid.   (319)

Everything has been turned on its head. First, Cooper calls Native American language not only "melodious" but also "comprehensive"; it has not only sound and music but also sense. Probably the principal sense of "comprehensive" is "containing much in small compass, compendious"; but present also is "characterized by mental comprehension . . . that grasps or understands (a thing) fully" (OED). And a comprehensive language cannot communicate without being comprehended; elsewhere in the novel, Cooper would have written that "though the words were unknown to the listeners, nothing could have been clearer than the martial spirit and valiant nobility of the speaker," but here that topos is not in force, and translation is both necessary and difficult.

Cooper's actual "translation" – he was of course making up Uncas's song, not translating a Delaware original – makes that necessity and difficulty clear. Consider, by way of comparison, a celebrated translation made by Cooper's contemporary Henry Rowe Schoolcraft, a recognized European American authority on Native American life. In his 1845 *Oneota*, he presents as an example of Native American poetry the Ojibwa "Chant to the Fire-Fly."[29] He describes it as follows: "metre there was none, at least, of a regular character: [the lines were] the wild improvisations of children in a merry mood" (61). He then presents a transcription of the poem, what he calls a "literal" translation of it, and, in a footnote, a verse translation:

Wau wau tay see!
Wau wau tay see!
E mow e shin
Tshe bwau ne baun-e wee!
Be eghaun–be eghaun–ewee!
Wau wau tay see!
Wau wau tay see!
Was sa koon ain je gun
Was sa koon ain je gun.

Flitting-white-fire-insect! Waving-white-fire-bug! give me light before I go to bed! give me light before I go to sleep. Come little dancing-white-fire-bug! Come little flitting-white-fire-beast! Light me with your bright white-flame-instrument – your little candle.

Fire-fly, fire-fly! bright little thing,
Light me to bed, and my song I will sing.
Give me your light, as you fly o'er my head,
That I may merrily go to my bed.
Give me your light o'er the grass as you creep,
That I may joyfully go to my sleep.
Come little fire-fly – come little beast –
Come! And I'll make you to-morrow a feast.
Come little candle that flies as I sing,
Bright little fairy-bug – night's little king;
Come, and I'll dance as you guide me along,
Come, and I'll pay you, my bug, with a song.

The transcription and "literal" translation, together with some explanatory notes, present the poem as a complex artifact. The transcription reveals

---

[29] Henry Rowe Schoolcraft, *Oneota, or Characteristics of the Red Race of America* (New York: Wiley and Putnam, 1845), p. 61.

   See on this celebrated example John Greenway, *Literature among the Primitives* (Hatboro, PA: Folklore Associates, 1964); Dell Hymes, "Some North Pacific Coast Poems: A Problem in Anthropological Philology," in *'In vain I tried to tell you': Essays in Native American Ethnopoetics* (Philadelphia: University of Pennsylvania Press, 1981; page numbers for subsequent quotations from this essay will be given in the text); and Arnold Krupat, "On the Translation of Native American Song and Story: A Theorized History," in Brian Swann (ed.), *On the Translation of Native American Literatures* (Washington, DC: Smithsonian Institution Press, 1992), pp. 3–32.

unfamiliar but evidently ordered sound patterns, the translation unfamiliar but intelligible ways of naming. But Schoolcraft hides these truths. For one thing, even before we get a look at the poem he has told us that it has no regular meter, that it is "wild," that is, not cultured or disciplined; we are being discouraged from seeing the intricate formal patterning that the transcription reveals. For another, even his "literal" translation blurs the formal order evident in the transcription; for instance, lines 1–2 and 6–7 are identical in the transcription but different in the translation. Schoolcraft's explanatory notes defend this; but the effect of the blurring is still to say that the evident formal order of the poem does not matter.

The inept verse translation goes further in that direction. It substitutes regular meter for irregular, and familiar sound patterns and ways of naming for unfamiliar ones; its implicit argument is that if the Ojibwa chant is a poem, it is a poem of a familiar English sort. Moreover, the verse translation has material that the transcription and literal translation do not; the only "complete" version, that is, is the verse translation – which suggests that the chant is either an English poem or no poem at all.

Cooper's "translation" suggests a different vision. It is, if not great poetry, at least unfamiliar poetry. The lines of unrhymed anapests, the unashamed repetition of the divinity's name, the recurring numerical structures (the first two lines of each quatrain comprise three sense-units, the third two, the fourth one), the complex syntax of the second quatrain all suggest what Cooper elsewhere seems to deny: that Native American languages have complex, artificial, and unfamiliar structures and require complex, artful, and unfamiliar translations. The makers of such poems are not identical to white makers of poems; they are not undeveloped versions of such makers; they are adult, artful, social, and different.

Cooper here is in line with the best of his contemporaries – with, for example, Heckewelder's translation of "The Song of the Lenape Warriors Going Against the Enemy":

> O poor me!
> Who am going out to fight the enemy,
> And know not whether I shall return again,
> To enjoy the embraces of my children
> And my wife.
> O poor creature!
> Whose life is not in his own hands,
> Who has no power over his own body,
> But tried to do his duty
> For the welfare of his nation.   (211)

Both anticipate some of the best anthropological translators of our own time. Dell Hymes, for example, has reshaped the translation of Native American poetry and storytelling through his passionate attention to "the structure of the original poem." By structure he means "particularly the form of repetition and variation, of constants and contrasts, in verbal organization" (42); and his re-translation of the firefly song, animated by his concern with such matters, is more Cooper's sort of text, or Heckewelder's, than it is Schoolcraft's:

> Flitting insect of white fire!
> Flitting insect of white fire!
> Come, give me light before I sleep!
> Come, give me light before I sleep!
> Flitting insect of white fire!
> Flitting insect of white fire!
> Light me with your bright white instrument of flame.
> Light me with your bright white instrument of flame.   (41)

Hymes's concern with structure has been complemented by Dennis Tedlock's concern with performance, with the circumstances in which poems are enacted and the theatrical and rhythmical details of the enactment. Here, for example, is Tedlock on "voice quality in Zuni narratives":

When a character is trying to pull some tough blades loose from a yucca plant, the narrator may render "He pulled" with the strain of someone who is trying to speak while holding his breath during great exertion. When a passage involves intense emotion, the narrator may combine . . . softness . . . with a break in his voice, as if he felt like weeping.[30]

Cooper, going further here than Heckewelder, follows the text of Uncas's song with this Tedlock-like commentary on its performance:

At the end of what might be called each verse, he made a pause, by raising a note louder and longer than common, that was peculiarly suited to the sentiment just expressed. The first close was solemn, and intended to convey the idea of veneration; the second descriptive, bordering on the alarming; and the third was the well-known and terrific war-whoop, which burst from the lips of the young warrior, like a combination of all the frightful sounds of battle. The last was like the first, humble and imploring. Three times did he repeat this song, and as often did he encircle the post, in his dance. (319–20)

Cooper's account of performance takes its meaning from being joined to an account of the text performed. By itself, as noted earlier, an account of

---

[30] Dennis Tedlock, *The Spoken Word and the Work of Interpretation* (Philadelphia: University of Pennsylvania Press, 1983), p. 47.

performance can reduce language to music or gesture. Joined to an account of text, it becomes the thick description of a speech-act. Uncas's tones and gestures do not have to do all the work here; they are illustrating the texts they accompany, not, as in Hawk-eye's earlier speech, replacing them.

The other important scene here is Uncas's funeral. Some Delaware "girls" sing a dirge for the dead warrior; Hawk-eye, Heyward, and Colonel Munro sit and listen.

The scout, to whom alone, of all the white men, the words were intelligible, suffered himself to be a little aroused from his meditative posture, and bent his face aside, to catch their meaning, as the girls proceeded. But when they spoke of the future prospects of Cora and Uncas, he shook his head, like one who knew the error of their simple creed, and resuming his reclining attitude, he maintained it until the ceremony . . . was finished. Happily for the self-command of both Heyward and Munro, they knew not the meaning of the wild sounds they heard. (344)

Here, if anywhere, one would think that meaning might be expressed by gesture and communicated across language barriers. But Cooper says just the reverse. The words are "intelligible" only to Hawk-eye; and even Hawk-eye has to "bend his face aside, to catch their meaning," on what may be the only occasion in the novel when Cooper dramatizes a native speaker's difficulty in understanding a Native American utterance.

"Wild" is changing meaning. It is a stock adjective for describing Native American culture; ordinarily it means "savage," and is the antonym of "ordered in a civilized way." That is what it means in the Schoolcraft passage discussed above. But in Cooper's sentence, when the sounds of the dirge are called "wild," their being called that is associated only with Heyward and Munro, not with Hawk-eye. This suggests that "wild" here means something like "incomprehensible." Heyward and Munro find the sounds "wild" because they know no Delaware. "Wild" is on the way to losing its Eurocentric political charge. Every sound can be wild for the hearer who does not understand it, and every sound can cease to be wild for the hearer who does. "Wild" in this sense is an epitome of cultural relativism.

Colonel Munro then asks Hawk-eye to do some translating for him; he wants to tell the Delaware women that in the world to come, all may assemble around God's throne "without distinction of sex, or rank, or colour" (347). But Hawk-eye declines:

"To tell them this," he said, "would be to tell them that the snows come not in the winter, or that the sun shines fiercest when the trees are stripped of their leaves!"

Then turning to the women, he made such a communication of the other's gratitude, as he deemed most suited to the capacities of his listeners. (347)

Why is Hawk-eye refusing to translate Colonel Munro's message? Because he himself does not think that it is true? Because the Delaware women will hold that view? The narrative sentence after Hawk-eye's speech argues for the second alternative; otherwise Cooper might have written, "he made such a communication . . . as he deemed most suited to the facts." The probable meaning of Hawk-eye's speech is something like this: "what you're asking me to tell them, they won't believe; so I'll tell them something they will."

The problem with Hawk-eye's decision is that it keeps translation from being what it often has been, namely, a way of bringing something new into the community of the target language. Hawk-eye's translation leaves everyone's "capacities" intact. But that is precisely why Cooper's scene is so revelatory: it *dramatizes* Hawk-eye's bad translation. Eric Cheyfitz has written, "our imperialism historically has functioned (and continues to function) by substituting for the difficult politics of translation another politics of translation that represses these difficulties" (xvi). Cooper is doing just the opposite. We see what Hawk-eye is doing, and at the moment when we say to ourselves, "wait a minute, why doesn't he just translate Colonel Munro's message?", we imagine, even without wanting to, the need for a faithful translation, and its possible cultural consequences. What would happen, we're led to wonder, if Hawk-eye just did the translator's job? Would the women regard the Colonel as a fool? A hypocrite? What set of attitudes would they bring to evaluating the remark? What effect might the remark have on those attitudes, offered as it is at this moment of vulnerability? Dramatizing bad translation opens up the multicultural world.

We ought not to make too much of these late scenes. They are not revolutionary. They do not make a case against Indian Removal in the way that *Uncle Tom's Cabin* makes a case against slavery. They are the exception rather than the rule. They come at the end of the book, under the shadow of Uncas's death and of the extinction of the Mohican line asserted in the book's title, and their placement affects their meaning; Cooper seems able to recognize his Native American characters' linguistic maturity only when they are doomed or dead, and such a recognition cannot have any present political meaning. Just so, perhaps, do Benjamin Whorf's celebrated arguments in the 1920s for the linguistic excellence of Hopi and Navajo follow, rather than avert, the capture of Geronimo in 1886, and the end for a while of significant Native American political resistance to American control.

But it would be arrogant to dismiss these scenes altogether. If they did not teach readers to resist Indian Removal, they at least encouraged them to doubt the idea of savagism. Cooper's account of Uncas's war-song raises the questions we would ask about any complex linguistic performance: What are the formal patterns and conventions of such songs? Where and how has Uncas learned them? Raising these questions helps readers see how Cooper's novel, in its truncated representation of Native American linguistic performance, has made it impossible to answer them. Reading the account of Hawk-eye's bad translation can make readers skeptical of all translations. What else, they may wonder, has Hawk-eye gotten wrong? What distortions might characterize the "translations" of Delaware utterances that Cooper has been offering them throughout the novel? By asking these questions, readers are at least led to Duponceau's noble and productive uncertainty: "What a subject for reflection, and how little do we know, as yet, of the astonishing things that the world contains!" (405).

EPILOGUE: POLYGLOTS AS JEKYLL, POLYGLOTS AS HYDE

Christopher Columbus dealt at first with the problem of interlingual communication by denying his interlocutors had a language. Hernán Cortés dealt with it by using two interpreters. One was Jerónimo de Aguilar, a Spaniard who had been shipwrecked in Yucatán in 1511, and there had learned to speak Mayan by the time that Cortés ransomed him, eight years later. The other was La Malinche, also called Doña Marina,[31] a native of the Gulf Coast who spoke both Mayan and Nahuatl, the language of the Aztecs, and is said to have joined Cortés's expedition not only as his translator but also as his mistress.

Aguilar is mostly forgotten, but Doña Marina became famous. Images of her are to be found in early paintings, in the illustrations for Bernardino de Sahagún's *Florentine Codex*, and "in murals, on calendars, in comic books" (2). She is associated with snakes and volcanoes. For Octavio Paz, she is the symbol of the Conquest: "Doña Marina becomes a figure representing the Indian women who were fascinated, violated or seduced by the Spaniards... This explains the success of the contemptuous adjective *malinchista* recently put into circulation by the newspapers to denounce all those who have been corrupted by foreign influences."[32] She is identified with La Llorona,

---

[31] Karttunen, *Between Worlds*, pp. 5–6 and 321, explains the names as follows: in 1519, the woman in question, who may or may not have been previously called "Malinalli," was baptized as "Marina." "Doña" is an honorific. In the ears and on the tongues of Nahuatl speakers, "Marina" became "Malina," then "Malintzin," with "tzin" as an honorific corresponding to "Doña." In the ears and on the tongues of Spanish-speakers, "Malintzin" became "Malinche." Page numbers for subsequent quotations from Karttunen's wonderful account of this woman will be given in the text.

[32] Octavio Paz, *The Labyrinth of Solitude*, trans. Lysander Kemp (New York: Grove, 1962), p. 86.

"a ghost in the form of a beautiful woman who leads men to death in dark out-of-the-way places and is heard weeping loudly in the night" (2).

But she is also, Karttunen notes,

indigenous intelligence personified, the equal of the great Cortés, the person without whom he would have been led into a trap and defeated. Hers is indigenous beauty that captivated the European conqueror. In folklore about Iztaccihuatl, she goes to sleep rather than submit to being married, and as long as she sleeps, she protects her people. (3)

She was an exceptional woman in a world that offered such women few opportunities. Her own mother gave her to a neighboring people, who gave her to the Chontal Maya, who gave her to Cortés. She made a place for herself by being a virtuoso of interpretation, reliable and multi-talented. She was skilled in languages, the Mayan and Nahuatl she started with, and the Spanish she learned later; she was skilled also in modes of rhetoric, from Cortés's adroit bluntness to Montezuma's high diplomatic circumlocution. The Spanish chronicler Bernal Díaz del Castillo tells us that when, on a journey with Cortés, she had occasion to speak with her mother and half-brother, she told them that

God had been very gracious to her in freeing her from the worship of idols and making her a Christian, and letting her bear a son to her lord and master Cortés and in marrying her to such a gentleman as Juan Jaramillo, who was now her husband. That she would rather serve her husband and Cortés than anything else in the world, and would not exchange her place to be Cacica [ruler] of all the provinces in New Spain.[33]

We cannot help being skeptical about this; but given the alternatives her reported speech identifies, is her preference impossible?

Whatever its meaning, the story of La Malinche is a story about a translator, a polyglot. It evokes our fears – and our hopes – of what translators can do to us and to themselves. It is the founding American story for thinking what it means to be, in Karttunen's beautiful phrase, "between worlds," the first in a long series of American stories on the ambivalent figure of the interpreter.

Cooper's novel is one such story, though in some ways a simpler one. Cooper cannot, it seems, bear the unresolvable ambiguity we see in La Malinche's story, the interpreter who is both traitor and guardian. Instead

---

[33] Quoted in Karttunen, *Between Worlds*, p. 18. For a complex analysis of Bernal's account of La Malinche, see Margo Glantz, "Doña Marina and Captain Malinche," in Doris Sommer (ed.), *Bilingual Games: Some Literary Investigations* (New York: Palgrave Macmillan, 2003), pp. 149–61.

he splits the figure in two. He gives Hawk-eye every good trait that an interpreter might have. Pure White as he is, "a man without a cross," he is an exemplary bilingual, natively fluent in English and Delaware, solidly reliable, trustworthy. (He does refuse to translate Colonel Munro's message for the Delaware mourners, but even there he states his refusal candidly.) He has, as Cooper presents him to us, a generous, critical, and expert understanding of both speech communities he belongs to, is as sharp a critic of White practices as of Red. But he is, as interpreters are asked to be, a servant and not a revolutionary. Chingachgook is his closest friend, but Hawk-eye defers to the European prejudice against intermarriage. He will mourn, but not obstruct, the increasingly oppressive dominion of one community over the other. He is trusted by everyone, but changes nothing. We might want him to be different in this respect; for Cooper, though, these limitations are marks of wisdom and self-knowledge.

Magua is Hawk-eye's nightmarish mirror image, La Malinche as Mr. Hyde. Like Hawk-eye he is a polyglot (by adult study, not by childhood rearing), fluent without apparent limitation of expressive power in his own Huron, in Delaware, in French, and in English. No other character in the book can match him. By his linguistic gifts, he makes himself a place among the French, the English, the Delawares; then he betrays them all. He has no complexly multicultural perspective. He has no cultural perspective at all. He is both more and less terrifying than La Malinche; less, because his ambitions are less grand, less political, more personal; more, because there is, it would seem, no group he belongs to, or has assimilated to, to which he will remain faithful. His gifts are used for power, for victory, for destruction, for the infliction of pain. He betrays Heyward and his party at the beginning of the book; later he sets in motion the massacre of Fort William Henry, kidnaps Cora Munro, demands that she become one of his wives, threatens to beat her whenever he wants vengeance for the abuse he himself has suffered at the hands of the Whites.

What is a polyglot? In La Malinche's case, a traitor, a woman of power, a ghost. In Hawk-eye's case, a clear-sighted but faithful servant of empire. In Magua's case, a monster.

CHAPTER 2

Alfred Mercier, George W. Cable, and Louisiana French Creole

Enter even briefly the domain of creole studies, and one becomes aware of numerous passionate disputes. How should creole languages be written? Do they constitute a distinct class on linguistic grounds and not only on social and historical ones? What roles are played in their development by the native languages of the speakers developing them? Are their grammars simple or complex? Is African-American English a creole or not?

The disputes matter, the stakes in them are high. But beyond them and before them there is also a clear, tragic, and heroic truth. Creoles have often been created by slaves, and slaves have created them because they have been ripped away from their original language communities, thrown together with other slaves ripped from other communities, robbed not only of liberty but also of the use of their own language, made infantile or mute. "I had no person to speak to that I could understand," wrote Olaudah Equiano,[1] and spoke for many. Then, in that anguished and oppressed state, slaves forged new languages, cobbling them together from the versions and bits of their slave-masters' languages they had access to, from their own languages, from necessary and playful linguistic invention, from their deep human need to communicate. Creoles created by slaves bear witness both to the crime and practice of slavery and to the almost inexhaustible, untamable power of the linguistic imagination. "Creole," write Jean Bernabé, Patrick Chamoiseau, and Raphaël Confiant in *Éloge de la créolité*, "is the original bearer of our deep self, our collective unconscious, our people's genius; and the language remains the river of our alluvial creoleness."[2]

Writers of literature who undertake to represent these languages face a formidable challenge but draw on a rich resource. There is so much risk: condescension, ignorance, inexactness, sentimentality, oversimplification,

---

[1] Olaudah Equiano, "The Life of Olaudah Equiano, or Gustavus Vassa, the African, Written by Himself," in Arna Bontemps (ed.), *Great Slave Narratives* (Boston: Beacon Press, 1969), p. 34.

[2] Jean Bernabé, Patrick Chamoiseau, and Raphaël Confiant, *Éloge de la créolité* (Paris: Gallimard, 1993), p. 43. My translation, as are all translations in this chapter not otherwise attributed.

mistranslation, cultish admiration. There is also so much of interest in the languages, the human dramas they emerge from, the richness of imagination they reflect, their ingenious and economical fusing of diverse materials into a single, sufficient expressive instrument. When a great writer attends to a creole, great things can happen – for example, to take two writers dealing with different creoles in different ways, Chamoiseau's *Texaco* everywhere and Derek Walcott's *Omeros* in some of its most beautiful passages:

> And this was the hymn that Achille could not utter:
> *"merci, Bon Dieu, pour la mer-a, merci la Vierge"* –
> "Thank God for the sea who is his Virgin Mother";
>   *"Qui ba moin force moin"* – "Who gave me the privilege
> of working for Him. Every bird is my brother";
> *"Toutes gibiers c'est frères moin', pis n'homme ni pour travail"* –
> "Because man must work like the birds until he die."[3]

Among the nineteenth-century writers of Louisiana, Alfred Mercier was the best in French, George W. Cable the best in English, and one reason for their eminence was precisely their willingness to deal with Louisiana French Creole. They had different and unequal gifts, different backgrounds, different strategies of linguistic representation: Mercier the hedgehog, holding steadfastly to the single practice of direct representation, a transcriber and sociolinguist, soberly telling lurid stories; Cable the fox, varied and supple, quoting and paraphrasing and commenting and insinuating, polyphonic and self-contradictory. But they had in common a stubborn, undogmatic willingness to do the hard work of representation, and their successes in that work, imperfect and intermixed with failures as they were, distinguish their writing from that of their contemporaries.

This chapter consists of two prefatory notes, a reading of Mercier, a reading of Cable, and a brief assessment of the two writers together, weighing their merits as portraitists of language in general and Louisiana French Creole in particular. At the outset, the chief point to make about the two writers is that we need them both; the linguistic scene they sought to portray was dizzyingly complex, a multilingual carnival but also a set of linked, tense language dramas, with French and English competing for mastery and Louisiana French Creole coming into being, finding an identity, being manipulated to serve conflicting political purposes, somehow surviving and flourishing.

---

[3] Derek Walcott, *Omeros* (New York: Farrar Straus and Giroux, 1990), p. 160.

TWO NOTES

(1) The word "Creole" will turn up a lot in this chapter, and in multiple meanings: a language, a language type, a geographical origin, an ethnic ancestry, a mixture of Black and White, a Whiteness unmixed with Blackness. It is not practical to use the word in only one of its meanings, so it is important to state the principal meanings and how they are related.

Comidas chinas y criollas, the name for the cuisine of Cuban Chinese restaurants in New York, means "Chinese and home cooking," and that contemporary meaning was for a long time the dominant one. Joseph Tregle's magisterial "Creoles and Americans" quotes Garcilaso de la Vega, writing in the early 1600s:

The name was invented by the Negroes . . . They use it to mean a Negro born in the Indies, and they devised it to distinguish those who come from this side and were born in Guinea from those born in the New World . . . The Spanish have copied them by introducing this word to describe those born in the New World, and in this way both Spaniards and Guinea Negroes are *criollo* if they are born in the New World.[4]

Others see a different origin but a similar history; Gwendolyn Midlo Hall, for example, claims that the word's root is the Portuguese *crioulo*, "meaning a slave of African descent born in the New World. Thereafter it was extended to include Europeans born in the New World."[5]

The earliest sense, then, connotes Blackness. But the immediately subsequent sense that both accounts acknowledge has no racial connotation at all; it simply distinguishes homegrown people and products from foreign, whether White or Black or mixed. And it was that sense, Tregle tells us, "which took root in colonial Louisiana" (137) and was the dominant sense there for a long time. It could stay dominant because the antebellum racial hierarchy had no need to limit the word's meaning along racial lines. The racially neutral sense of the word had "evolved in a society which knew only White men as political persons . . . Unchallengeable White supremacy . . . had made it possible to accommodate a pan-racial creolism" (172).

Not surprisingly, a secondary sense existed, by way of a slippage from the primary one. Since "creole" could refer either to Black or White, it was sometimes taken to mean "having some mixture of Blackness," "not pure

---

[4] Joseph G. Tregle, Jr., "Creoles and Americans," in Arnold R. Hirsch and Joseph Logsdon (eds.), *Creole New Orleans* (Baton Rouge: Louisiana State University Press, 1992), p. 137. Page numbers for subsequent quotations from this work will be given in the text.

[5] Gwendolyn Midlo Hall, *Africans in Colonial Louisiana* (Baton Rouge: Louisiana State University Press, 1992), p. 157.

White." Hence Lafcadio Hearn's observation (which he himself does not document), that "Ladies at Washington have been known to faint while conversing with Southern Senators at a reception, because the honorable and distinguished gentlemen accidentally observed in the course of conversation that they were Creoles" – that is, were part Black.[6]

In the years after the Civil War – that is, in the period in which Cable and Mercier are writing, as distinct from the periods in which their fictions are set – the political situation changed, and the word's meaning did too. Blacks had become "political persons," in theory at least, and White supremacy had been challenged during Reconstruction. Most Louisiana Whites were seeking, in Cable's words, "how to get back to the old semblance of republican State government, and – allowing that the freedman was *de facto* a voter – still to maintain a purely arbitrary superiority of all Whites over all Blacks."[7] White Creoles of French and Spanish descent in particular, no longer having the institution of slavery to maintain their distinctness from, and their superiority over, their Black and mixed-race fellow citizens, sought to reassert both distinctness and superiority by redefining the word that named them. They succeeded. "Henceforth," writes Tregle, "to be creole was to be White" (173).

A twentieth-century Louisiana State Court of Appeals in due time ruled that "when a person is called a creole this evidences an absence of any negro blood," and the Louisiana Historical Society in 1915 sealed the question by proclaiming that "the definition of 'creole' as stated by Prof. [Alcée] Fortier is the correct one." . . . The degree to which the memory of antebellum reality had been extinguished in the enveloping acceptance of fantasy emerges clearly in this excerpt from a New Orleans newspaper editorial of 1922: "Here in Louisiana a 'creole' has never been anything but a descendant of the original French and Spanish settlers born in Louisiana instead of in France or Spain . . . One dictionary says that the term was once applied to negroes born here to distinguish them from negroes brought from Africa. We have never heard it used in that sense." (183)

A word invented by Blacks to describe New World Blacks, then generalized to describe all people and things born or created in the New World, then sometimes understood as referring only to things containing some quantum of Blackness, then made to refer only and polemically to Whites "untainted"

---

[6] Lafcadio Hearn, "Los Criollos," in *Occidental Gleanings*, 2 vols. (Freeport: Books for Libraries, 1967, repr. of original 1925 edition), vol. I, p. 195. See also Tregle, "Creoles and Americans": "the creoles added to the common white man's rejection of the black this additional spur to hatred: they might be confused with blacks" (173).

[7] George W. Cable, "The Freedman's Case in Equity," in Arlin Turner (ed.), *The Negro Question: A Selection of Writings on Civil Rights in the South by George W. Cable* (New York: Norton, 1958), pp. 12–13.

by Black ancestry. Maybe not quite a primal word as Freud defined that term, but pretty close.

(2) One notable thing "born or created in the New World" was Louisiana French Creole, that is, the French-based creole[8] language created by Black slaves working on French-run plantations. It was in 1719 that French colonists[9] began importing slaves, and by 1731 we have attestations of the French-based language the slaves created – significantly, in an account of the Pointe Coupée slave revolt that same year. Written texts date from around 1850. Many of these are songs and *contes créoles*, fables created by Black storytellers, lively and subtle. Others are satires created by Whites; Blacks created the language, but Whites learned it, often as a first language taught to them by Black nurses, and used it for their own literary purposes. The language is still spoken, by some twenty to thirty thousand people in four areas of Louisiana; but there are few unilingual speakers, and no great prospects for a revival.[10]

"Louisiana French Creole," sometimes simply "Louisiana Creole," is what linguists call this language now. It was called *créole or* "creole" (without any indication of region or lexifying language) in nineteenth-century texts in French and English. But it had other names as well, more tendentious ones: *Nèg* ("Negro"), *Français Nèg* ("Negro French"), "Nigger French," *Gombo* (literally okra, then the soup made with okra, then the language), and *couri vini*, "go-come," which became a name for the language because *couri* and *vini* were used in serial verb constructions, a structure falsely regarded as typical of the language, and probably also because it contained the verb *couri* ("run," "go,"), which Cable himself, in a notable essay on the language, singled out as expressing the language-creators' mentality: "for the verb to go [the "Louisiana Negro"] oftener used a word that better signified his slavish pretense of alacrity, the verb to run."[11]

---

[8] How "creole" came to be the standard term for a language type is unclear. The first use of the word to refer to a specific language occurs in 1739, "when the very youthful Dutch-lexifier creole Negerhollands was referred to as *carriolsche* by a Moravian missionary" (Jacques Arends *et al.* [eds.], *Pidgins and Creoles: An Introduction* [Amsterdam and Philadelphia: John Benjamins, 1995], p. 8). According to the OED, the formal adaptation of the term (and of the related term "pidgin") as a linguistic term of art took place in Jamaica in 1959.

[9] "French" is an oversimplification. See Hall, *Africans in Colonial Louisiana*, pp. 1–28 on the demography of the first European settlements in Louisiana; the first census of Biloxi lists French, Canadians, and racially unspecified Caribbean pirates.

[10] See on this Margaret M. Marshall, "The Origin and Development of Louisiana Creole French," in Albert Valdman (ed.), *French and Creole in Louisiana* (New York: Plenum Press, 1997), and the rich introductory material in Valdman *et al.* (eds.), *Dictionary of Louisiana Creole* (Bloomington: Indiana University Press, 1998).

[11] Cable, "Creole Slave Songs," in Arlin Turner (ed.), *Creoles and Cajuns* (Garden City: Doubleday, 1959), p. 396. Page numbers for subsequent quotations from this work will be given in the text.

Cable's essay was one of several written about the language in the nineteenth century and afterwards. All the essayists were White. Mercier was one of them, and the best of them. Whites dealt with the language in other ways as well. They collected, edited, annotated, and translated tales and songs composed by Blacks. They also translated European texts *into* this American language, from La Fontaine's fables to the *Chanson de Roland* to Homer. They portrayed and commented on the language in fictions.

Blacks created and spoke the language, Blacks created the songs and tales that Whites translated and commented on. But there are no nineteenth-century Black works in Creole in which Creole is a theme or subject. Here, as with the discussion of Native American languages in Chapter 1, we are looking from the outside in.[12]

THE HEDGEHOG

It's hard to get a feel for Alfred Mercier; even his diaries are impersonal, and his motto, *Allons toujours!* ("Ever onward!"), says something about his cheerfully dogged activity but not much about his character.

Still, the facts of his life are suggestive.[13] He was born in Louisiana, in 1816, but spent much of his early and middle life in France; he went there in 1830 for his education, and from then until the end of the Civil War lived more in Europe than in Louisiana, marrying a Frenchwoman named Virginie Vezian there in 1849 and beginning the study of medicine shortly afterwards. During the war itself he practiced medicine in Paris. A learned man, well-traveled, half an outsider to his birth community.

After the war, the outsider came home; he returned to Louisiana and stayed there, busy with medicine, busier still with writing, busiest of all as the guiding spirit of the Athénée Louisianais, founded in 1875 to "maintain the French language in Louisiana . . . to be engaged in, and to safeguard,

---

[12] See Ingrid Neumann-Holzschuh (ed.), *Textes anciens en créole louisianais* (Hamburg: Helmut Buske, 1987), the standard collection of nineteenth-century Louisiana Creole texts. Professor Neumann-Holzschuh confirmed my sense of this matter in a personal communication.

[13] For Mercier's life see the detailed notes in Réginald Hamel's edition of *L'Habitation Saint-Ybars* (Montreal: Guérin, 1989); George Reinecke, "Alfred Mercier, French Novelist of New Orleans," *Southern Quarterly* 20:2 (Winter 1982), pp. 145–76; Edward Larocque Tinker, *Les écrits de langue française en Louisiane* (Paris: Honoré Champion, 1932), pp. 351–64; Tregle, "Creoles and Americans"; Auguste Viatte, *Histoire littéraire de l'Amérique française des origines à 1950* (Quebec: Presses Universitaires Laval, 1954), pp. 286–91; and above all, Gloria Nobles Robertson's admirable introduction to her edition of Mercier's diaries ("The Diaries of Dr. Alfred Mercier: 1879–1893" [master's thesis, Louisiana State University, 1947]; page numbers for subsequent quotations from Robertson's work will be given in the text).

works of science, literature, and art . . . to function as a mutual aid society"
(Robertson, "Diaries" 46). By the end of his life, the proceedings of the
Athénée consisted almost entirely of Mercier's own writings. He died in
1894. He wrote, during his last illness, "Must I then live without reading?
Is that indeed living? No; it is not even existing" (73).

A medical quality marks Mercier's writing, an exactness and colorlessness
of observation. Sometimes he seems amateurish. But sometimes he shows
a stubborn willingness to push against limits, as in an astonishing dream-
sequence in his last novel, *Johnelle*, where the tormented Tito Metelli, his
sister murdered at birth by their mother, imagines a wailing universe of
infanticide and abortion victims:

Tito saw that [the first bank of clouds] was composed of countless small beings,
themselves unmoving and silent, driven by a force tending in the direction of the
winds . . . As he was wondering what this might be, he heard a long, bitter sigh
rise from the depths of the sea.
     A head, apparently lifeless, floated by on the eddying water; from its blue-black
lips came these words:
     "You see the embryos that their mothers destroyed in their womb . . ."
     Tito was surrounded by a spiral rising into the highest regions of space. He was
frozen with horror as he saw, swirling about him, innumerable legions of children,
each one bearing, on its skull or torso, the mark of a wound . . . [14]

L'Habitation Saint-Ybars ("The Saint-Ybars Plantation") reflects
Mercier's stubbornness at its best. He refused, in writing it, to use any
of the usual, indirect strategies for representing language difference – no
"he said in language X," no quaint, literal "translation" of heterophone
idioms, no narrative characterization of heterophone languages, no footnoted translations of passages readers might not understand. (In *Johnelle*, he
gave in and provided such translations.) Instead, he quoted his characters
speaking the languages he judged they would have used.[15] When he judges

---

[14] Alfred Mercier, *Johnelle* (New Orleans: Eugène Antoine, 1891), pp. 153–55.
[15] I use this elaborate phrase because it is hard to say with confidence whether Mercier's judgments in
   this matter are sound; we cannot get an independent view of what the novel is showing us. Consider,
   as a telling demonstration of that impossibility, an article by the noted creolist Albert Valdman, "La
   diglossie français-créole dans l'univers plantocratique," in Gabriel Manessy and Paul Wald (eds.),
   Plurilinguisme: normes, situations, stratégies (Paris: L'Harmattan, 1979), pp. 173–85. Valdman takes
   Mercier's novel as raw sociolinguistic data, and uses it as the chief source for his account. To justify
   this strategy, he claims, as he must, that "stereotyping and caricature seem totally absent from the
   creole dialogues" (177). But how, except in relation to other trustworthy sources, can he know this?
       The fact is, there *are* no other trustworthy sources. Mikael Parkvall, at the University of Stockholm,
   used to maintain a comprehensive collection of texts in numerous creole languages; when that site
   was running, passages from Mercier's novel made up 99 percent of the Louisiana French Creole
   material collected there.

they would have spoken French, they speak French. When he judges they would have spoken Creole, they speak Creole.[16]

In some respects the novel is a typical *roman-feuilleton*, full of lurid events, scheming villains, and tragic outcomes. The hero is Antony Pélasge, a Parisian-born, French-trained, revolutionary Huguenot intellectual. He has been on the Paris barricades, has been wounded and imprisoned and deported, has escaped from an Algerian prison; now, in 1851, at the age of twenty-three, seeking refuge from the political turmoil of Europe, he arrives in Louisiana and finds employment as a tutor. His employer is the proud and moody plantation-owner, Saint-Ybars; his charges are the two children, the daughter Chant-d'Oisel ("Birdsong") and the son Démon ("Demon").

These facts once established, the novel tells Pélasge's subsequent story: his successes in tutoring, and his affection for his two students; his friendship with Vieumaite, Saint-Ybars' Jekyll-and-Hyde father (the two sides of his face are sharply different, and the plantation slaves call them "sunside" and "shadeside");[17] his participation in the family's furious quarrels; his love for Chant-d'Oisel, who marries him on her deathbed; his visits to a magnificent tree called "The Old Sachem"; his grief at Démon's suicide, occasioned by racial prejudice; his growing isolation; and his return to a life of political activity in Europe. We sense other, greater stories in the background, but they matter less; the chapter on the Civil War takes only three pages, one page fewer than the chapter recounting the departure of the Russian music tutor.

The real drama of the novel, its intellectual inner life, is linguistic. Its great theme is the relationship between French and Creole, between the language created by Whites and the language created by Blacks.

One aspect of that relationship is hierarchical: French is presented as being superior to Creole. The superiority in question is not, to be fair, that of a language to a non-language. Mercier's essay on Creole prefigures his

---

[16] Unambiguous names for the two languages are "Louisiana Standard French" and "Louisiana French Creole." Using those names all the time would be cumbersome, using acronyms would be obscure. In most of this chapter Louisiana Standard French is referred to as "French," Louisiana French Creole as "Creole."

[17] "Vieumaite" is the Creole version of the French "vieux maître," "old master"; its effect would be something like "olemassa'," though Saint-Ybars's father is called by this name by everyone, not just by the Saint-Ybars slaves and freed Blacks, and the novel does not tell us any other name for him.

There is a striking reciprocity here. Vieumaite creates most of the epithet-names in the book, e.g., "Chant-d'Oisel" and "Démon," and creates them in French; but his own name is created by the slaves and freed Blacks in Creole.

novel in this respect. The essay is more exact, and freer of prejudice, than any other essay on the subject in his time or for a good while afterwards.[18] We encounter little condescension in it, no comic adjectives, no sense that Creole is sub-linguistic. The word "savage" excepted, the following crucial passage is exemplary:

> It is a curious thing to attend to the intellectual operations by which the savage of the African coast, transported to another continent, composes himself [*se compose*] a grammar from the foreign words that strike his ear. We use the word "grammar" intentionally; yes, the Negro makes himself one; the words he has heard emerge from the Whites' mouths are combined in his brain in such a way as to create there all the parts of speech necessary for the expression of his thought.[19]

That same vision animates the novel. Creole is rendered with a consistent, non-comic orthography. It is not mocked. Its range is not restricted; speakers of it plot, implore, bargain, make allusions, reprove, dispute, sing, threaten, command, bless, reflect. It has not only a general vocabulary but at least one technical one (made use of to discuss blacksmithing). No bilingual speaker of it switches into French for lack of a Creole word. It is not compared with any non-linguistic system, gesture or music or the noises made by animals. The differences of value asserted between the two languages are not differences of kind.

But they are differences of value. French is superior to Creole, in the novel's theory, because Creole is a language with limitations. It is, for one thing, associated with childhood. At the beginning of the novel, Démon prefers the company and conversation of Mamrie, the Black nurse and cook, to those of his parents; he is always running off to her kitchen to hear her stories. When he speaks to her, he speaks to her in Creole, and calls her *vou* rather than *to*. After the Civil War, when he

---

[18] Of the other essays in question, Cable's "Creole Slave Songs" has already been cited. To it I would add Cable's own "The Dance in Place Congo," in Arlin Turner (ed.), *Creoles and Cajuns* (Garden City: Doubleday, 1959); Alcée Fortier's "The French Language in Louisiana and the Negro-French Dialect," *Transactions of the Modern Language Association of America* 2 (1884–85), pp. 96–111; James Harrison's "The Creole Patois of Louisiana," *American Journal of Philology* 3 (1882), pp. 285–96; Lafcadio Hearn's 1877 remarks in "The City of the South," in *Occidental Gleanings*, 2 vols. (Freeport: Books for Libraries, 1967, repr. of original 1925 edition), vol. I, pp. 186–91, and his 1886 "A Sketch of the Creole Patois," reprinted in *The American Miscellany* (New York: Dodd, Mead, and Co., 1924), pp. 154–58; and Edward Larocque Tinker's "Gombo: The Creole Dialect of Louisiana, with a Bibliography," *Proceedings of the American Antiquarian Society* 44 (April 1935), pp. 101–42.

[19] Mercier, "Étude sur la langue créole en Louisiane," *Comptes-rendus de l'Athénée Louisianais* 4 (1880), p. 378. Page numbers for subsequent quotations from this work will be given in the text.

returns from Europe, he speaks to her in French, and uses *tu*. Mamrie approves:

To blié parlé créol; mo oua ça; tapé parlé gran bo langage de France; épi asteur, effronté to tutéié to Mamrie. Mo palé grondé toi pou ça; an contraire, ça fé moin plésir to tutéié moin, to acé gran pou ça.[20]

Her speech reveals the conventions at work here. It is appropriate for Démon in his boyhood to speak Creole with Mamrie, and to treat her with the respect implied by *vou*; it is equally appropriate for Démon in his manhood to speak to her in French, and to treat her with the intimacy and mastery implied by *tu*.[21]

Knowing this can help us read one of the novel's tensest scenes. The young Démon quarrels with his father; his father attacks him, striking him several times in the face; Mamrie is told of what is going on, comes to Démon's aid, and tells his father to let him go. When Saint-Ybars continues his attack, she throws an axe at his head. Saint-Ybars resolves to punish Mamrie, ordering a slave named Jim to whip her. But before the whipping starts, Démon comes up to Jim and tells him, "si tu as le malheur de donner un seul coup de fouet à Mamrie, tu es mort" (187; "should you be so unfortunate as to give Mamrie even a single lash, you are a dead man"). Démon is still a boy; but at this crucial moment, needing to exercise the adult authority he has so far been at odds with, he adopts the linguistic persona of a man. Like his own father, he now addresses a slave in French, and with *tu* rather than *vous*. Jim obeys; he refuses to do the whipping, and in the end no one gets whipped by anyone.

French is also superior to Creole, the novel teaches us, because the former is associated with reason, the latter with storytelling.

During the war, Pélasge and Chant-d'Oisel undertake the education of Blanchette, the illegitimate daughter of the slave Titia and an unnamed White planter's son. In that education, says Mercier's narrator, "they always spoke to her in the language of reason, and carefully avoided filling her head with tales and legends" (216). Clearly that is a good thing to do, and

---

[20] Mercier, *L'Habitation Saint-Ybars, ou, Maîtres et esclaves en Louisiane (Récit social)*, ed. Réginald Hamel (Montreal: Guérin, 1989), p. 246; page numbers for subsequent quotations from this work will be given in the text. "You've forgotten how to speak creole. I can see that – you speak the big, beautiful language of France. And now, you insolent thing, you say *tu* to your Mamrie. I won't scold you for that; just the opposite. It pleases me that you say *tu* to me. You're big enough for that."

[21] Part of the pathos of Chant-d'Oisel's later bilingual deathbed scene, in which she speaks Creole to Mamrie and French to everyone else, is precisely that she dies before making Démon's linguistic *rite de passage*.

it follows that "the language of reason" is better than "tales and legends."
But there is a strong association in the novel between "tales and legends"
and Creole. When Démon runs off to talk with Mamrie in her kitchen,
Chant-d'Oisel defends him, saying that "he loves to hear the Negroes tell
their stories" (109). Vieumaite carries the defense further, saying,

He likes the Negroes' tales? That's natural. Who of us at his age did not listen to
them with pleasure? And let us not fool ourselves – there is sometimes a very subtle
irony in these stories, not just the intrigue of the plot. (109)

Vieumaite rightly sees in the Creole *contes* something more than entertain-
ment. But even for him, they are *contes* and not treatises. Mercier amplifies
the point in his essay: "when thought rises into the sphere of abstractions,
Creole speech can no longer follow it; the presence of metaphysics afflicts
it, one might say, with a sudden paralysis" (Mercier, "Étude" 381).

Such a hierarchy is predictable; what White Louisiana intellectual at this
time – what White intellectual anywhere, in 1881 – would have taken a
Boasian position on the relative merits of French and Creole? Less predictable is the second principal aspect of the novel's linguistic system: that
the Saint-Ybars plantation is a place, not only of strict linguistic hierarchy,
but also of free linguistic circulation. Most of the characters, both Black
and White, are bilingual; they choose to speak French or Creole for reasons of temperament or decorum or situation, but they understand both
languages, often speak both languages, and language difference is almost
never a barrier to communication.

Pélasge is the one character who understands no Creole, and that only
at the beginning of the novel. His ignorance is dramatized in two scenes;
in neither, though, does it keep him from seeing to the heart of the matter.
Rather it sets his new community's universal bilingualism in motion.

Consider the first of these scenes, the one in which Creole makes its first
appearance:

The young stranger slowed his pace, to see more clearly; but at first he did not
understand what he was seeing. He turned, therefore, towards a Negro woman
coming his way, and said,
"Tell me, Madame, I beg you: what is going on?"
On hearing herself called "Madame," the woman gave vent to one of those expansive, joyful laughs that are peculiar to the African race, and which no European
can imagine before actually hearing them; then, partially regaining her decorum,
she answered,
"Vou pa oua don, Michié? Cé nég pou vende."[22]

---

[22] "So you don't see, Sir? They're Negroes for sale."

She saw that she was not understood; so, presuming that she was dealing with a foreigner, she continued in good French,

"They are Negroes for sale, Monsieur."

"Ah," said the stranger, and asked nothing further. (79–80)[23]

A Black woman sees a White man in the streets of New Orleans. He asks her a question in French – his own language, and so far as he knows the language of the community. The question suggests that he might be a stranger; he does not understand the locally familiar institution of the slave auction, and he addresses the woman as "Madame." The woman laughs at the unfamiliar form of address, but then answers the question in Creole; that, presumably, would be the language normally used by a Black for speaking with a White, in the absence of any cue to the contrary, and the White would normally understand.

In this case, though, the White does not understand; seeing this, the woman realizes that he is a stranger, and addresses him in his own language.[24] She plays the cosmopolitan to Pélasge's outsider, and thus enacts the claim Mercier makes in his essay:

whoever speaks the creole here can also speak good French; any ordinary [*petit*] Black man or woman, in the most remote streets of the city, will make it a point of honor, if you pose a question in French, to answer you in the language that you speak. (Mercier, "Étude"378)[25]

This free circulation of language is accompanied by an equally free circulation of culture – and in all directions, Creole not always being the raw material, nor speakers of French always its consumers or refiners. Mamrie composes a *complainte* in Creole to the tune of the French song "Malbrouck s'en va-t-en guerre" (143). (A *complainte* is a recognized French literary genre; Littré's dictionary defines it as "a popular song dealing with a tragic event or a devotional legend.") Chant-d'Oisel sings European opera arias to the old slave Ima, who later plays them, "with motifs and variations of his own" (127), on the African banjo. Mamrie's creolophone letters to Démon, who is waiting out the Civil War in France, are published in

---

[23] On the challenges raised by translating Mercier's novel – the quoted passage shows one way of dealing with them – see below, pp. 126–28.

[24] Mercier wrote "en bon français" ("in *good* French," emphasis added). I think he means by that, not that Creole is bad French, but that the unnamed woman speaks Standard French without error.

[25] According to Mercier's essay, the unnamed woman in his novel should have answered Pélasge's French question in French rather than in Creole. Perhaps Mercier in his essay is referring to the situation in 1880, not in 1851?

It is impossible not to want to see this scene as suggesting a connection between an unfamiliar language and an unfamiliar institution, between the Creole and slavery. What a novel Mercier might have made had he developed this connection!

a French philological journal, with commentary by Pélasge;[26] and for a while, writes Mercier, "Mamrie was a subject of discussion among certain men of letters" (201). Mamrie makes use of French literature in developing her unservile ideas about freedom and slavery; the scheming Black page, M. le duc de Lauzun, makes use of other works of that same literature in developing his ideas about intrigue and seduction.

The richest example of such circulation turns up in Chapter VII, when Pélasge and Démon go for a walk and encounter Man Sophie, a harmlessly demented Black woman who carries two dolls around with her in the belief that they are her children. She and Démon talk for a while, Démon translating their conversation for Pélasge; then she leaves, singing what Mercier calls "la vieille romance de Saint-Domingue" (124; "the old Santo Domingo love song"):

> Lisett' to kité la plaine;
> Mo perdi bonhair à moué;
> Ziés à moué semblé fontaine;
> Depi mo pa miré toué.
> Jour là can mo coupé canne,
> Mo chongé zamour à moué;
> Lanouitt' can mo dan cabane,
> Dan droumi mo tchombo toué.[27]

What Man Sophie is singing is a Louisiana Creole version of the famous Haitian Creole song, "Lisette quitté la plaine," composed by the White planter Duvivier de la Mahautière in an effort to prove Haitian Creole capable of artistic nuance. The song was then printed by Moreau de Saint-Méry in 1797, in his *Description topographique, physique, civile, politique et historique de la partie française de l'isle Saint Domingue.* Probably that is where Mercier read it. It is not clear how the Haitian text was rewritten in Louisiana Creole; perhaps Mercier himself did the work, perhaps the White planter's song became a Black folk song, then made its way to Louisiana with the Haitian slaves who came there towards the beginning of the nineteenth century, and was adapted by Blacks from the Haitian Creole into the Louisiana one.

In any case, a song artfully composed by a White planter is presented as a Black folk song and the expressive utterance of a Black woman; is perceived

---

[26] Given that Creole is understood so often as an essentially oral language, it is a bold choice on Mercier's part to imagine Mamrie writing it.

[27] Lisette, you left the plain;/ I lost my happiness./ My eyes are like fountains/ since I stopped seeing you./ Daytimes, when I cut cane,/ I think of my love;/ at night, in my cabin,/ in my sleep I dream of you.

by Pélasge as a document of the Black culture that he is coming to know; and is finally translated for his benefit into his own French, which is also the language of the planter who wrote the song in the first place. The sequence of events evokes White exploitation and expropriation of Black linguistic creativity, but also the unstrained, productive circulation of culture and language that marks this novel everywhere.[28]

The points made so far are points about a multilingual system, points about rules. The remaining points concern two individual users of those rules, the novel's two most vivid and most sharply opposed language users: Mamrie, the faithful Black nurse, and M. le duc de Lauzun, the scheming Black page. The novel's multilingual system is one of benevolent orderliness, freedom within a hierarchy of difference. The linguistic behaviors we see in Mamrie and De Lauzun complicate that image. Evoking a sharp opposition between cosmopolitanism as treason and cosmopolitanism as fidelity, they show us something of the system's underlying, sometimes erupting tensions. They also suggest that at crucial moments, the two languages are essentially alike.

Mamrie is the good cosmopolitan. She is bilingual and literate. She may be trilingual; during the war she goes to New Orleans to make money for Démon in Europe, and what she does to make it is sell sweets to Union officers. Presumably she would speak English to them, though Mercier doesn't say so explicitly. She composes poetry and has musical gifts. Her taste in French literature is excellent: Rousseau and Voltaire, Lamartine and Hugo.

In the novel, though, she speaks only Creole, and that makes her cosmopolitanism strange. Many cosmopolitans practice what we might call cosmopolitanism as chameleonism. Citizens of the world rather than of any particular place, chameleonic cosmopolitans adapt their language, diction, frame of reference, eating habits, religious practices to those of their hosts or interlocutors. When in Rome, they do as the Romans do. Mercier knows this pattern, and gives us an example of it: Man Miramis, the freed Black who rules tyrannically over the Saint-Ybars servants, consistently

---

[28] I owe this account of "Lisette" to personal communications from George Lang and Mikael Parkvall; my thanks to both for extraordinary generosity in sharing extraordinary learning. For further information see George Lang, "Islands, Enclaves, Continua: Toward a Comparative History of Caribbean Creole Literatures," in A. James Arnold (ed.), *A History of Literature in the Caribbean*, 3 vols. (Amsterdam: John Benjamins, 1997), vol. III, pp. 29–56.

Several traits of the chapter on Man Sophie anticipate Kate Chopin's 1893 story, "La Belle Zoraïde." Like the chapter, the story tells of a delusional Black woman who treats a doll as her "piti," and quotes lines from "Lisette." It seems likely that Chopin read Mercier's novel and borrowed from it without acknowledging it.

adapts her language to her interlocutor's, speaking French with Whites and Creole with Blacks.

One alternative to such cosmopolitanism is parochialism: knowing only one's own language and habits, contentedly ignorant of the languages and habits of others. Mamrie's way of being is a different alternative, a cosmopolitanism of a different sort. She understands other people's languages and habits perfectly well. In particular she understands other people's modes of being polyglots, the rules of the bilingual system she functions in, which she defines more clearly than does anyone else in the novel. It is by choice and not by incompetence, in awareness and not in ignorance, that she chooses to speak only one language, only her own. One point of her freely moving compass is fixed; her cosmopolitanism is rooted.[29]

Mamrie's opposite and antagonist is Saint-Ybars's quadroon page and illegitimate grandson, M. le duc de Lauzun (sarcastically named by Vieumaite after a seventeenth-century French courtier).[30] He is the novel's chief villain, its language traitor, and his scheming brings about three suicides.

De Lauzun represents linguistic dissimulation. We know from what he says in his last scene that he speaks Creole, we have every reason to think that Creole is his native language, but until that scene we never see him speaking it. Inverting Mamrie's linguistic code, he speaks French all the time, to Blacks and Whites alike: cosmopolitanism as apostasy, we might say, always preferring one's adopted language or languages to one's own. He speaks French with the slave Titia, whom he is attempting to seduce. He also speaks it to himself: "'Quand on est maître d'un secret, on est toujours fort,' se disait-il" (203–4; "'who holds a secret is always in a position of strength,' he said to himself").[31] Unlike all the other Black speakers of French, he has a particular French literary style, what Mercier calls "the bombastic language of M. le vicomte d'Arlincourt" (202). D'Arlincourt was an early nineteenth-century pamphleteer; that De Lauzun admires him makes his taste as bad as Mamrie's is good. De Lauzun is also a diarist, and no doubt his diary is written in D'Arlincourt's language as well. Every trait of his use of language and languages is presented in a bad light: excessive verbal

---

[29] On "rooted cosmopolitanism" see Kwame Anthony Appiah, *The Ethics of Identity* (Princeton: Princeton University Press, 2005), especially pp. 213–72.

[30] Mercier does not tell us what De Lauzun was called before Vieumaite named him. Mamrie's "nom primitif" (115), presumably her baptismal name, was Marie. But her twin nurslings, Démon and Chant-d'Oisel, rename her; unable or unwilling to say "Maman Marie" ("Mother Marie"), they combine the two nouns into one. One might say that we have here two Black slaves renamed by Whites, one by a White elder, one by White children. But probably both "Marie" and whatever De Lauzun was named at birth were also names chosen by Whites.

[31] He is not the only Black character to do this; the aged slave Lagniape does also (219).

facility, self-conscious wit, forgetting or denying one's linguistic roots and history, pomposity of style, linguistic opportunism.[32]

But the language traitor is also a linguistic virtuoso, the most literary and literarily productive of all the Black speakers of French, the most linguistically ambitious. He is also the novel's most skilled polyglot, just as the villain Magua is in Cooper's *The Last of the Mohicans*. After the war, he goes about making speeches, "haranguing the freed slaves and exciting them against their former masters, whom he made a point of calling *Bourbons*. He spoke only English now; he swore he had forgotten French" (261–62).

In this context, his grotesque death makes perfect sense. Towards the end of the novel, his scheming brings about the double suicide of Démon and Blanchette. Mamrie, now blind, resolves to unmask and punish him. As she says to him, "tan pou réglé to conte vini" (298; "time come to settle your account"). And time come, at last, to speak Creole; Mamrie has unmasked not only his crimes but also his language. His last words are in that language: "Mamrie, pa tranglé moin comme ça . . . ou sinon ma cognin vou" (298; "Mamrie, don't choke me like that, or I'll hit you"). No more scheming, no more fine manners or sentences, no more French, no more English; and after his revelation of self and language, Mamrie stabs him to death.

This opposition between nurse and page feels condescending. Mercier celebrates the slave who is loyal to her masters and her subordinated native language, modest in her ambitions, active in private but not in public. He condemns the slave who plausibly calls slave-owners *Bourbons*, learns and uses the language first of his francophone masters and then of his anglophone ones, has large political ambitions, oratorical gifts, public influence. Mamrie looks a little like Aunt Jemima, M. le duc de Lauzun like a southern slaveholder's image of Frederick Douglass.

That is part of the truth, part of who Mercier was, but not all. For one thing, Mamrie is aggressively unservile. She has no respect for slavery, she tries to kill Saint-Ybars with an axe, she does not repent of having done so, she plots as well as De Lauzun does, and the last act of her life before her despairing suicide is a murder. It's hard to imagine a White supremacist who wouldn't find her terrifying.

Mercier lived comfortably in a racist society, but he was not a White supremacist of any typical sort. His spokesman Pélasge is a sharp critic of slavery and his portrait of White Creole society is devastating; he quotes

---

[32] Mercier seems to dislike people who make a cult of playing with words. Certainly the three characters who do so are all fools or knaves: the fatuous M. Héhé, Démon's previous and unsuccessful tutor; Héhé's bigoted and cowardly consort, Mlle Pulchérie; and the murderous duelist, M. des Assins.

Voltaire's remark that prejudices are "kings of the common herd" (285). His great cause, as he wrote the novel, was sustaining French in Louisiana. His chief sphere of activity was the Athénée Louisianais, and more generally the doomed struggle for Louisiana francophone culture in a world increasingly dominated by the anglophone north. All around him, he saw people deserting their native French, failing to support the organization founded to nurture it. By 1900, wrote Edward Larocque Tinker, "the use of French in Louisiana [became], not a necessity, but a mere sentimental addiction, indulged in by a rapidly decreasing few" (quoted in Robertson, "Diaries" 23). Mercier could see that happening in 1879: "The Athénée has done something remarkable in lasting beyond its first three years. But what pains we have taken, a few faithful spirits and I, to keep it from falling by the wayside [*en deliquium*]! Will we manage to keep it upright much longer? Truly I doubt it" (Robertson, "Diaries" 91).

For Mercier, then, Mamrie's language loyalty is a great moral quality, the quality that he seeks in his fellow Creoles and cannot find. For him, the opposition between Mamrie and De Lauzun represents not just two ways of being a Black servant, but also two ways of living in a multilingual world, not just the difference between subordination to one's masters and rebellion against them, but also that between nurturing one's culture and abandoning it.

After killing De Lauzun, Mamrie has nothing left to live for. She places the point of her knife "between [her] collarbone and neck," then drives it home; "the blade disappeared, and only the hilt could be seen" (299). Before that, though, we get her last speech, and the last Creole utterance of the book: "Chant-d'Oisel, Démon, Blanchette, cher piti, zote apé attane Mamrie: alà li!" ("Chant-d'Oisel, Démon, Blanchette, my dear little ones, you have been waiting for Mamrie; now behold her!") Not a great speech, but outside the range of the picturesque; not folksy, not a proverb, not a story of how Miss Calinda had to choose between Mr. Hare and Mr. Tortoise. If not metaphysical, it is at least the same sort of high, over-literary speech that French-speaking characters use – for example, Blanchette when she finds that Démon has taken poison and wishes to join him in death: "non, non; cela ne peut pas être, je m'en irai avec vous" (295; "no, no, that cannot be; I shall depart with you"). Whatever notional hierarchy Mercier has constructed in his novel, at the end of it the two languages in which the novel takes place are at the same high pitch, equally the instruments of melodrama. We could wish that both languages were used more vividly; but we note with pleasure and admiration that at these crucial moments of the novel, both languages are used alike.

THE FOX

George W. Cable was born in New Orleans in 1844, fought for the Confederacy during the Civil War, and until the early 1870s, by his own retrospective account, "had no views at variance with those his neighbors held on the problems of the South."[33] The stories he wrote during those years were warmly received by Southern readers. So at first was his novel *The Grandissimes*, published in book-form in 1880. But Cable's views had been changing, had been turning upside down in fact, and in the 1880s he stated his new views in some noble essays on the situation of Blacks in the post-Reconstruction South, nuanced and passionate demands that Blacks obtain the civil rights guaranteed them by national law. Many White Southerners then turned against him, coming in the process to see even his earlier fictions as in accord with the views later stated by his essays, and Cable became "the most cordially hated little man in New Orleans" (Tregle, "Creoles and Americans" 131).

It took courage and intelligence to do what Cable did, broad imaginative sympathy, freedom from prejudice. So we are likely to be taken aback when we come across Cable's 1886 translation of a Louisiana Creole comic song, published one year after his bold essay, "The Silent South"; it looks like the worst sort of minstrel-show parody of Black speech, and we wonder what on earth is going on.

C'est Miché Cayetane,	Dass Cap'm Cayetano,
Qui sorti la Havane,	W'at comin' fum Havano,
Avec so chouals et so macacs.	Wid 'is monkey' an' 'is nag'!
Li gagnein ein nhomme qui dancé dans sac;	An' one man w'at dance in bag,
Li gagnein qui dancé si yé la main;	An' mans dance on dey hand' – cut shine'
Li gagnein zaut', à choual, qui boir' di vin;	An' gallop hoss sem time drink wine!
Li gagnein oussi ein zein, zoli mom'selle,	An' b'u'ful young missy dah beside,
Qui monté choual sans bride et sans selle!	Ridin' 'dout air sadd' aw brid'e;
Pou' di' tou' ça mo pas capab';	To tell h'all dat – he cann' be tole.
Mé mo souvien ein qui 'valé sab'!	Man teck a sword an' swall' im whole!
Yé n'en oussi tou' sort' bétail.	Beas'es? ev'y sawt o' figgah!

---

[33] Arlin Turner, *George W. Cable: A Biography* (Durham, NC: Duke University Press, 1956), p. 41.

Yé pas montré pou la négrail';	Dat show ain't fo' no common
	niggah!
Gniapas là dotchians dos-brilé,	Dey don't got deh no po' White cuss'
	–
Pou 'fé tapaze et pou' hirlé;	Sunbu'nt back! – to holla an' fuss.
Cé gros madame et gros miché,	Dass ladies fine, and gennymuns
	gran',
Qui ménein là tous pitits yé,	Fetchin' dey chilluns dah – all han'!
'Oir Miché Cayétane,	Fo' se Cayetano,
Qui 'rivé la Havane	W'at come fum Havano
Avec so chouals et so macacs.	Wid 'is monkey' an' 'is nag'!
	(Cable, "Creole Slave Songs" 411–13)

There is tremendous verbal energy here, the sort of energy often released when White writers avail themselves of Black languages, and John Hollander was right to include Cable's translation in his great anthology of nineteenth-century American poetry. But there is also a false and condescending sense of the dialect in which the translation is made.

We see it in the orthography. What justifies non-standard orthography is the notion that it helps the reader to hear non-standard pronunciation. That is not a perfect justification, but it has some force.[34] Success in rendering non-standard pronunciation is certainly one thing that William Labov and David Carkeet admire in Mark Twain's rendering of Jim's English in *Huck Finn*.[35] But the two linguists would hardly admire Cable's rendering here. Can we believe that a speaker who says "sawt" for "sort" (11) will pronounce the "r" in "sword" (10), or that a speaker who cuts the final "d" of "told" (9), even at the end of the line and the sentence, will pronounce the final "t" in "don't" (13) and "ain't" (12), even in the middle of a sentence and before a following initial consonant? Will the same speaker say "w'at" for "what" (beginning, that is, with [w] rather than with [hw]) and "White" (beginning with [hw])? Cable chooses a non-standard orthography even where it has nothing to do with representing pronunciation; what Southern speaker, White or Black, would aspirate the "h" of "him" after "swallow" (10)? What need, therefore, to delete that "h"? Getting rid of the "h" does not mean, "that's the way a Black man speaks"; it means, "here's a comic character; laugh at him!"

Consider, by way of paradoxical contrast with Cable's burlesque, the translations of Creole fables by Alcée Fortier. Fortier was an eminent

---

[34] For a fuller account of orthography see above, Introduction, pp. 8–11.
[35] David Carkeet, "The Dialects in *Huckleberry Finn*," *American Literature* 51 (1979), pp. 315–32; Labov, a regrettably unpublished lecture, summarized in a personal communication.

White Creole and an eminent scholar of Louisiana Creole texts. He was also a racist; even Edward Larocque Tinker, who admired him, wrote that his "personal prejudices too often mar[red] his historical discoveries."[36] In introducing his translations of those texts, mostly beast fables, he gives rein to those prejudices. He ascribes to "the negroes of Louisiana . . . humor and a naïveté bordering on childishness." Their language, he continues,

partakes necessarily of their character, and is sometimes quaint, and always simple . . . we may also observe in the language of the negroes a great many examples of abbreviations due entirely to the want of energy of the person speaking.[37]

But his prejudices do not mar his translations: carefully done, in unaffected prose, prefaced by sober commentary, accompanied by helpful glosses. Reading them, we might think we were reading something published by Franz Boas's Bureau of American Ethnology. Fortier was a racist, Boas an apostle of cultural relativism; when it came to translating, however, the two men were doing the same thing, and something quite different from the enterprise of their civil rights activist contemporary Cable.

We can explain Fortier's surprising translations by remembering that translating can lead the translator into a freer space, where conscious prejudice plays a diminished role. Sherry Simon writes, "we limit too narrowly the powers of translation if we do not take account of the elements of resistance that it can bring into play."[38] She is thinking of people without power, not those holding power and abusing it; but arguably her point holds good for the latter as well, for people like Fortier.

Cable's surprises are more complicated. He was no more a cultural relativist than Fortier was; he wrote of "how strangely the French language is corrupted on the thick Negro tongue,"[39] accepted the possibility that the "colored" were an inferior race, and deplored "social confusion," that is, race-mixing, which in "The Negro Question" he said had "already brought about the utter confusion of race and corruption of society in the West Indies and in Mexico."[40] A part of Cable probably thought that minstrel shows were just fine, and liked an occasional chance to put one on – free for a moment from his public political views as Fortier was free of his.

---

[36] Tinker, *Les écrits de langue française*, p. 204.
[37] Fortier, "The French Language in Louisiana," p. 102.
[38] Sherry Simon, *Le trafic des langues: traduction et culture dans la littérature québécoise* (Montreal: Boréal, 1994), p. 23.
[39] Cable, "The Dance in Place Congo," p. 380. Note the complexity of the insult: French for Cable is a "language," but "Negroes" have only "tongues," the physical rather than the more general linguistic capacity.
[40] Cable, *The Negro Question*, ed. Arlin Turner (New York: Norton, 1958), p. 145.

But only an occasional chance; because the deeper explanation, I think, is that unlike Fortier or Boas, unlike most translators in Western history for that matter, Cable liked to be all over the translational map. Whatever we think of his mode of dealing with the Cayetano poem, we have to acknowledge that it is not his only mode, not even his characteristic mode. Nor is any of his other modes. As a translator Cable is an improviser, a protean opportunist, undeterred by the hobgoblin of inconsistency, in love with the range of possibility that the translator's task presents. In "Creole Slave Songs" we encounter that range in full: translation as absence – that is, the Creole text untranslated; translation as annihilation – that is, the English translation without the Creole text; scholarly translations like Fortier's; literary translations into Black English; literary translations into Standard English, as full of energy as the circus broadside but unfettered by its minstrel-show limitations, somber and lofty and beautiful. Hollander is right to see the energy in Cable's burlesques; he is still more right to see it in Cable's grander efforts, for example, his rendering of *Ourrâ St. Malo*:

Ourrâ St. Malo	*The Dirge of St. Malo*
Aïe! zein zens, vini fé ouarrâ	Alas! young men, come, make lament
Pou' pôv St. Malo dans l'embas!	For poor St. Malo in distress!
Yé ç'assé li avec yé chien,	They chased, they hunted him with dogs,
Yé tiré li ein coup d'fizi,	They fired at him with a gun,
* * *	* * *
Yé halé li la cyprier,	They hauled him from the cypress swamp.
So bras yé tassé par derrier,	His arms they tied behind his back,
Yé tassé so la main divant:	They tied his hands in front of him;
Yé marré li apé queue choual,	They tied him to a horse's tail,
Yé trainein li zouqu'à la ville.	They dragged him up into the town.
Divant michés là dans Cabil'e	Before those grand Cabildo men
Yé quisé li li fé complot	They charged that he had made a plot
Pou' coupé cou à tout ye blancs.	To cut the throat of all the Whites.
Yé' mandé li qui so compères;	They asked him who his comrades were;
Pôv St. Malo pas di' a-rien!	Poor St. Malo said not a word!
Zize là li lir' so la sentence,	The judge his sentence read to him,
Et pis li fé dressé potence.	And then they raised the gallows-tree.
Yé halé choual – ç'arette parti –	They drew the horse – the cart moved off –
Pôv' St. Malo resté pendi!	And left St. Malo hanging there.

Eine hèr soleil deza levée	The sun was up an hour high
Quand yé pend li si la levée.	When on the levee he was hung;
Yé laissé so corps balancé	They left his body swinging there,
Pou' carancro gagnein manzé.	For carrion crows to feed upon.
	(Cable, "Creole Slave Songs" 418–19)

Who is Cable now? He retains the rhythm and jettisons the rhyme, translates line by line so as to retain the expressive order of the narrative, chooses a diction neither over-elevated nor willfully vulgar, allows the song to tell its harrowing story. Not the same translator, we might think, who produced the circus broadside; but of course the same translator who produced the circus broadside, revealing himself as a translator who deals with Louisiana Creole not by preferring one strategy to another, but by trying them all.[41]

It is this same protean Cable, impostor and perceiver, whom we feel at work in his great language novel, *The Grandissimes*, called by Lafcadio Hearn "the most remarkable work of fiction ever created in the South."[42] It was published a year before Mercier's *L'Habitation Saint-Ybars*, is as intelligent as that book, and as severely critical of Creole society, but is a world away from it in its strategies of linguistic representation, and a world more complicated and ambitious.

The novel's central character, though not its most vivid, is Joseph Frowenfeld: American, of German parents, a pharmacist. He comes to New Orleans with his parents and two sisters in 1803, the year of the Louisiana Purchase. Shortly after their arrival, all except Joseph die of the fever. Joseph lies ill, recovers, grieves; then, when the first intensity of his grief has eased, he resolves "to begin at once the perusal of this newly found book, the Community of New Orleans."[43]

Among the chief characters in that unwritten book: the two Honoré Grandissimes, one White and one of mixed race (a "free man of color," abbreviated FMC); Aurore and Clotilde Nancanou, widowed mother and daughter, charmingly impoverished White Creoles (the mother ends up marrying the White Honoré, the daughter Frowenfeld); Agricola Fusilier,

---

[41] Patrick Chamoiseau's great novel *Texaco* makes use of a similarly creative instability in dealing with the Creole of Martinique – a similarity worth noting, not to trace some line of filiation from the earlier author to the later, but to establish that such a strategy can be chosen by Black authors as well as White, and by native speakers of Creoles as well as outsiders. See my "Sur quelques aspects de la traduction de textes créoles louisianais du xixème siècle," *Études Créoles* 25:2 (2002), pp. 153–71.

[42] Arlin Turner (ed.), *Critical Essays on George W. Cable* (Boston: G. K. Hall, 1980), p. 8. Page numbers for subsequent quotations from this work will be given in the text.

[43] Cable, *The Grandissimes* (New York: Hill and Wang, 1957), p. 103. Page numbers for subsequent quotations from this work will be given in the text.

eminent White Creole, polyglot, orator, defender of racial hierarchy; Clemence the *marchande de calas*, a Black woman born in Virginia, employed by Honoré FMC, singer and storyteller; Palmyre Philosophe, a free woman of color, first-generation African, practitioner of voodoo, in love with White Honoré and beloved of Honoré FMC, feared by Agricola and hating him because of his treatment of Bras Coupé, an African king sold into slavery and brought to Louisiana in 1795; and Bras Coupé himself, whose story of rebellion, defeat, and triumph, though over by the time the novel begins, haunts it till it ends.

Mercier's novel is neatly bilingual: French, Creole, and the relations between them. Cable's is messier and richer, abundantly multilingual and multidialectal, and the relations among dialects and languages cluster together into patterns. So we cannot look at his portrait of Louisiana Creole in isolation, or in relation only to French; we have to see it as part of a large account of Black–White language relations generally, dealing not only with French and Creole but also with English and Black English and "Creole English" – that is, the English spoken by francophone White Creoles as they learned the language of the new American government.

Cable's representation of Creole English was controversial right from the start, and the controversies illuminate what is at stake here. William Dean Howells loved that English, treating it as if it were a new toy: "Oh the charm of their English! We speak nothing else now but that dialect."[44] An anonymous reviewer in the *Atlantic Monthly* found "the broken English of the [Nancanou] ladies . . . often delicious" (Turner, *Critical Essays* 13). Charles Gayarré, a noted White Creole historian and politician, saw Cable's Creole English as instancing the "overpowering and incomprehensible . . . perversion or depravity of his intellect."[45] Gayarré was a less sophisticated reader than Howells, and the quoted critique is all heat and no light; but the question of Creole English mattered more to him than to Howells, and he saw more clearly what was at issue. In his widely celebrated, apocalyptically denunciatory 1885 lecture on the novel, he set out the essential claim: that Creole English was being presented as similar to the "broken, mutilated africanized English of the Black man" (Ekström, *George Washington Cable* 176n). G. H. Clements quoted an unnamed Creole woman making the same claim in 1891: "Not for Meester Cable make de creole to talk so – is's

---

[44] Turner, *George W. Cable*, p. 99. Note also Turner's remark that "like Mark Twain, William Dean Howells, and others afterwards, [Cable's friend and discoverer Edward King] spoke in Creole, he said, and he scattered Creole expressions through his letters" (54).

[45] Kjell Ekström, *George Washington Cable* (Lund: Carl Blom, 1950), p. 176. Page numbers for subsequent quotations from this work will be given in the text.

think we is niggers!" (Ekström, *George Washington Cable* 178). The theses minus the epithets are two: that Cable had represented Creole English as being like Black English, and that in doing so he was getting it wrong.

The first thesis is true. William Evans's "French-English Literary Dialect in *The Grandissimes*" goes into the matter carefully. Evans acutely notes some of the particular points in common – for example, "the absence of /r/ or /t/ in final clusters, and of the –s verb inflection."[46] He finds that "much Black English resembles Cable's French-English in other characteristics" as well.

The second thesis seems to be false. Most of the testimonies carefully collected in Kjell Ekström's biography of Cable praise Cable for having gotten Creole English right. "The careful rendering of the dialect reveals patient study of living models," wrote a New Orleans *Picayune* reviewer of *Old Creole Days*. The New Orleans journalist Charles W. Young wrote to Cable: "'The Grandissimes' is immense . . . And the dialect. I could almost fancy I was once more among my old friends in the Second District." G. H. Clements seconded that, writing to Cable in 1881: "'Tis amazing how you catch their idioms" (Ekström, *George Washington Cable* 177).

So Creole English resembles Black English in Cable's novel, and resembled it also in the real world that Cable lived in. But what does that mean? Once we have noted the real and literary similarities between Creole English and Black English, how should we understand them? Behind the linguistic question is a racial and political one, and Gayarré raises it most clearly:

Was it [Cable's] intention to produce the impression on his readers in his own sly and covert ways that the creoles are instinctively attracted, by a sort of magnetic influence, to every thing that is low, base and impure, as a natural effect of that Gallic recklessness which, since the foundation of the colony, was the cause of their ignoble descent from the ill specimens of three races – Indian, African and French prostitutes? (Ekström, *George Washington Cable* 176n.)

The underlying question is this: should the fact that Creole English is like Black English be taken to mean that White Creoles are part Black?

Gavin Jones's 1999 *Strange Talk* gives one answer to that question, and a brilliant one: that "Cable's work . . . demonstrates what a powerful tool of counterhegemonic subversion dialect could be."[47] Why? Because in a

---

[46] William Evans, "French-English Literary Dialect in *The Grandissimes*," *American Speech* 46:3–4 (1971), p. 215.

[47] Gavin Jones, *Strange Talk: The Politics of Dialect Literature in Gilded Age America* (Berkeley: University of California Press, 1999), p. 133. Page numbers for subsequent quotations from this work will be given in the text. *Strange Talk* is a terrific book, and offers the most illuminating account I know on the material of this chapter.

society in which relations of power were so tightly linked to differences of color, claims of hybridity were potentially revolutionary. If Whites *were* Blacks, Blacks Whites – if "we *is* niggers" – what could it mean to raise Whites *above* Blacks?

One sphere of White culture that was clearly, empirically Black was Southern English. Lafcadio Hearn wrote generally of "the motley clamor of a semi-tropical land in which even the sharp accents of European tongues lose their firmness, and old languages obtain a new softness and sweetness and languor" (Turner, *Critical Essays* 8). Jones does not quote that phrase; he does, though, tellingly quote James Harrison, who in 1884 acknowledged that "to the shame of the White population of the South . . . they perpetuate many [Black English] pronunciations in common with their Negro dependents; and that, in many places, if one happened to be talking to a native with one's eyes shut, it would be impossible to say whether a Negro or a white person were responding."[48] Jones also quotes L. W. Payne's 1901 statement that "the speech of the White people [in east Alabama] . . . is more largely colored by the language of the negroes than by any other single influence" (Jones, *Strange Talk* 105). The English that White Creoles were learning to produce was part Black. Gayarré was right about the implications of Cable's Creole English; he was wrong only about the facts.

Jones shows us an important truth about Cable here, and a strength in Cable's work. But it is not the whole truth, and the strength is accompanied by subterfuge – operating, as is often the case, in the representation not of dialect but of what we are to take as standard.[49] There are four characters in *The Grandissimes* whose quoted speech is represented in standard orthography: Frowenfeld, the White Honoré Grandissime,[50] Agricola

---

48 James Harrison, "Negro English," in J. L. Dillard (ed.), *Perspectives on Black English* (The Hague: Mouton, 1975), p. 143.

49 Jones quotes some illuminating remarks on this by William Cecil Elam, published in 1895: "In actual life the negro talks more or less like the white persons he serves or comes most frequently in contact with; but when some of our accomplished literary artists attempt to delineate him, this likeness utterly disappears, and his 'English as he is spoke' is exaggerated in all its features by elision and every literal device, *while that of his white interlocutors is revised according to Noah Webster and Lindley Murray*" (Jones, *Strange Talk* 106–7; emphasis added). See also my comments on *Huck Finn* in "American Anglophone Literature and Multilingual America," in Werner Sollors (ed.), *Multilingual America: Transnationalism, Ethnicity, and the Languages of American Literature* (New York: New York University Press, 1998), pp. 338–41.

50 Honoré's speech is less standard in the serial version of the novel, and in the 1880 edition; it was made more standard for the 1883 version of the novel, and for every subsequent version I have seen.
    It is not clear what to make of this. The 1880 version reflects Cable's original intention, the 1883 version his subsequent one, so both have authority. In 1880, Cable indicated both French r-lessness and a French rolled /r/. The results are hard to read and typographically hideous: "My-de'-seh, rhecollect that to us the Grhandissime name is a trheasu'e." So Cable's choice to make the 1883

Fusilier, and Charlie Keene, the local doctor and Frowenfeld's great informant about New Orleans Creole society. It is implausible, maybe preposterous in fact, to represent the speech of these characters in this way.

For one thing, three of the four are speakers of Southern English, one native and two accomplished polyglots. Now Southern English has, as noted, numerous features in common with Black English; that is why showing the Blackness of Southern English in relation to most of its White Creole speakers makes sense. But that is also why singling out three of those speakers and presenting their English as not affected by Blackness does not make sense.[51]

Still less does it make sense to have the speech of these three characters be so similar to Frowenfeld's. He comes, Cable tells us, from a "far northern home" (8). His English pronunciation and cadence cannot be Southern, and must differ from the English of the three White Creoles. But they don't.

What Cable is up to here, probably, is something other than representing pronunciation. His aim is to establish a social and moral hierarchy. Dickens's Oliver Twist speaks Standard not because he is likely to have learned it at the orphanage, but because that is the language spoken by Dickens's heroes. Cable's four Standard-speakers are not all his heroes; but they are all part of his inner circle, well-bred, educated, thoughtful, eminent. The standardness of their speech reflects those traits but obscures their likely dialect.

This mode of differentiating characters' speech has a lofty tradition. But it is at odds with Cable's other mode of differentiating characters' speech, the one at work in his depiction of Creole English, where sociolinguistic accuracy is the goal and justification. Cable's point about Creole hybridity is a revelation. His exempting certain Creole characters from that hybridity, linguistically at least, blurs that revelation. It even gives Gayarré's critique a certain legitimacy.

---

changes was a good one. Still, in Cable's original intention Honoré's English was to be discernibly less standard than that of the other three Standard-speakers. See on this William Evans, "French-English Literary Dialect in *The Grandissimes*," *American Speech* 46:3–4 (1971), pp. 216–17.

[51] Ekström tells us that a Chicago woman named Katharine Girlin wrote to Cable about a lecture delivered by Alcée Fortier, as learned and intellectually distinguished a White Creole as one would want. But even Fortier's speech "showed the scars where odd branches had been lopped off. Rob [sic; "rub"?] away his polish and the sound of the Creole dialect would evidently follow . . . He omitted the 'penult' in such words as *seats, parts*, and the final t in *most*, the ch sound overcame him in *such* and *much*, the r was torn out of 'pobably,' the u of monument became i, cruelty was cooelty . . . It was natural that his English should sound like the English of a Frenchman but he said it didn't" (*George Washington Cable* 179). If Cable were rendering everyone's speech according to its sound, the speech of both Honoré and Agricola should resemble Raoul Innerarity's more and Frowenfeld's less; education and breeding would count less, region would count more.

The same dynamic, the same fruitful mix of subterfuge and sharp perception, is at work in Cable's depiction of Louisiana Creole, "the creole patois"
as he liked to call it, and the same questions of purity and hybridity are being
explored. But the linguistic situation is different. Unlike Southern English,
Louisiana Creole was uncontestedly Black. Blacks created it, and Blacks
created at least one of the names for it; its other names imply its Blackness,
tell us that it is a Black creation, even tell us that it is Blackness itself.
But unlike the dances on Congo Square that one of Cable's great essays
describes, unlike voodoo, Louisiana Creole is not Black-and-not-White.
Louisiana Creole is hardwired into White minds. Whites participate in
the use of it. They grow up with it, liberal Mercier and conservative Kate
Chopin alike;[52] they are native speakers of it; they compose in it; and their
pronunciation even of Standard French is by some accounts shaped by it:
"their organs – larynx, speech-chords, pharynx, uvula – are so habituated
to the drawling utterance of the kitchen and scullery that they chant rather
than speak the cultivated French," writes James Harrison in 1882.[53] For francophone White Creoles seeking to establish superiority over Blacks, and
thus needing to assert separateness from Blacks, Louisiana French Creole
is a nightmare.

   Given the different linguistic situation, we expect different strategies
of linguistic representation, and we find them. Creole English in Cable's
novel is represented almost exclusively by means of quotation, by direct
presentation. Louisiana French Creole is sometimes represented by those
means, but not often.[54] Rather Cable uses numerous strategies of indirect
representation, half-lies that contradict one another but point towards deep
truths.

---

[52] The suggestion that Creole was Chopin's native language is reported in Per Seyersted's *Kate Chopin:
      A Critical Biography* (Baton Rouge: Louisiana State University Press, 1969), p. 15. Emily Toth's *Kate
      Chopin* (New York: William Morrow, 1990) is more equivocal; Toth reports that Chopin's great-
      grandmother, Madame Victoire Verdon Charleville, who was Chopin's first important teacher,
      "spoke the soft Creole patois, less sharp than the French of Paris" (35), but cites no source and does
      not make clear whether the "patois" in question was Louisiana Standard French or Louisiana French
      Creole.
         That Creole was Mercier's native language we have from Mercier himself: "there are in fact some
      among us who use only the Negroes' dialect until the age of eleven or twelve; I am one of them,
      and I remember the reward I was given, the day I promised my parents not to speak anything but
      French with them thenceforward" (Mercier, "Étude" 378).
[53] Harrison, "The Creole Patois of Louisiana," p. 287.
[54] That may be because Cable wasn't capable of direct representation, or because even he, audacious
      transcriber of non-standard dialects in English as he was, couldn't nerve himself to present extended
      passages in a language neither English nor French. But given how far he went to represent non-
      standard English in the first edition of *The Grandissimes*, and how much farther he went in *Dr.
      Sevier*, I myself would see artistic choices here rather than practical ones.

The first is naming. "There is occasional confusion," Jones writes, "whether, by 'Creole dialect,' Cable intends the English of his White Creoles or the creole French of his African Americans – a confusion that suggests further uncertainties in racial definition" (Jones, *Strange Talk* 124–25). True enough, but too restrained. The fact is that there is *systematic* confusion in the book about what language is being spoken, and the confusion bears on all the languages being spoken, not just on Creole English vis-à-vis Creole French, and above all on French and Creole.

Such confusion is an irritant, a cloud of squid ink, for any reader seeking to understand the linguistic situation Cable is representing. Why not make clear what language is being spoken when? That is what most great language novelists do, however widely they differ from one another in other respects.

But there is a deep political and linguistic point to the confusion. It begins, appropriately enough, at a masked ball, in the novel's opening chapter. We follow four maskers and hear the "cries of delight" of those who look on at them – "all, of course, in Louisiana French" (3). Meaning what, exactly? If the language Cable wants us to imagine as being spoken is Louisiana Standard French, then why not just call it "French"? The differences between Louisiana Standard French and Parisian French were minimal; a haughty review of Mercier's *L'Habitation Saint-Ybars* by the French Consul Paul d'Abzac asserted that the French reader would find some "provincialisms" there (Robertson, "Diaries" 71), and some evidence suggests that Louisiana pronunciation differed somewhat from Parisian, but that's it. D'Abzac himself spoke of Mercier's *"expression toujours correcte,"* and what links Mercier's French with Victor Hugo's is much, much more than what separates them. Moreover, at this point in the novel Cable has named just two other languages: the "slave dialect" and the "unprovincial" French of Agricola Fusilier. "Louisiana French" cannot be Agricola's "unprovincial" French, so if it has to be one or the other, it has to be the "slave dialect." And if it is the "slave dialect," then Cable, by calling it "Louisiana French," is asserting that the essential French of francophone Louisiana is, precisely, Louisiana Creole – an equivocation, but aimed expertly at White Creole self-esteem and self-definition.

These are some of Cable's language names: the "soft dialect of old Louisiana" (4), the "corrupt French of the old Creoles" (60), "colonial French" (65), the "peculiar French" (66) of the Nancanous, "the French of the late province" (88), "Creole French" (162 and 164), "Louisiana French" (202), "the French of the province" (235). Absent any sample of speech, each name can point either to Louisiana Standard French or to Louisiana Creole, and that fact is full of meaning. If "Louisiana French" is Louisiana

Creole, then Louisiana Standard French becomes unimportant, uncharac-
teristic of the state, peripheral. If "the peculiar French" of the Nancanous
is Louisiana Standard French, then that language becomes second-rate –
"peculiar," "corrupt," "colonial," "provincial" not, after all, being epithets
of praise. (And if, as Cable seems half the time to be suggesting, the supposedly Olympian French of the Creole aristocracy is "peculiar," then the
likely cause of its being so is the Creole it is supposedly distinct from.)

Cable's mix of equivocation and perception sometimes produces absur-
dities, incidents and patterns in which plausibility is subordinated to effect.
Frowenfeld is a cultivated man and the child of polyglot Germans; living
in trilingual New Orleans, he would have learned French and probably
Creole as well. Palmyre is a gifted polyglot; her not having learned French
or English makes no sense. Their ignorance of each other's languages con-
tributes to some intense scenes between the two characters, full of meaningful looks and blocked verbal communication, but the implausibility of
that ignorance makes the scenes less convincing.

Again, early in the novel, as the Frowenfeld family is making its way
towards New Orleans, the elder Frowenfeld gets to talking with a Creole,
and asks him, "Who was Bras Coupé?" The elder Frowenfeld is German;
he asks his question in French. The Creole answers "in a *patois* difficult,
but not impossible, to understand" (10). Since the *patois* is different from
French, it must be Louisiana Creole; and probably it is Louisiana Creole
because, as Jones points out, Cable seeks to associate both storytelling and
Bras Coupé with that language. That makes sense, but probability is being
stretched too far for the point to feel compelling. A cosmopolitan German
addresses a francophone Creole in French; surely the Creole should respond
in French, that being a language his interlocutor can understand. Nor is
Cable's claim credible that the *patois* is "difficult, but not impossible, to
understand." Mercier got it right here; even Antony Pélasge, a native rather
than a second-language speaker of French, cannot in his first encounter with
Louisiana Creole understand the simplest utterance in it. Cable's intended
point is wrecked by the hard facts.

More often, though, his points hold. Consider a striking fact about
Cable's representation of Louisiana Creole: how much of the speech directly
quoted, as opposed to the speech asserted to be taking place, is not speech
but song, and not created by Cable but borrowed by him. Examples are: a
stanza from the "well-known song of derision" associated with the Calinda
dance (95) and *Dé 'tit zozos* ("Two Little Birds"), both sung by Clemence;
La prémier' fois mo té 'oir li (167; "The First Time I Saw Her"), and *Dé zabs*
(168; "The Trees," probably, though "Two Devils" is also possible), sung

by Raoul; *En haut la montagne* (178; "Up in the Mountains"), sung by Bras Coupé; *Anoqué, Anobia* (188, meaning uncertain), sung by an unnamed White Creole "bearer of good tidings." The scenes of presentation vary much as Cable's translations do. Sometimes we get a translation, sometimes we don't, sometimes commentary and sometimes not, sometimes musical notation – a rarity in literary texts, and so doubly striking – and sometimes not. The songs are witty and suggestive and full of pathos, sometimes incantatory, always free of self-pity. The quantity is imposing, and the scenes are full of interest.[55]

There are no comparable repertories of anglophone or francophone song in the novel. Why not? There are anglophone and francophone songs in the world, and not including them conceals that. The unparalleled abundance of creolophone song might be taken to mean that Creole is not only rich in song but also restricted to it. More than half the quoted Creole passages in the book are songs, and in no real language does that ratio hold. We know that one way of denying linguistic status to a language is to restrict its domain of expression; this is so even when the domain is a rich and praise-worthy one – gesture or musicality in Cooper, song in Cable.[56] If Creole is exclusively song, then it is also exclusively musical rather than discursive, already composed rather than improvised, folk rather than individual, not capable of doing all the things that real languages do.

In fact, though, the distinction Cable makes here is linked not to prej-udice but to comparative analysis. Frowenfeld says that "the shadow of the Ethiopian" (156) has hampered White Creole artistic activity. On the evidence of the novel, he's right. One manifestation of that activity is Raoul Innerarity's picture, his "pigshoe," of "Louisiana rif-using to hanter de h'Union" (114). Frowenfeld says of it that "to a judge of paintings it is ten dollars' worth of paint thrown away" (116), and that it would be worth its asking price of $250 only "if it could become the means of reminding this community that crude ability counts next to nothing in art, and that nothing else in this world ought to work so hard as genius" (115–16). The other manifestation is Agricola Fusilier's *Philippique Générale*, left unfin-ished at his death. Whatever genius Agricola may have brought to it did not lead him to hard work: "I wrote it myself in one evening" (326), he says on his deathbed. That's pretty much it for White Creole cultural produc-tion. Creole creativity is flourishing, French and English creativity mori-bund, not because Blacks have good rhythm and Whites don't, but because,

---

[55] See in particular Jones's excellent account of the "Two Little Birds" scene, *Strange Talk*, pp. 126–27.
[56] See above, Introduction, p. 18.

as Cable shows us, one community fosters artistic activity and the other impedes it.

Nor in revealing the richness of Creole song does Cable obscure the richness of Creole speech. In the great Creole passage of the book, which is also the greatest passage of the book in any language, Cable shows us not song but speech, not a speech community but an individual, not a prefabricated text but an improvisation. Clemence is the speaker, and her speech is a desperate plea for mercy, the improvised argument of a Black woman alone.

It has been found out that Clemence has been Palmyre's agent, delivering her voodoo charms to Agricola Fusilier, with dreadful effect on him. "Some rods within the edge of the swamp," accordingly, at the foot of "a big and singularly misshapen water-willow . . . the younger and some of the harsher senior members of the Grandissime family" put Clemence on trial – not a trial in the strict sense, but not quite a lynching either, since she is asked, at its beginning, "in the negro French" (one of the novel's relatively few unambiguous references to what language is being spoken, and importantly so), "have you any reason to give why you should not be hung to that limb over your head?" (321)

Clemence answers in the longest speech in the book, going on for a full page and interrupted only by narrative that functions as stage directions: pleading, excusing, apologizing, warning, threatening, in Black English, in Creole, in Louisiana Standard French. We might at first be skeptical: her Grandissime judges are francophones, address her in Creole, are as a group largely ignorant of English; her speaking so much English to them is fruitless. Maybe, we think, Cable didn't have the nerve to let her speak Creole for a whole page, maybe he didn't have the expertise, maybe he again subordinated probability to effect.

But English is Clemence's native language, our native language is what we turn to when in need, and her speech is magnificent:

"Oh, god 'a' [sic] mussy on my wicked ole soul! I aint fitt'n to die! Oh, gen'lemen, I kyan' look God in de face! *Oh, Michés, ayez pitié de moin! Oh, God A'mighty ha' mussy on my soul!* Oh, gen'lemen, dough yo' kinfolks kyvaeh up yo' tricks now, dey'll dwap f'um undeh you some day! *Solé levé là, li couché là!* Yo' t'un will come! Oh, God A'mighty de God o' de po' nigga wench! Look down, oh God, look down an' stop dis-yeh foolishness! Oh, God, fo' de love o' Jesus! *Oh, Michés, y'en a ein zizement!* Oh yes, deh's a judgmen' day! Den it wont be a bit o' use to you to be White! Oh, oh, oh, oh, oh, oh, fo', fo', fo', de, de, *love o' God! Oh!*"
They drew her up. (322–23)

Much of this is in Black English. Two phrases are in Creole. Both of them are sternly commanding, warning respectively of the impending judgment by human beings and of impending judgment by God. In both cases these warnings are echoed by English phrases that don't quite reproduce them; both languages are needed for Clemence's full range of thought and feeling. The English "Yo t'un will come!" is less vividly pictorial than *solé levé là, li couché là* ("sun rise there, set there"). The English "Oh yes, deh's a judgmen' day" makes unambiguously theological what in the Creole has just a hint of being secular: *y'en a ein zizement* ("there is a judgment") echoing a creolophone threat from earlier in the speech, *mo dis la zize* ("I'll tell the court"). The central plea is in a mix of Creole and Standard French: *Oh, Michés, ayez pitié de moin!* ("Oh sirs, have mercy on me"). "Michés" and "moin" belong to the Creole, "ayez" (and maybe the standard spelling of "pitié") to French. Again the English echoes the French without quite imitating it – the French appeal is to the Grandissimes for mercy on her body, the immediately following English one to God for mercy on her soul.

Facing his death and trying to avert it, Mercier's polyglot De Lauzun can hardly talk. Clemence in a similar situation draws on all her eloquence, unimpededly articulates her despair, her resourcefulness, her toughness, her wit. She first pleads for mercy; she is not fit to die, she says, slightly varying this central theme with each restatement. But she is not only begging for mercy; she turns next to proclaiming judgment. What courage she has, to threaten her threateners! She threatens in two ways: with the betrayal of their kinsfolk, and with the judgment of God – the God, she says, of the Black woman, "o' de po' nigga wench," an audacious theological claim in the face of such persecutors. When she speaks to that God, she has a surprising name for what is being done to her: not wickedness, not injustice, but "foolishness." Moralists see sin, satirists foolishness; even in the face of death Clemence remains the sharp-eyed satirist she has always been.

Afterwards, Clemence is set free, told to run for her life, then shot dead (we are not told by whom). That makes her speech seem an allegory of creole genesis. In the face of murderous persecution, against all odds, she uses whatever means she has to communicate: her native English, her persecutors' French, the slaves' Creole, notions of God and notions of law, self-abasement and threats of vengeance, narrative, argument, ejaculation, repetition, variation. The slaves of Louisiana did likewise; survivors of trauma, under long-enduring oppression, needing to communicate, over some fifty years they created a language. Like Clemence, they used all there was to use. Like her, they created something of power and beauty. Like her, they found that their creation could not deliver them.

CONCLUSION

Cable was a better writer than Mercier; his sentences are more vibrant, he had a more distinctive voice and a better ear for speech, he was more ambitious. But assessing the two novelists here means not only judging their literary gifts, but also thinking about how those gifts are used to represent the multilingual world. Dickens was a greater novelist than Elizabeth Gaskell; but in dealing with the dialect of Lancashire, writes Norman Page, "the lesser writer achieves the greater success: not even Dickens can make a few days in Preston an effective substitute for a long and affectionate awareness of a dialect as the expression of a way of life."[57]

In this context, some apparently dry facts turn out to be of great significance. First, no one in Mercier's novel (no one in *Johnelle* either) is ever shown switching linguistic codes. Each speech is solidly in one or the other of the two languages of the book.[58] Nor is there any linguistic variation between one person's French and another's, between one person's Creole and another's. In Cable's novel, on the other hand, people code-switch frequently, a linguistic continuum links all the languages spoken in the novel, and speakers move around that continuum rapidly and fluently. Clemence's final speeches are the most dazzling performances, but modulation is everywhere. So are the dialectal, socioeconomic, and regional variations of speech that in Mercier's novel are not to be found.

Mercier's exactness of recording goes well with his characters' exactness of language choice; Cable's protean inconstancy with his characters' linguistic mobility. But at issue here is not only temperament but also accuracy. Surprising at it may seem, it is Cable's strategy, evasions and all, which gets at the exacter truth. We know from our own experience how much variation is to be found from one person's speech to another's, even from, say, one American professor's speech to another; we know also how much variation is to be found within any one person's speech, as we move from one register to another, one variety to another. The historical record tells us the same thing, that Creole was and is "highly variable,"[59] that different speakers of it spoke different versions of it, some more like French (what linguists call "acrolectal"), some less so (what linguists call "basilectal"). We know the same thing about Louisiana French and about Louisiana English. The language continuum of Louisiana contained not only multiple

---

[57] Norman Page, *Speech in the English Novel* (Atlantic Highland: Humanities Press, 1988), p. 70.

[58] To be exact, since exactness is at issue here: there is one phrase in English, "business is business" (81), and one brief scene in "un jargon composé d'indien et de créole" (144; "a jargon composed of Indian and Creole"). But that's it.

[59] Valdman *et al.* (eds.), *Dictionary of Louisiana Creole*, p. 3.

languages but also multiple varieties of those languages, multiple moves among those languages, multiple improvised, skilled blendings of those languages. Cable's novel gets at the exacter truth not because he was a better linguist than Mercier was, not because he never played fast and loose with linguistic truth, but because he was more open to the linguistic plenitude of the world he sought to portray, less bent on a Linnaean classification of it, more ready to look at how, in Edward Sapir's phrase, "all categories leak."

Early in *The Grandissimes* there is a wonderful passage describing the costume of Queen Lufki-Humma, the "Diana of the Tchoupitoulas":

The queen sat down with [her captives], clothed in her entire wardrobe: vest of swan's skin, with facings of purple and green from the neck of the mallard; petticoat of plaited hair, with embroideries of quills; leggings of fawn-skin; garters of wampum; black and green serpent-skin moccasins, that rested on pelts of tigar[sic]-cat and buffalo; armlets of gars' scales, necklaces of bears' claws and alligators' teeth, plaited tresses, plumes of raven and flamingo, wing of the ping curlew, and odors of bay and sassafras. (21)

Exoticizing, yes, and probably invented rather than documented; but a brilliant image of the messiness, the variety, the plenitude that the world is full of, which Cable rejoiced in, and the depiction of which, along linguistic lines among others, makes his novel both so varied and so exact.

CHAPTER 3

More than an echo, or, English in Yiddish in America

THREE PREFATORY NOTES

Language encounters between Europeans and Native Americans were represented in writing almost exclusively by Europeans. Language encounters in Louisiana between White francophone slave-masters and Black creolophone slaves were represented in writing almost exclusively by Whites. But language encounters in America between immigrants and residents are different; they have been represented in writing mostly by the immigrants themselves.

There is something to regret in that; any encounter takes two, and understanding it means exploring both perspectives. But there is more to rejoice at. Too often we have to see language encounters through the languages of the more powerful: invaders, colonizers, and slave-masters. Here we can see them through the languages of the aspiring citizen, the refugee, the petitioning outsider, the "homeless, tempest-tossed," the alien.

The linguistic experiences of Jewish American immigrants were chiefly represented in literature in two languages, Yiddish and English. The present account focuses almost exclusively on literature written in Yiddish. Why?

The first reason is practical. The territory is vast, and mapping both the English and Yiddish regions would be a vast undertaking. The English domain, moreover, has been fully and brilliantly explored. Henry Roth's *Call It Sleep*, for example, arguably the greatest Jewish American language novel and certainly the most ambitious and the greatest in English, has been the object of fine studies by Werner Sollors and Hana Wirth-Nesher.[1] Wirth-Nesher's recent book, *Call It English: The Languages of Jewish American Literature*, is an illuminating account not only of Roth's book but also of a good number of other distinguished Jewish American writers in English.

---

[1] Both in Hana Wirth-Nesher (ed.), *New Essays on Call It Sleep* (Cambridge and New York: Cambridge University Press, 1996).

The second, deeper reason is conceptual. Writing in Yiddish rather than English, or the reverse, has no single, determinate meaning for Jewish American writers. Writing in Yiddish need not mean fidelity or authenticity or parochialism, nor writing in English opportunism or cosmopolitanism or betrayal. But the fact of writing in one or the other language is not meaningless. Other things being equal, the Jewish American writer writing in English has taken one step towards assimilation – I use the term not negatively but in the joyous, complex sense given it by a recent essay of Michael Kramer's[2] – towards Americanness. In Jewish American writing in English, Yiddish is the Other. The reverse is true of writing in Yiddish. Other things being equal, the writer is one step farther from assimilation, one notch more strongly identified as an immigrant, a Jewish outsider, a person about to make a choice about assimilation and Americanization rather than one carrying out a choice already made. America itself is one notch stranger, more bewildering. English, not Yiddish, is the Other.

From one door comes the sound of Lithuanian Yiddish, from another Polish Yiddish; in one hallway a man and a woman are conversing in the Yiddish of Volhinia and, in another, a woman is cursing in the Yiddish of Galicia . . . More often Americanized Yiddish is heard, and very frequently Yiddishized English, seasoned with the coarse language of the streets, and not infrequently the noble diction of Shakespeare and Byron and, sometimes, even the beautiful literary Russian of Turgenev.[3]

My utopia in the world would be the sort of place the American Yiddish writer Leon Kobrin is describing here, with all its realized and potential linguistic polyphony. My utopia in literature would be a work that justly and richly represented such a place. Kobrin doesn't do quite that, since the various languages being spoken in the tenement house are named rather than dramatized. But naming is a good first step. Even by itself it evokes the linguistic plenitude of the Jewish American immigrant world: Yiddish and English; the Americanized Yiddish and Yiddishized English that result from their encounter; the multiple dialects and registers within Yiddish; the multiple registers within English, from lowest to highest; even, as a kind of complicating adornment, the presence and literary nobility of Russian. Kobrin's vignette suggests the sort of linguistic material that a great Jewish

[2] Michael Kramer, "The Art of Assimilation: Ironies, Ambiguities, Aesthetics," as yet unpublished.
[3] Leon Kobrin, "The Tenement House," in Henry Goodman (ed. and trans.), *The New Country: Stories from the Yiddish about Life in America* (New York: YKUF, 1961), p. 31. Page numbers for subsequent quotations from this anthology will be given in the text.

American language fiction would seek to animate.[4] It thereby helps create a high standard of literary judgment – a standard of judgment I have tried to keep firmly in mind in writing the present essay, both the general considerations on Jewish American writing in Yiddish with which it begins, and the extended analysis and celebration of Sholem Aleichem's *Motl the Cantor's Son* with which it concludes.

WORDS, WORDS, WORDS

The portrait of American English in American Yiddish literature is a portrait of something existing in the real world, namely, the linguistic relations between American English and American Yiddish. We cannot understand or judge the portrait without knowing something about what it's portraying.

Some data regarding those linguistic relations are furnished by glossaries. The most important is Abraham Cahan's *Verter-bukh far nit amerikanishe lezer* ("A Dictionary for Non-American Readers"), a glossary of English elements in American Yiddish that Cahan appended to the second volume of his autobiography, published in 1926. It fills almost twelve double-columned pages, and no other glossary is on its scale. But there are other glossaries to supplement it. Some are smaller than Cahan's but equally explicit – for example, the list of ninety-four *farenglishte verter* ("Englished words") that the editors of the 1921 Folksfond edition of Sholem Aleichem put at the end of volume XXI, to explain the English-based terms in "Mr. Green Gets a Job" and "A Tale with a Greenhorn." Some are less explicit – for example, the English words that Cahan italicizes in his novel *Yekl*, characterizing them as "the five or six score English words and phrases which the omnivorous Jewish jargon has absorbed in the Ghettos of English-speaking countries."[5] Many are wholly implicit: the sets of English-based words that

---

[4] Kobrin seems to like this sort of image. In "The Pest," he writes that "the words of the Russian *Dubinushka*, of the Bundist Pledge and of popular Yiddish theater songs mingled under the clear blue sky and then blended with the passionate outcries of the relaxed picnickers and the joyful sounds of the pavilion . . . *Od lo ovda tikvoseynu*, came the words of the Zionist anthem, ardently sung by a duet, a man and a woman" (ed. and trans. Max Rosenfeld, *New Yorkish and Other American Yiddish Stories* [Philadelphia: Sholom Aleichem Club Press, 1995], p. 72; page numbers for subsequent quotations from this anthology will be given in the text). See also Kobrin's "A Common Language," in Max Rosenfeld (ed. and trans.), *Pushcarts and Dreamers* (Philadelphia: Sholom Aleichem Club Press, 1967); page numbers for subsequent quotations from this anthology will be given in the text.

[5] Abraham Cahan, *Yekl and the Imported Bridegroom, and Other Stories of Yiddish New York* (New York: Dover, 1970); *Yekl: A Tale of the New York Ghetto* (New York: D. Appleton and Co., 1896); *The Imported Bridegroom and Other Stories of the New York Ghetto* (Boston and New York: Houghton

particular writers in Yiddish use in their narratives of American life, or put into the mouths of their characters in American scenes.

These glossaries make up a significant lexicon. How is it to be read?[6] One approach, probably the dominant approach as long as American Yiddish was a flourishing language, was to consider the English-based lexicon as raising a question about the nature of good or correct Yiddish, and then to argue for or against the use of these words just as English-language usage critics do today. The advocates of Americanized Yiddish include Cahan himself, his contemporaries H. L. Mencken and George L. Wolfe, the noted lexicographer Alexander Harkavy, and at least two eminent critics of Yiddish literature, Shmuel Niger in Cahan's time and Benjamin Harshav in ours.[7] They all argue for a lively, demotic, egalitarian Yiddish, and against a set of claims they characterize as purist and elitist. "Though Dr. [Chaim] Zhitlowsky and his fellow Yiddishists may rail against [the] potato-chicken-kitchen language," writes Mencken, "it is the Yiddish of the overwhelming

---

Mifflin, 1898), p. 38. Page numbers for subsequent quotations from the Dover anthology will be given in the text.

    Unlike most of the literary texts considered in this essay, *Yekl* was written in English. That should, in theory, rule it out of consideration, since the point here is to get a sense of how English is imagined in Yiddish. But the situation is complicated. Though written in English, *Yekl* marks and comments on English elements in its characters' Yiddish speech. That by itself makes it distinctly more like a Yiddish-language fiction than an English-language one. Moreover, Cahan wrote *Yekl* both in English and in Yiddish. I quote the English version for convenience (the Yiddish one was never published in book form), but the Yiddish-language one provides pretty much the same data. See on this Aviva Taubenfeld's excellent "'Only an L': Linguistic Borders and the Immigrant Author in Abraham Cahan's *Yekl* and *Yankel der Yankee*," in Werner Sollors (ed.), *Multilingual America: Transnationalism, Ethnicity, and the Languages of American Literature* (New York: New York University Press, 1998), pp. 144–65.

6 In the ensuing analysis, the glossaries will be treated collectively. In fact they differ considerably. We can see this even by comparing their titles. Cahan's, "A Dictionary for Non-American Readers," denies legitimacy to any argument against the use of the words it records. They are, it suggests, simply part of the Yiddish spoken in America; readers of Yiddish in other countries may not be familiar with some of them; this glossary is therefore provided. Cahan thus positions himself as an expert guide to an unfamiliar but uncontested vocabulary. The Folksfond title more frankly calls the words *farenglisht* ("Englished"), and reveals their ambiguous status. They are Yiddish, yes, they are written in Hebrew characters, they are used by the leading Yiddish writer. But they are also "Englished," they have been transformed, they have been made more English and therefore less Yiddish; they have, then, become peculiar and unfamiliar, not just to a non-American reader of Yiddish, but to any reader of Yiddish anywhere.

7 See H. L. Mencken, *The American Language* (New York: Knopf, 1937); George L. Wolfe, "Notes on American Yiddish," *American Mercury* 29 (August 1933), pp. 473–79; Alexander Harkavy, *Yiddish-English-Hebrew Dictionary*, introduced by Dovid Katz (New York: Hebrew Publishing Company, 1928, repr. New York: Schocken, 1988); Shmuel Niger, "Lomir zey kashern" ("Let's make them kosher"), *Yidishe shprakh* 1 (1941), pp. 21–24; Benjamin Harshav, *The Meaning of Yiddish* (Berkeley: University of California Press, 1990). Page numbers for subsequent quotations from these works will be given in the text.

majority of American Jews" (634).[8] Niger compares suspect words to immigrants detained at Ellis Island, and pleads, "lomir zey kashern" (21; "let's
make them kosher"). Harkavy does just that, including such words in his
dictionary without any invidious classification of them.

The issue, for these writers, is how a language depicts the outside world,
that is, the world as something external to the language the writer uses to
depict it. That is why Cahan writes at the beginning of his autobiography
that he will use a different Yiddish for the first volume, which recounts
events in Europe, than for the subsequent volumes, which recount events
in America.

> With the exception of the first volume, these "pages" are written in American
> Yiddish – the Yiddish in which I have been accustomed to speak and write for
> more than forty years.
> In the first volume, such a language would be unnatural, because there the story
> is about the old country.[9]

He thus implies that European and American Yiddish will inevitably differ,
and that the differences between them will result simply from the different
situations they are used to describe. A similar conception animates Niger's
argument for accepting the Americanism *trobl*, that is, "trouble":

> How long will we continue to have "*trobl*" with . . . a word like "*trobl*" itself?
> How long will we continue to have it enclosed in quotation marks, as if in some
> sort of linguistic Ellis Island? There are cases when we have, not *tsores*, not *dayges*,
> not *zorgn*, not even *unongenemlikhkeytn*, but rather just *trobl*. So let us stop being
> ashamed, and just say that we have *trobl*. (22)

Those on the other side, those who insist, in Wolfe's phrase, "on a Yiddish
pure and undefiled," have in mind a different goal: not depicting the outside
world, but maintaining the language's internal integrity:

> [They] are vitally interested in the perpetuation of Yiddish wherever Jews are.
> They ridicule the indiscriminate use of English loan words. From the platform, in
> the press, and in conversation they deplore the development of a bastard Yiddish
> in America. They call it the potato-chicken-kitchen language, the barbaric lan-
> guage, the language of the streets, and so forth. "When one thinks of Yiddish in

---

[8] Mencken got his information and opinions on these matters from Cahan; he is not offering an
independent competent judgment on Yiddish usage. But even his second-hand views matter. He was
a more widely known language critic than any of the Yiddish-language writers, and the prestige of
his unborrowed views about English gave credibility to his borrowed views about Yiddish.

[9] Abraham Cahan, *In der alter heym* ("In the old country"), *Bleter fun mayn lebn* ("Pages from my life"),
5 vols. (New York: Forward Association, 1926), vol. I, p. 3, my translation, as are all translations not
otherwise identified. Page numbers for subsequent quotations from this work will be given in the
text.

America," says Dr. Ch[aim] Zhitlowsky, the theoretician of the Yiddishist movement, in the *Day*, "one must not forget that we have here two brands of Yiddish.
One brand is the wild-growing Yiddish-English jargon, the potato-chicken-kitchen
language; the other brand is the cultivated language of Yiddish culture all over the
world." (Wolfe, "Notes on American Yiddish" 478)

Sometimes, though, the "Yiddishists" make more complex arguments.
Consider Max Weinreich's remarkable 1941 essay, "Vegn englishe elementn in undzer kulturshprakh" ("On English Elements in Our Culture-
Language"). Weinreich begins by noting that what is at issue is not just
vocabulary but also grammar. He then establishes a troubling association
between the use of English vocabulary and that of non-standard grammar –
that is, between something Cahan and Niger are defending and something
they would surely disdain. He investigates and annihilates the argument
that new English words are introduced only to describe new American
phenomena.

His demolition work finished, Weinreich makes some surprising maneu-
vers. He argues for the legitimacy of certain English-based phrases that are
clearly not introduced for that reason. Is it correct to use *trobl*? There is,
says Weinreich, no single answer. Making the right choice depends on
context. Accordingly, he distinguishes among speech registers – for example, "correct Yiddish"; "the American Yiddish culture-language," "general
literary Yiddish"; and among speech situations – for example, a private
conversation among friends, a speech at a meeting, a newspaper article, an
editorial, a scholarly book. He reflects thoughtfully on what usage might
be appropriate in each register and situation.[10]

Compared with most English-language usage debates, these Yiddish
debates are more intelligent, less dogmatic, less self-righteous. But they
have an important limitation: the writers' focus on whether particular
words should be used kept them from investigating what happened when
they were used. Perhaps it was good that speakers and writers of American
Yiddish were using this or that individual English-based word or group of

---

[10] Max Weinreich, "Vegn englishe elementn in undzer kulturshprakh," *Yidishe shprakh* 1 (1941),
pp. 33–46. Page numbers for subsequent quotations from this work will be given in the text.
   An extreme position on these matters is that of Isaac Bashevis Singer, whose 1943 "Problems of
Yiddish Prose in America" was, David Roskies writes, "so controversial in its cultural pessimism
that it carried a disclaimer from the editors. What Singer argued is that Yiddish as a modern secular language was dead" (David Roskies, *A Bridge of Longing: The Lost Art of Yiddish Storytelling*
[Cambridge, MA: Harvard University Press, 1996], p. 281). For Singer's essay, see "Problemen fun
der yidisher proze in Amerike," *Svive* 2 (March–April 1943), pp. 2–13, and the English translation,
"Problems of Yiddish Prose in America," trans. Robert Wolf, *Prooftexts* 9 (1989), pp. 5–12.

words. Perhaps it was bad. In any case, they were using them. What were the consequences?

Emerson wrote, "a new fact makes a new system." A new word is a new fact. A whole vocabulary of new words is an abundance of new facts, a collective new fact on a large scale, and the system has to change to accommodate it. Uriel Weinreich brilliantly describes the process in *Languages in Contact*.[11] Even at the level of the individual word, he writes, "the consequences of a word transfer or a word reproduction on the miniature semantic system . . . of which the new word becomes a member are as much a part of the interference as the transfer or reproduction themselves" (53). At the highest level,

every enrichment or impoverishment of a system involves necessarily the reorganization of all the old distinctive oppositions of the system. To admit that a given element is simply added to the system which receives it without consequences for this system would ruin the very concept of system. (1)

Consider, as an example of how the process works in a particular case, the case of the word "smart." There is a perfectly good Yiddish word of approximately the same meaning: *klug*. *Klug*, though, is less likely than American English "smart" is to refer to people who ruthlessly exercise their intelligence for their own interest.[12] So what happens when "smart" comes into Yiddish? Weinreich states the three possibilities: "confusion in usage, or full identity of content between the old and the new word"; the discarding of the old word; and "specialization in content" – that is, the development of a felt difference between the old word and the new, in reference or style or both (55). In the case at hand, the first possibility was

[11] Uriel Weinreich, *Languages in Contact* (The Hague: Mouton, 1970). Page numbers for subsequent quotations from this work will be given in the text. See also on this subject the writings of Joshua Fishman, especially *Yiddish in America*, Indiana University Research Center in Anthropology, Folklore, and Linguistics, publication 36, *International Journal of American Linguistics* 31:2(2) (Bloomington: Indiana University Press, 1965); and Sol Steinmetz, *Yiddish and English: A Century of Yiddish in America* (Birmingham: University of Alabama Press, 1986).

This English-in-Yiddish bilingualism is related to, but also distinct from, the long history of what Max Weinreich called "Jewish internal bilingualism," i.e., the bilingualism constituted by the simultaneous presence in some Jewish communities of two specifically Jewish languages – Yiddish and Hebrew. See Max Weinreich, *History of the Yiddish Language*, trans. Shlomo Noble, assisted by Joshua A. Fishman (Chicago: University of Chicago Press, 1980), pp. 257–314.

[12] The *Oxford English Dictionary* notes that "smart," in the morally ominous sense of "quick at devising, learning, looking after oneself or one's own interests," is in its later use chiefly American; the *Dictionary of Americanisms* defines "smartness" as "extreme cleverness or shrewdness, especially to one's own advantage." When Dickens's Martin Chuzzlewit asks the scoundrel Colonel Driver whether "smart" is "American for forgery," he is getting at this connotation (Charles Dickens, *Martin Chuzzlewit* [New York: Penguin, 1986], p. 326).

not realized; this, Weinreich says, "is probably restricted to the early stages of language contact." Nor was the second; Yiddish retains *klug* till this day. What happened was the realization of the third possibility, specialization in content: "smart" took on the sense of "unethically intelligent," and *klug* was restricted to the legitimate uses of intelligence. A similar distinction seems to have arisen between English-derived *biznes* and standard European Yiddish *gesheft*; as George Wolfe writes, "*business* is reserved for an enterprise of a questionable character; otherwise the purer and dignified *gescheft* is employed" (474). Max Weinreich substantiates this, writing that the word is usually used "with a flavor of scorn" (40).[13]

The two examples are strikingly similar: the Yiddish word is honorable, the English one is not. A wider sampling yields a more complicated portrait. The English elements gathered in the glossaries focus most strikingly on the commercial world. Almost every list has the word "business."[14] The Folksfond list adds a few idioms that put that word to use: "attending to business," "settling the business," "business-broker." Cahan's list adds "busy," "business card," and "businessman." Other words name particular aspects of business: "advertisement," "agent," "appointment," "boss," "cash," "commission," "deposit," "expenses," "job," "salary," "shop," "success," "trade," "wages." Some words describe particular businesses and occupations: "bookkeeper," "bricklayer," "butcher," "custom tailor," "druggist," "garbageman," "laundry," "newsboy," the almost omnipurpose "operator," "peddler," "stationery," "waiter." It is no accident that Cahan cites *makhn a lebn* ("making a living") as the first phrase that gave him a taste – and a sour taste, at that – of American Yiddish: "when I would hear a phrase like '*er makht a lebn*,' I'd barely keep from gnashing my teeth."[15]

---

[13] Wolfe writes *gescheft*, I write *gesheft*. My own transliterations of Yiddish words are mostly in accord with YIVO guidelines. When I quote other writers, I quote their transliterations as I find them.

[14] Most words taken from the glossaries will be given in the standard spelling of the English words they are derived from. Their Yiddish spelling is interesting, especially as reflecting the New York pronunciation of English at the time when the glossaries were compiled, e.g., "furniture" rendered as *foyrnitsher*, but reproducing it here would slow the argument.

[15] Cahan, *Bleter*, vol. II: *Mayne ershte akht yor in amerike* ("My first eight years in America"), p. 109. For a published English translation, see Abraham Cahan, *The Education of Abraham Cahan*, trans. Leon Stein, Abraham Conan, and Lynn Davison (Philadelphia: Jewish Publication Society of America, 1969) p. 242.
   Why Cahan had such a negative reaction to the phrase isn't clear, though the context suggests that what he disliked was both the grammar of the expression and its implicit greediness. After the sentence quoted in the text, we read, "I remember this expression specifically, and also the expression, 'he is worth ten thousand dollars'."

A related group of words evokes the sharp and slippery uses of commercial intelligence. "Smart" is of course one of them. Others are "bluffer,"[16] "bargain," "scheme," and "trick." Other words in the same group have a different relation to sharp business; they are not terms for describing it but part of the verbal repertory of those who practice it, elements in the repartee of con men: "leave it to me," "never mind," "sport" (in the sense of a "good fellow"). Sholem Aleichem's Mr. Baraban the Business Broker, scheming to ruin a young man by selling him a laundry instead of a stationery store, deploys the first of these phrases expertly:

". . . *leave it to me*, I'll give you a better *business*, a *laundry* in the Bronx, you'll work *regular* hours and live like a king!" . . .
"What will that cost?"
I tell him, "a bargain at a thousand dollars, but *leave it to me*, I'll get it for you for eight hundred." (Sholem Aleichem, "A Tale with a Greenhorn" 254)[17]

But American English-in-Yiddish also has a vocabulary of resistance to business – that is, for describing the world of labor and union organizing. Cahan's list is especially rich in these: "association," "chairman," "dues," "grievance committee," "handbill," "headquarters," "labor," "labor day," "labor lyceum," "lock-out," "picket," "rank and file," "strike," "trade and labor alliance," "trade union." ("Union" itself does not appear there, though both Cahan and many other writers use the word frequently.) A related group of words describes the political institutions that those who sought to resist the pressures of business would have to understand: "assemblyman," "association," "board of education," "district attorney," "governor," "legislature," "nomination," "politician," "Tammany," "trial," "vote." Another related group describes the grimmer side of immigrant life, especially working-class immigrant life: "breadline," "gambling house," "jail,"[18] "pawnshop," "prison," "riot," "sack" (in the sense of "to fire"), "sweater" (in the sense of a sweatshop boss), "sweatshops."

---

[16] A particularly interesting example. *Blofer*, "bluffer," is glossed by Cahan as *ligner*, "liar." Fair enough, if what matters is only to understand what the word refers to. But using the former in place of the latter means emphasizing deceitful craft over moral dishonesty.

[17] In translating Yiddish literary passages for this chapter, I have usually used italics to indicate words that are in English in the Yiddish original. I have also sometimes used italics for Yiddish words that I have chosen to retain in the English translations. In theory, this risks creating ambiguity. In practice it seems not to.

[18] In "Notes on American Yiddish," *Journal of English and German Philology* 37 (1938), J. H. Neumann suggests that "jail" gets used in American Yiddish because, for "words for which there exist in Yiddish many local and dialectal terms, . . . American Yiddish substitutes a single English word understood by all" (412). Page numbers for subsequent quotations from this work will be given in the text.

These are the principal categories.[19] They evoke conflicting aspects and values of immigrant life, not just its American-style commercial villainy. But they consistently define English-in-Yiddish as belonging to secular life rather than sacred, daily life rather than ceremonial, and, though less consistently, public life rather than private. No glossary proposes to replace *khazn* with "cantor," *khosn* with "bridegroom," *kheyder* with "religious school." Rather these Yiddish words, and others like them, regularly turn up in another sort of glossary, that is, the glossaries of Yiddish words retained in English-language narratives. The glossary of Mary Antin's *Promised Land*, for example, includes not only these words but also *dayen* (a judge in a religious court), *goles* (exile, diaspora), *khumesh* (Pentateuch), *lamdn* (scholar), *mikve* (ritual bath), *treyf* (ritually forbidden).[20] To describe religious and ceremonial life, immigrants held fast to Yiddish even when they had turned to writing in English.

The few exceptions to the generalization strengthen it. Consider the word "reverend." For once, Cahan's definition suggests skepticism: "someone venerable; used of a rabbi, a cleric, chiefly of a rabbi or another *klekoydesh* [Yiddish term for a Jewish cleric] in 'modern' dress" – that is, a sartorially assimilated rabbi. J. H. Neumann notes that "rabbi" itself "invariably means a reform or conservative minister, not an orthodox rabbi of the old school" (413). Sholem Aleichem's Huck Finn-like Motl the Cantor's son cheerfully sharpens the skepticism:

A *rov* [European Yiddish for "rabbi"] has to be able to *poskenen shayles* [give authoritative responses to technical and practical legal questions]. And yet, there are *rabonim* [plural of *rov*] in America. Here they're called "reverends" – at home they were butchers. My brother Elye met a *moyl* [a ritual circumciser], a *reverend*, whom they call for brisses. At home he was a tailor, in fact a ladies' tailor! Elye says to him: "can it be?" He answers: "America!"[21]

Yiddish borrows American English words to refer to the religious world when it wants to describe second-rate clerics and religious impostors.

None of this is surprising. Its being unsurprising, though, does not make it neutral, nor keep it from having wide-ranging consequences. It is one thing to take two nearly synonymous words, one borrowed and

---

[19] The glossaries do describe other areas of life as well, e.g., the geography of New York City, the public schools, the architecture and furnishings of a tenement house.

[20] Mary Antin, *The Promised Land* (New York: Penguin, 1997), pp. 289–94.

[21] Sholem Aleichem, *Motl Peyse dem khazns*, ed. Khone Shmeruk (Jerusalem: The Magnes Press, 1997), p. 241. Page numbers for subsequent quotations from this work will be given in the text.

Note that Motl has a certain admiration for the way people can, as he believes, learn absolutely anything in America. It's the writer and reader who are skeptical.

one traditional, and distinguish between them by specializing both. It is another thing to do this with two languages. When we step back from the particular American encounter between English and Yiddish, we know perfectly well that English has a rich vocabulary for talking about religious practice and ceremony, and Yiddish a rich vocabulary for talking about daily life, heroic labor, and rapacious management. When Yiddish writers borrow English terms for describing the secular life and retain Yiddish ones for describing the religious life, when writers in English reverse the process, both languages risk being diminished in their self-sufficiency and splendor. Casting English as a secular language is stereotyping it. So is casting Yiddish as a religious one.[22]

STEREOTYPES AND LANGUAGE TRAITORS

Many images of English in Yiddish writing simply dramatize the stereotypes the glossaries imply. Cahan's *Yekl* tells us that America is the land where "*a shister vet a mister un a mister vet a shister*" (25; "a cobbler [*shister*] becomes a gentleman [*mister*, i.e., the English word "mister"] and a gentleman a cobbler") – that is, an English word speaks of success, a Yiddish one of labor.[23] Leon Kobrin's "*Aktyorn*" ("Actors") makes the same sociolinguistic point more flamboyantly:

The cashier of the theater, who spoke only English when "business was booming" and only Yiddish when "business was rotten" – he too, hearing what the actors were saying, stuck his black curly head out of the booth whenever he saw me and greeted me enthusiastically in English: "A double-G!" he predicted, which meant, I assumed, Good with a capital G. (*New Yorkish* 54)

Numerous American Yiddish fictions present a class of Jewish language traitors: villains who use English villainously, on its own or through the incorporation of English terms into their Yiddish, immigrant companions to history's Doña Marina, Cooper's Magua, Mercier's De Lauzun, Cable's

---

[22] This scheme, in which Yiddish is religious and English secular, is ironically related to an aspect of the Jewish internal bilingualism mentioned above, in which Hebrew is religious and Yiddish secular. Figuring out how that relation works is beyond the scope of this essay.

For a sharp-tongued critique of a similar position regarding a different language pairing, see Doris Sommer, *Bilingual Aesthetics: A New Sentimental Education* (Durham, NC: Duke University Press, 2004): "Speakers of Lakota object to a 'thingness' about English because it allegedly reifies spiritual meanings into objects. The 'sweat house,' for example, is a wooden translation for a mystical ceremony called *inikagapi* ('with it they make life'). But the contrast between sacred Lakota and secular English is bogus. It ignores the heated mystical tradition in Standard English, where, for instance, communion means much more than wafer eating. The Lakota case shows only that one tradition doesn't easily understand another" (xviii–xix).

[23] I take this point from Taubenfeld, "'Only an L'," p. 151.

Palmyre.[24] If the glossaries associate English with what is secular and commercial, the stories, some of them at least, more sharply associate English
with what is wicked.

Sometimes these characters are evoked only briefly. The quickest learner
of English among the greenhorns depicted in Chaver Paver's *Tsen Landslayt*
("Ten Landsmen")[25] is the one criminal, Berele the Pickpocket: "on the way
from Ellis Island to his brother Herschel's house on Prospect Avenue in the
Bronx, Berele Pickpocket learned a few English words: 'Hello, how are you,
thanks, all right'" (*The New Country* 95). Miriam Raskin's Lily, in "In the
Shadows," appears only as "a young, pretty girl who spoke only English,
[and] seemed to have become extremely attractive" (*New Yorkish* 85); her
English and her attractiveness together endanger the relation between the
sympathetic protagonist Annie and the poet Isaac Lev. Tashrak's James
Pussy ("[I] thought to myself that his Jewish name probably was Zushe
Katz" [*The New Country* 120]), with his English name, English vocabulary,
and mildly fraudulent real-estate "bargains," would be a successful language
traitor if he were smarter; instead, the narrator to whom Pussy makes
his pitch decides, at his wife's suggestion, that he himself will turn real
estate agent, and concludes the story by offering to sell the reader "half
of New York!" (124) The landlady in Jonah Rosenfeld's "Americanized" is
made sinister and alien by three traits: being fat, having frequent sex with
her husband, and speaking English, which the disgusted narrator cannot
understand.[26]

[24] Immigrant characters of this sort are not restricted to Yiddish. I myself first came across the type
in *Die Emigranten*, an anonymous 1882 German play from St. Louis, and I have read of other
examples in Scandinavian-language immigrant fiction; see Orm Overland, "From Melting Pot to
Copper Kettles," in Werner Sollors (ed.), *Multilingual America: Transnationalism, Ethnicity, and
the Languages of American Literature* (New York: New York University Press, 1998), p. 55, and my
"Language Traitors, Translation, and *Die Emigranten*," in Winfried Fluck and Werner Sollors (eds.),
German? American? Literature? New Directions in German-American Studies (New York: Peter Lang,
2002), pp. 250–56.

[25] *Landslayt* are groups of Jewish immigrants in America who come from a single *shtetl* in eastern
Europe.

[26] Other, related characters in these stories are marked not by their English nor by the English words in
their Yiddish, but by other aspects of their Yiddish speech. These are sometimes simply incompetent
speakers of the language, e.g., Avrom Reyzn's "The American Europeans": "she would not voice her
opinions in Yiddish because she feared they would laugh at her pronunciation" (*The New Country*
211); sometimes speakers of the language with a more egalitarian, less respectful politeness code;
sometimes speakers whose particular version of the language suggests a general rejection of Judaism,
as in Kobrin's "Door #1": "'it seemed to me,'" says the protagonist Moishe of his two sons, "'these
were two Polish priests who had come for us – and to listen to their Yiddish! It sounded to me like
Stephan, the policeman, talking. Don't you remember, we surely thought at that time, that they had
actually gone over?'" (186).

Sometimes the portraits are richer. Consider Sholem Ash's[27] "American," a "biznes-man" long in America, traveling with a group of green immigrants to New York. One of the immigrants is a pianist, a virtuoso with grand ambitions. But then the businessman gets hold of him:

Well, Mr. Paderevski, I want to tell you something . . . kunst, shmunst ["art, shmart"]. We've heard this sort of thing before, and with your piano-playing there you're not going to surprise anyone. *No, sir.* America needs *business, and that's all!*[28]

Then, with a wealth of convincing detail and an abundance of English, the businessman proposes an alternative scenario: not New York but a city in the Midwest, say Memphis or Kansas City; not a grand public concert, but private lessons, friendships with the ladies, connections with the local *"reverend"* and his pretty daughter, good clothing, perhaps a concert in a private house at a *"five o'clock dinner,"* a music school ("it's a *business!*"); at the end, money in the bank, a car, a house, a young wife and two children playing in the garden.

Ash's intelligence here lies in the precise details and the sadly realistic conclusion. The young man is no hero. He does not turn away from the American's appeals to assert the cause of art. Instead, he is seduced by them: "suffused with joy, a song in his heart, the young man listened to the American's speech, and it resounded in his ears like the most beautiful of concerts."

Jake in Abraham Cahan's *Yekl* is a language traitor on a bigger scale, and *Yekl* as a whole is a story about language treason.[29] The better a character speaks English, and the more English elements a character incorporates into his or her Yiddish, the more assimilated the character is, and the worse his or her behavior. Jake is the protagonist, a Yiddish-speaking Jew come to America to make a living. Gitl, his Old World wife, is the person in relation to whom the other characters' behavior can be charted. Jake's co-worker Mr. Bernstein cannot speak English, and speaks a Yiddish mostly free of English elements; he continues to say the traditional blessing over bread, and in the end he seems likely to become Gitl's new and faithful husband. Jake's neighbor Mrs. Kavarsky speaks some English and incorporates some English elements into her Yiddish; she is Gitl's friend and supporter against

[27] "Ash" is the scholarly transliteration of Ash's name. But it is more usually transliterated as "Asch."

[28] Sholem Ash, *Der amerikaner* ("The American"), recorded by Chaim Ostrowsky on *Jewish Classical Literature* (New York: Folkways Records, 1960). I have been unable to find the story in printed collections of Ash's works.

[29] For a wonderful commentary on *Yekl* from a different but equally language-centered perspective, see Hana Wirth-Nesher's *Call It English: The Languages of Jewish American Literature* (Princeton: Princeton University Press, 2006), pp. 32–51.

Jake, but she also presses Gitl to stop covering her hair in the traditional way, and in a burst of passion first combs, then cuts Gitl's unfashionably long hair with scissors and curling iron – which Gitl experiences as "instruments of torture" (67), though the result is "a pair of rich side bangs" (67). Jake himself speaks a Yiddish thick with English elements, and likes speaking English.[30] He delays purchasing tickets to bring Gitl and their son Yosselé to America, preferring boxing-matches and dances and his "general life of gallantry" (25). He does bring them in the end; but then he deserts them, albeit remorsefully, for the thoroughly Americanized Mamie Fein, arranges for both rabbinical and civic divorces, and leaves with Mamie for Philadelphia. Mamie, who speaks English "like one American born" (52), takes Jake away from Gitl and feels no remorse at all.

This linguistic pattern is dramatized in a pivotal scene in which Mamie comes to reclaim Jake from Gitl, and in which her strategies for reclaiming him are enacted in and facilitated by the use of English. Before the scene, Jake seems to be working his way back into his marriage; afterwards, he's clearly moving away from it. Mamie enters, "preceded by a cloud of cologne odors" (49). She exchanges English greetings with Jake, which Gitl tries unsuccessfully to participate in. When she speaks to Gitl in Yiddish, she deliberately makes herself unintelligible, speaking

with an overdone American accent in the dialect of the Polish Jews, affectedly Germanized and profusely interspersed with English, so that Gitl, whose mother tongue was Lithuanian Yiddish, could scarcely catch the meaning of one half of her flood of garrulity. (49–50)

The actual actions of concealment and betrayal are then performed in English. Mamie has lent Jake $25. Gitl does not know of the loan, which implies an intimacy between Mamie and Jake that Jake has concealed. Mamie threatens in English to tell Gitl of the loan "in Jewish" (50) – that is, in Yiddish; but the threat is itself an intimate conspiracy with Jake, in that it takes place in Gitl's presence but without her comprehension. Then Jake, fearing justly that their continuing to speak in English will make Gitl uneasy, makes a crucial concession:

"For Chrish'[31] shake, Mamie!" he entreated her, wincingly. "Shtop to shpeak English, an' shpeak shomet'ing differench. I'll shee you – ver can I shee you?" (51)

[30] Cahan's exact rendering of that English in its Yiddish-influenced grammar and pronunciation makes it hideous and nearly unintelligible on the page – so hideous, in fact, that one wonders whether he intends the repellent orthography to be a critique of the language it is representing.

[31] Jake's allusion to Jesus here suggests a religious assimilation that Cahan probably wants us to read as running in parallel with his linguistic assimilation. (My thanks to my colleague Bill Cain for calling my attention to this point.)

Speaking English thus enables Jake and Mamie both to conceal their previous relationship and to arrange for its continuation.

The subtlest of these language traitors is Sholem Aleichem's Mr. Baraban
the Business Broker. What makes him subtle is partly his virtuosic scheming.
He settles on a victim, a young man with a pretty wife and $1,000 that
the wife has brought to the marriage. The young man wants to buy a
business, a stationery store. Mr. Baraban, in envy (his wife is "a freak to
look at and a Xantippe besides"[32]) or in motiveless malignity, sets out to
ruin him. He sells him a laundry instead of a stationery store, and at an
inflated price ($800); terrifies the young man by making him believe that
another laundry is opening around the corner; buys the laundry back from
the young man, for $500 (minus a broker's commission!); then entices the
young man into buying a laundry again, to compete with the laundryman
from whom Mr. Baraban had acquired the original laundry in the first
place. A fierce competition arises between the two laundries; the young
man goes broke and is put in jail; and Mr. Baraban finishes the comedy
by finding the young man's wife a lawyer, to help her sue her husband for
her dowry, for a divorce, and for support payments until the divorce comes
through.

The other thing that makes Mr. Baraban subtle is his self-presentation.
His language itself is familiar, a particularly vigorous, three-card monte
style of Americanized Yiddish.

"What's the use to you," I say, "of *bothering* yourself with a *stationery-store*, eighteen
hours in twenty-four, peering about in case a *schoolboy* runs through to get *candy*
for a *penny* and so forth? So *leave it to me* – I'll get you a better *business*, a *laundry*
in the *Bronx*, you'll work *regular* hours and live like a king!" (254)

When we first meet him, though, what he is doing with this language is
shamelessly crusading against the unregulated passion for American-style
business. Mr. Baraban's opening monologue could be a critique of Sholem
Ash's *Amerikaner*:

You say: America is a country of *business*. *Never mind*. That's the way it has
to be. But *after all*, going to get married and selling yourself for *biznes* – that,
surely, *excuse me*, is a *khazeray* ["piggishness," general negative term derived from
the traditional Jewish prohibition of eating pork]. I'm not preaching a moral, but

[32] Sholem Aleichem, "A mayse mit a grinhorn" ("A Story with a Greenhorn"), in *Ale verk fun Sholem-
Aleichem*, 28 vols. (New York: Sholem Aleichem Folks-Fond, 1921), vol. XXI, p. 257. Page numbers
for subsequent quotations from this work will be given in the text. Published English translations by
Goodman, in *The New Country*, and by Ted Gorelick, in Sholem Aleichem, *Nineteen to the Dozen*
(Syracuse: Syracuse University Press, 1998).

I'm telling you, it's a *fact*, ninety-nine percent of all greenhorns get married here for *business* – and that bothers me, and when I meet a greenhorn like that, he's not getting away without something to remember me by, *leave it to me*. So let me tell you a story . . . (253)

Sholem Aleichem knows that the most skillful language traitors present themselves as righteous critics of all the rest.

MEANS OF RESISTANCE

These images of English-in-Yiddish are so powerful that they almost seem inevitable. In fact they are tendentious, and the vision they imply is an over-simplification. Speaking English, let alone simply incorporating English elements into one's Yiddish, does not mean abandoning Jewish religious values for American commercial ones. (Cahan himself was an advocate of Americanized Yiddish but an opponent of assimilation.) Speaking Euro-pean Yiddish does not mean adhering to Jewish values. Being American does not mean holding exclusively commercial and secular values; being Jewish does not mean holding exclusively ethical and religious ones.

A wonderful sketch by the humorist Moshe Nadir, called "I: As Echo," hints at a more complex view. The bohemian narrator takes a job with a friend, a farmer and country resort-keeper. A competing resort-keeper, seeking to attract nature-lovers, has hired a man to provide a picturesque echo. The narrator's friend hires him for the same purpose, at "$2.40 a day plus free laundry."[33] The narrator finds a hiding place by a picturesque bridge and waits. A wandering nature-lover happens by, then shouts a few phrases in the hope of hearing them echoed. The narrator imitates the nature-lover's first phrases almost perfectly. But soon he finds the job growing burdensome; and when the nature-lover calls out, "how are you doing?" the narrator steps out of his part and answers, "*thank you*! I'm *all right*. How are you doing yourself?" (58) He is, predictably enough, fired, and sent back to the city on the first available train.

Nadir's sketch is a genial parable about linguistic assimilation, and a lens for looking at the fictions so far discussed. Those fictions are concerned with the bad effects of what Nadir's sketch teaches us to call being an echo. They present the unreflective, mechanical, docile imitation of English words and phrases – that is, the echoing of them – as both profitable and corrupting. It

---

[33] Moyshe Nadir, "Ikh – als viderkol," in *Zeks bikher* (New York: Yidisher Farlag far Literatur un Visnshaft, 1928), p. 55. Page numbers for subsequent quotations from this work will be given in the text.

is profitable because it enables one to get ahead in anglophone America. It is corrupting because, the stories imply, echoing American English means echoing American commercial values.

Nadir knows the truths these stories know. His sketch, too, makes the association between echoing and commercial success. Before becoming an echo, the narrator is poor and unemployed. While being an echo, the narrator is paid $2.40 a day plus free laundry – a modest but not minimal salary at the time. After being an echo, the narrator is poor once again, with no prospects in sight. The sketch also resembles the stories in suggesting that being an echo isn't finally very satisfying. It's going too far to call the narrator a man of principle, who rejects the job of being an echo because it degrades him. Nadir's sketch doesn't sound such earnest notes. But something in the narrator – artistic boredom, vain eagerness to speak in his own voice, sheer impudence – pushes him, and pushes him quickly, to give up a good salary and situation.[34]

But Nadir knows other truths as well. In the stories, the implicit alternative to echoing English seems to be not to speak it at all – that is, to hold on to Yiddish against English as a means of holding on to Jewish ethical and religious values against American secular and commercial ones. This would be, in the terms of Nadir's sketch, either to refuse the job in the first place, or, on finding out what it entailed, to resign from it with dignity and nobly bear the privations of honest poverty – that poverty which, as Anzia Yezierska's autobiography reminds us, "becomes a wise man like a red ribbon on a white horse."[35]

That is not what Nadir's narrator does. He enjoys the prospect of $2.40 a day and free laundry. He enjoys echoing – for a while, at least. He continues to like certain aspects of echoing, for example, the form of call and response. What he doesn't like is always having to be an exact echo. Let him be free to improvise a little – enough, say, to make echoing into conversation, into two Jews talking – and he will be perfectly happy. This would be, in the terms of the stories, not to reject English but to play with it, to speak it but to speak it in one's own voice.

Where do we see this richer possibility realized? Sometimes in the language itself. A good example is *olraytnik*, with the Slavic suffix "nik" joining

[34] Maybe, of course, what pushes him to give up his salary and situation is the nature-lover's invitation: "how are you doing?" Even the nature-lover, that is, is asking for conversation more than he's asking for an echo. (My thanks to my friend and colleague Margery Sabin for this acute observation.)

[35] The epigraph to Anzia Yezierska, *Red Ribbon on a White Horse* (New York: Persea, 1987); identified as a "ghetto proverb." The oldest form of the proverb known to me is differently gendered: "Poverty is becoming to a Jewess, as a red ribbon on the nape of a white horse," quoted by Akiva, Leviticus Raba 35:6.

the American idiom "all right." The American idiom itself, says the *His-torical Dictionary of American Slang*, means "excellent, great; (of persons) dependable, trustworthy, friendly." The Yiddish word means pretty much the opposite. Cahan's glossary, often aimed at neutralizing the emotional or ethical charges of English elements in American Yiddish, defines "all right" simply as "*gut, rekht*" ("good, correct"). Weinreich's scrupulous dictionary makes the matter clearer; an *olraytnik* is an "upstart, philistine, parvenu." An English word of praise has been transformed into a Yiddish word of satire.

Writers of literature let us watch such transformations and resistances take place. Sometimes they do that simply by showing us characters who hold opinions about particular English words – that is, who do not receive them as inevitable facts:

The teacher teaches the class the skill of spelling "night," which is almost like the Yiddish "*nacht*" but which has that extra "g" in the middle: "Sister," which means "*shvester*," is a pleasure to spell, without any extra letters at all. But "knife," with the unnecessary "k" right smack at the beginning! (Chaver Paver, "Gershon," *Pushcarts* 213–14)

When the words are charged with meaning, the process of having an opinion about them is more intense, as in Chone Gottesfeld's "A Pleasure to Have a Beard," where "one old man, who had been in America a long time, interpreted the word ["kike"] in this way: 'kike is a word which a greenhorn who chews chewing-gum calls a greenhorn who does not yet chew gum'" (*The New Country* 230). Sometimes, to hold off the pressure of English, immigrants simply invent words. In Jonah Rosenfeld's "Vreplamrendn," for example, the narrator's landlady insults him in English, which he cannot understand; but he defends himself with "vreplamrendn," which she cannot understand, and prevails: "her eyes flared with such dislike for me that my sides almost burst with the laughter exploding inside me, and I repeated the word so I wouldn't forget it, in order to have it ready for similar situations" (*Pushcarts* 180).[36]

Sometimes it seems that simply reading English, rather than only speak-ing it, is enough to make one an unservile student of American values. Avrom Reyzn's story, "Mama Goes to the Library," presents us with Bessie, a thoroughly Americanized girl who regards her Yiddish-speaking mother as an embarrassment, so much so that when she's being visited by a girlfriend, she won't even ask for a snack for fear that her mother will speak to her

---

[36] Note, though, that in Kobrin's "A Common Language," *eylembeylemyamtsedreylem* is a means of attack (*Pushcarts* 34 and throughout the story).

in Yiddish. A thoroughly predictable generational split. But Bessie is also a reader, and loves taking English books out of the library. This fascination with the reading of English makes her less hostile to her mother, readier to join in fellowship with her when she too starts going to the library (though to take out Yiddish books). The sketch ends, not with some squabble or irremediable split, but with Bessie taking a didactic pride in her mother's literacy: "[Bessie] even talks about it with her *boy*, with whom she ventures to go for a *walk* as far as *Jackson Park* . . . Henry, did you know that my mother goes to the library? . . . and she looks at him triumphantly."[37] Or consider again Mr. Bernstein in Cahan's *Yekl*. We first see him "intent upon an English newspaper," (3), and looking up an occasional word in a "cumbrous dictionary" (3).[38] He does not speak English well; but his reading seems to have given him a richer sense of America and more complex American ambitions than Jake has, who speaks English but does not read it. And what he suggests to Jake, towards the end of the first scene, is not that Jake reject American values but that he study them:

"Look here, Jake; since fighters and baseball men are all educated, then why don't you try to become so? Instead of *spending* your money on fights, dancing, and things like that, would it not be better if you paid it to a teacher?" (7)

Appropriately enough, it is Bernstein and not Jake, but also Bernstein and not some Old World rejector of America and American English altogether, who is about to be Gitl's New World husband when the novel ends.

A more playful form of resistance is making puns. It would be wrong to make too much of this, but also wrong to ignore it. George Orwell's remark about dirty jokes describes these puns too: "a dirty joke is not, of course, a serious attack on morality, but it is a sort of mental rebellion, a momentary wish that things were otherwise."[39] It is no accident that Cahan's Gitl makes the one pun in *Yekl*:

"Don't say varimess," [Jake] corrected [Gitl] complaisantly; "here it is called *dinner*."
"*Dinner*. And what if one becomes fatter?" she confusedly ventured an irresistible pun. (38)[40]

[37] Avrom Reyzn, *Gezamlte shriftn*, 14 vols. (New York: Frayhayt Publishing Association, 1928), vol. XIV: *Tsvishn grenetsn: ertseylungen*, pp. 137–38.

[38] Wirth-Nesher writes, "it is tempting to see the avid reader as Cahan himself, who learned English by devouring works of literature, just as Bernstein is intent on his American newspaper" (Wirth-Nesher, *Call It English* 44).

[39] George Orwell, "The Art of Donald McGill," in *A Collection of Essays* (San Diego: Harcourt Brace & Company, 1981), p. 114.

[40] The sound of the English "dinner" is similar to that of the Yiddish *diner*, which means "thinner."

Jake is in a good mood, and this is one of his more amiable moments with Gitl. But what he is doing is imposing a word, the right word, the American word. Gitl defends herself by pointing out the wrongness, or at any rate the comic absurdity, of that right word; how, after all, can a meal that makes one fatter be named by a word that means "thinner"? She is not resisting the need to learn the English word, just refusing to treat it as a fact of nature.

A comrade of Gitl's in this line is Sholem Aleichem's Brokhe, in *Motl the Cantor's Son*. Like Gitl, Brokhe is allied with the Old World; like Gitl, but more aggressively, Brokhe expresses that allegiance in a pun on an English word. The word is "window," brought into Yiddish as *vinde*. "There's another word that my sister-in-law can't stand," says Motl. "That word is *vinde*. A vinde is what they call a *fentster* here. To which Brokhe says, 'wind and woe to all who speak so'" (240). Brokhe doesn't like the neologism, and resists it with a pun – a rhyming pun, in fact. *Vinde* is like *vind*, "wind," and that reminds her of the idiom *vind un vey*, "wind and woe"; she quotes it, then finishes the line with a rhyme, thus turning *vinde* against itself.

Or consider Henry Roth's Bertha in *Call It Sleep*,[41] striving to resist the tyranny of her brother-in-law Albert. That tyranny is not exclusively the tyranny of assimilation; Albert is a troubled and abusive man, and would be troubled and abusive anywhere. But assimilation seems to be one of the things his tyranny demands; even in the first scene, he is unable to contain his anger at his newly arrived wife and son's distinctively European attire, and throws his son's hat into the water. And Bertha's resistance, like that of Gitl and Brokhe, is associated with puns (and to some extent with dirty jokes as well):

"In Veljish," she continued, "they say that 'kockin' will clear the brow of pain. But here in America – didn't he call it that? 'Kockin'? – will clear the mouth of pain."
[Albert's] newspaper rustled warningly.
"Cocaine?" said her sister hastily.
"Oh, is that how you say it?"
'Kockin,' as [Albert's son] David had learned long ago, was a Yiddish word meaning to sit on the toilet.[42]

The point here is double. Gitl and Brokhe and Bertha stand out in their respective stories for holding to some Old World values, and their irreverent

---

[41] An English-language text, of course, but the example is too good to resist. For a related pattern in a German American play, see my "Language Traitors, Translation, and *Die Emigranten*," pp. 255–56.
[42] Henry Roth, *Call It Sleep* (New York: The Noonday Press, 1991), p. 160.

puns on words used zealously by enthusiastic Americanizers express those allegiances. But by punning on the words, rather than simply refusing to use them, they remain free. Nadir's narrator could echo the nature-lover, or refuse to echo him. He finds instead a third choice: to talk with him. And that, really, is what Gitl and Brokhe and Bertha are doing with their puns: finding a way to talk back to American English, instead of simply and oppressively being talked at by it.[43]

MOTL THE SOCIOLINGUIST IN AMERICA

These other modes of representing the encounter between English and Yiddish are ordered, dramatized, and illuminated in a single great work of literature: the American scenes in Sholem Aleichem's *Motl the Cantor's Son*. The remainder of this essay is a reading of that work.[44]

The American scenes of the book are only its second half. It begins in Kasrilevke, the meticulously invented *shtetl* where so many of Sholem Aleichem's stories take place. The opening scenes tell us of Cantor Peyse's illness and death, and introduce us to his wife and two sons: nine-year-old Motl, the narrator, and his older brother Elye. The following scenes recount Motl's life as an orphan; Elye's marriage to Brokhe; the bankruptcy of Brokhe's father and consequent impoverishment of Peyse's family; Elye's ingenious but unsuccessful attempts to make money (by making and selling *kvas*, ink, and mouse powder); and the family's decision to go to America. We meet, in these scenes, not only the principals but also a large cast of richly delineated secondary characters: Elye's friend Pinye and his wife Teybele; Brokhe's father Yone the Baker and his wife Rivl; Motl's neighbor Fat Pessi and her husband Moyshe the Bookbinder.

---

[43] The fact that Bertha, Brokhe, and Gitl are all women makes one wonder whether this mode of resistance is somehow characteristically female. It is not *exclusively* female; Sholem Aleichem's Motl and Roth's David Schearl participate in it. But many adult males seem deeply at odds with it.

[44] See on *Motl* Sidra Ezrahi, "By Train, by Ship, by Subway," in *Booking Passage* (Berkeley: University of California Press, 2000); Hillel Halkin, "Translator's Introduction" to *The Letters of Menakhem-Mendl & Sheyne-Sheyndl and Motl, the Cantor's Son* (New Haven: Yale University Press, 2002); Rhoda S. Kachuk, "Sholom Aleichem's Humor in English Translation," *YIVO Annual of Jewish Social Science* 11 (1956–57), pp. 39–81; Dan Miron, "Bouncing Back: Destruction and Recovery in Sholem Aleichem's *Motl Peyse dem khazns*," *YIVO Annual of Jewish Social Science* 17 (1978), pp. 119–84; Khone Shmeruk, "Sholem Aleichem un amerike" ("Sholem Aleichem and America"), *Di Goldene keyt* 121 (1987), pp. 56–77; and Seth Wolitz, "Sholem Aleichem's *Motl peyse dem khazns* and its Haggadic Masterplot" (regrettably unpublished manuscript, kindly sent me by the author). Of these distinguished essays only Shmeruk's and Halkin's touch on the linguistic questions treated in this chapter, and Shmeruk's remark still holds good: "it would be worthwhile to describe and study this phenomenon thoroughly" (69).

The final scenes of the first part show us Peyse's family, plus Pinye and Teybele, on their picaresque and indirect journey: over the border to Brod, to Lemberg, to Cracow, to Vienna, to Antwerp, and finally to London. The sequence concludes with Motl's justifiably anguished question: "Master of the universe! when will we ever be in America?" (164)

What matters here about the sketches of the first part is how they prepare the characters for the quasi-Platonic dialogues on language in the second. All the characters belong to a community where language matters. Everyone in that culture, Motl tells us on a couple of occasions, has both a name and a nickname. All the principal characters love to talk. When they seek help from emigrant aid agencies, they are asked to tell their story; and invariably each of them wants to do the telling, each insists on doing the telling, each does in fact do the telling, each in a different way but all with gusto. When they are reunited in New York, they talk themselves hoarse on the subway taking them to their new home, despite the strain on their voices and the impossibility of being heard.

Each principal character has a vividly defined individual relation to language. Pinye is a language enthusiast. He likes new places and new languages, learns them quickly, speaks Russian, has a reputation as a satiric poet (Motl quotes some of his verses), reads novels, uses big and formal words and resounding names. Motl says of him, "he can flood you with speeches" (186). (Motl likes this: "I like our friend Pinye just for his speeches" [234].) He is always stopping to look into a book or scribble some notes, and goes to newspaper offices to try to sell poems or articles.

Brokhe is a language skeptic, that is, a critic of linguistic innovation. Her speech is plainer than Pinye's (though she has a Homeric laugh and a great stock of proverbs), she distrusts new places and new languages, refuses to learn them, says they're absurd. She is quick to criticize, as Motl points out: "Is there some particular thing that's supposed to please her? She finds a flaw in everything" (188). She is especially quick to criticize new languages:

[English] is even worse than German. Brokhe says three Englishmen should drop dead for every single German. She says, how on earth can there be a street called *vaytshepl*, and coins called *aypeni, tapeni, tripeni*. (159)[45]

Yet Brokhe also speaks with great force, reveling in language even as she detests languages. In one critical situation, when a member of the traveling group is lost, and the situation has to be explained to an official, the remaining members of the group choose her as their spokesperson: "after

---

[45] The street is Whitechapel, and the coins are "ha'penny" (which Brokhe hears accurately as pronounced with a Cockney accent), "tuppenny," and "threepenny."

a good bit of time spent arguing, the bottom line was that the speaking should be done by my brother Elye's wife Brokhe" (214).

Elye's less vivid relation to language lies between these two extremes. He is Pinye's constant antagonist, so we presume that he shares Brokhe's skepticism about new non-Jewish languages rather than Pinye's enthusiasm for them. This accords with his being Jewishly learned – that is, with his having a linguistic expertise that, unlike Pinye's, reaches into the Jewish past rather than out to the Gentile present. He, and not Pinye, leads the Yom Kippur prayers on board the ship to America. But he is more curious than Brokhe is about the Gentile present; he is curious enough about new languages to get into a fight with Pinye over the German pronunciation of the Yiddish word *khrayn* ("horseradish").

The richest portrait is Motl's. He is nine or so – some four years younger than Huck Finn, that other great boy narrator of a great language novel, though just the age that Huck seems in the illustrations for Twain's book. Motl's relations to language are strikingly mixed. He has a lively curiosity and an exact ear. He's linguistically playful; the first sentence of the novel presents him inventing a name for a calf. He likes nonsense sounds, and sound generally – he takes great pleasure, for example, in the cacophony of the horse market (36). He puzzles over the fact that his employer, Old Luria, doesn't say *du* to him (170). He notes the differences between Yiddish and German, and between what women talk about and what men talk about (185). He reproduces with a playwright's precision whole dialogues conducted by his elders (59), performs some of these dialogues with his friends (144–46), is quick to learn *kaddish* by heart, zestfully (and a little cruelly) reproduces Yossi the Rich Man's inability to make a /sh/ sound (330), invents variants on the rhyme his brother Elye makes up for him to sell *kvas* with. Even his nickname is oral: Motl with the Lips, or just Lips (19). One of his favorite formulae implies a desire for verbal precision: "he's a baker. He's called Yone, Yone the Baker. That is, he doesn't do the baking himself. He only buys flour and sells bread" (41). He knows – and it is a liberating knowledge in this context – that "everything in the world is custom" (22).

On the other hand, Motl is a curiously limited understander of language. He is, in particular, repeatedly confused by the metaphorical and paradoxical language of idioms and proverbs:

[Elye's prospective father-in-law] is a baker, and is called Yone the bagelbaker. He bakes bagels. "May you lie in the ground and bake bagels." That's what Pesye says, probably for a joke. But maybe she really means it? I don't understand – how can you lie in the ground and bake bagels? Who will buy them there? (34)[46]

He is equally perplexed by "a lot of water will run down the hill [before Motl gets married]" (35); "you can't spit your soul out"(48); "even to be unlucky, one must have luck"(66); "has no gall in her" (79); and, most poignantly, "stealing across the frontier" (98).

Probably Motl's excellence as a witness is increased by his limitations in understanding. What we understand, or think we understand, we often overabstract or overgeneralize. We say, "she talked like a man with a lisp," and then, unlike Motl, we do not – and perhaps cannot – reproduce the speech that this condition generates, because our belief that we understand the phenomenon diminishes the intensity of our attention to it. Motl can hear so well because his curiosity is unhampered by his understanding.

In the first part of the book, all these traits have a psychological interest rather than a sociolinguistic one, because the challenges the characters are facing are not challenges of language. Initially, Motl and company are living in a familiar linguistic world; the challenges they face are dealing with the Cantor's death, staying solvent, keeping the family together. Later, the linguistic situation is less familiar; they are traveling from one unfamiliar country to the next, observing and responding to the new languages they encounter. But their principal goal is not learning languages; it is getting to America.

When they arrive in America, the linguistic aspects of their situation are crucial. English is the language of the world they have come to inhabit. Dealing with it is an essential rather than an ornamental part of their experience, and their various dealings with it reveal their various styles of learning to live in America: Elye and Pinye's endless, revelatory debates over etymology; Brokhe's stubborn, playful resistance to American Yiddish; and Motl's eclectic fashioning of an authentic Jewish American linguistic self.

ELYE, PINYE, AND ETYMOLOGY

Motl and his family talk and argue about the etymologies of English words from the moment they arrive at Ellis Island. In fact, Ellis Island itself is the first object of their analysis:

---

[46] Presumably Motl cannot figure out "may you lie in the ground and bake bagels" partly because it is associated with death. Here too he reminds us of Huck Finn, who famously says, "I don't take no stock in dead people."

. . . We're in America! That is, they say we're in America. America we haven't actually seen yet, because we're at the moment still in *Kestel-gartel*. That is, it used to be called that. These days it's not called *Kestel-gartel* any more, it's called *Elyes Ayland*. And why *Elyes Ayland*? "Because the patch of land belonged once to an Elye, who was a fool from head to belly." That's what our friend Pinye says to make a rhyme, the way he likes to do. (183)

This is not the richest of the book's etymological discussions, partly because everyone's in agreement; it does suggest, though, how etymological invention can reflect resistance to American injustice. Pinye doesn't like Ellis Island because, he says, they detain the poor emigrants and let the rich ones in – and that, he says, is unworthy of America, the free land where all must be equal. He expresses his anger by taking possession of the word that denotes the establishment he's angry at. He recognizes "-land" and a proper name, conjuring up, from a false understanding of the "s" of "Ellis," a possessor named Elye – which happens, not coincidentally, to be the name of his favorite debating partner, Motl's brother – and then taking possession of "Elye" by making him a fool. In the absence of this etymological play, *Elyes Ayland* is scarier and more enigmatic. The punning etymology cuts it down to size.

The same dynamic animates most of the book's etymological scenes, but these scenes are richer because the etymologies are contested, and because the competing attitudes towards etymologies are linked to competing views of America. Take an early argument about *tsobhey* and *eleveyter* (i.e., "subway" and "elevated").[47] Elye derives *eleveyter* from *leyter*, "ladder," and *tsobhey* from a call used to get oxen moving – something like, say, "giddy-up." Pinye says that that's ridiculous; oxen crawl, whereas the *tsobhey* flies. Elye says that's the point, that in America things fly, that flying is in fact what America is about. Then Brokhe breaks in and says she doesn't like the whole business – that is, the means of frighteningly rapid transport that the words refer to. She expresses her view with a proverb: "lift me not up and throw me not down" (219). Motl, taking no position on the etymological question, takes a position on the practical one; he would like nothing better, he says, than to be riding the subway and elevator all day long.

Here we see Elye and Pinye in their typical roles. Elye invents etymologies, and Pinye criticizes them.

---

[47] It is a mark of Motl's exact hearing, and of Sholem Aleichem's commitment to having his character hear exactly, that Motl reports here, not the English words as English-speakers know them ("subway" and "elevated"), not the English words as Yiddish immigrants came to use them (*sobvey* and *eleveyted* in Abraham Cahan's glossary), but deformations of those English words such as newly arrived immigrants would be likely to utter and hear: *tsobhey* and *eleveyter*.

We know already that Elye is also the most Jewishly learned member of the family, the one who leads services on ship for Yom Kippur. We know also that he is skeptical about America. We know that Pinye is less learned Jewishly, more learned in the ways and languages of the secular world, readier to admire the lands through which the family travels, more enthusiastic about America. He makes great speeches in praise of America, argues with those who criticize it, learns English quickly, stuffs his Yiddish with English words. Making etymologies is associated here with a rootedness in the Old World, rejecting them with an allegiance to the New.

When we seek the etymology of a word in a new language on the basis of words in our old language, we are insisting that the word, and the new language in general, make sense on our terms. We want to understand the word or phrase we're learning, not just take it as given. This desire can hinder us in learning the language. But it is a powerful desire, and Sholem Aleichem's decision to associate it with skepticism about America is artistically right. Wanting to understand is a gesture of resistance, not just one of contemplative curiosity.[48] It says, I can't just accept this new word; I have to figure out how it works, why it is the way it is. It is not a refusal to use the word – that seems to be Brokhe's position, to be explored later – but a refusal to use it unexamined. As an expression of the need to examine, to analyze, it belongs more to skeptics than to enthusiasts.

All of this is vividly dramatized in a later comment of Moyshe the Bookbinder's. Elye and Pinye, on the same side for the moment, are trying to figure out the word *dayningrum* ("dining room"). *Bedrum* ("bedroom") they understand – there are beds in it. (Yiddish *bet* is close enough to English "bed" to make the etymology transparent.) But *dayningrum*? They rack their brains trying to understand. Then Moyshe, who probably doesn't understand either, intervenes:

Why are you wearing yourselves out for nothing? As long as I'm a *balebos* in New York, God be thanked, and my children are all working, with God's help, and we're making a living in America . . . (227)

Which is to say, words don't matter if one is, to use the single most revelatory American Yiddish idiom, making a living. (Motl acutely notes Moyshe's

---

[48] It may be significant that "subway" and "elevated" are etymologically transparent for native speakers of English – unlike, say, "automobile" or "pistol." "Why is the thing we're riding in called the 'elevated'? Because it's elevated above the ground etc." With regard to these particular words, that is, the etymological knowledge Elye seeks is not utopian but realistic.

new verbal authority and freedom. In Europe, he was meek and silent. In America, he is a new man. America lets him speak about the unimportance of speech.)

These debates between Elye and Pinye lead to some wonderful moments. Consider their conversation about *brekfish*, that is, "breakfast." Elye thinks it's from *fish*; he points out that one does, after all, eat "fish or herring" at that meal. Pinye objects – why not *brekhering*? Elye has a good answer – what, after all, is a herring if not a fish? Pinye has one remaining strategy – let's go out and ask an old hand, he says. And they do: why, they ask, do Americans call *onbaysn* (European Yiddish for "breakfast") *brekfish*? The old hand responds as follows:

The guy looks at them and says, "who told you that for *onbaysn* we say *brekfish*?" "Well, what do we say?" "*Brekfest*! *Brekfest*! *Brekfest*!," he shouts three times right in their face, and calls them dumb greenhorns. (244–45)

They thus learn the word's pronunciation. But the quest to figure out its etymology is thwarted; in the end, having lost its one intelligible component, the word is even more mysterious than when they started.

Both characters' positions are flawed. The flaw in Pinye's position is obvious: it keeps him from scrutinizing things. Elsewhere Sholem Aleichem satirizes his trust in what he reads – for example, his belief in the rags-to-riches stories of America's robber barons, his belief that Charlie Chaplin is dumb, his general reliance on novels for historical information. In these scenes we see his unthinking trust in what he hears; the new words mean what they mean, and his acceptance of them keeps him from finding out how they mean. He has no alternative to offer to Elye's impatient curiosity. He is simply echoing English.

But Elye's view is equally narrow. He is eager to understand, but only on the basis of what he knows already; he is not ready to learn anything new. He sees in some English word a part that he recognizes, or thinks that he recognizes, and doesn't think he needs to inquire about the part that he doesn't recognize. (Just as here he derives *brekfish* from *fish*, so later he derives *foyrnitsher* ["furniture"] from *tsher* ["chair"].[49]) He is, in a way, making English the echo of Yiddish. Neither he nor Pinye is open to the possibilities this encounter of languages presents.

---

[49] Probably Sholem Aleichem forgot the earlier exchange when he wrote the later one. But the repetition of the incident suggests the importance of the theme.

BROKHE AND NEOLOGISMS

We turn with relief to Brokhe's caustic but lively conservatism, which we first encounter in a scene that both mocks and justifies it. The whole family are in the subway for the first time, on the way to Yone the Baker's house. He tells them that at the next *steyshn* ("station") they'll have to *stapn* ("stop," "get off"). The family do not understand, Yone translates, and Motl's mother asks, "since when did you start speaking the local language?" (222). Yone's wife Riveleh answers, "you'll start speaking it in a week yourself. Because if you go out in the street and ask where the *katsef* [European Yiddish for "butcher"] is, you can go *katsefing* from today till the day after tomorrow, and no one will answer you . . . you'll have to say '*butsher*'." To which Brokhe replies, "may they be sick for so long! . . . they can swell up and burst, for all I care, I'll still say *katsef, katsef, katsef*."

Brokhe's position is parochial. But there is something poignant in the image of a woman forever intoning *katsef* in the street, and something tyrannical in Riveleh's prediction of that event. It is not, after all, as if Brokhe were proposing to ask where the *katsef* was on a street in Madrid, or even in Gentile New York. The street where she is going to go is a street where everyone speaks Yiddish. The first thing Motl notices about the street, in fact, is that "the signs are in Yiddish, and all sorts of Jewish [*yidishe*] things are on display . . . probably a Jewish city" (223–24). So the imagined unwillingness of these Yiddish-speakers, all of whom probably know the word *katsef*, to admit that knowledge, is as extreme as Brokhe's parochialism, and goes some way towards justifying it.

The even-handed ambiguity of this early scene prepares us for a dazzling later one:[50]

[Elye and Pinye] come home every day exhausted and hungry. And we sit down to have **vetshere**. Here it's called *sahper* ["supper"]. Brokhe hates that particular word, the way a good Jew hates pork. There's another word that my sister-in-law can't stand. That word is *vinde* ["window"]. A *vinde* is what they call a **fentster** here. To which Brokhe says, "wind and woe to all who speak so." Today she can't bear to hear people say *stahkings* ["stockings"]. You'll never guess that *stahkings* are socks. Or for example, what would you say about the word *dishez* ["dishes"]? It

---

[50] Discussed above, p. 101. See also Kenneth Wishnia, "'A Different Kind of Hell': Orality, Multilingualism, and American Yiddish in the Translation of Sholem Aleichem's *Mister Boym in Klozet*," *AJS Review* 20:2 (1993), pp. 333–58. Wishnia notes that the scene does not appear in the first published translation of the whole work: Sholem Aleichem, *Adventures of Mottel the Cantor's Son*, trans. Tamara Kahana (New York: Henry Schuman, 1953). Hillel Halkin bravely translates it, and brilliantly, though not precisely enough for my purposes here.

On the translation of multilingual works generally, see below, pp. 122–45.

seems that **posude**, Brokhe says, is a lot prettier. Or what can be simpler than a **lefl** ["spoon"]? Wrong. They won't buy it. With them it turns out that a **lefl** is a *spun*. It's not for nothing that Brokhe says her **vertl** ["proverb"] (she has her own **vertlekh** ["proverbs"]): "America is a country, *steyk* is a **maykhl**, fork is a **gopel**, and *Eynglish* is a tongue." (240)[51]

Elye and Pinye are here at an early point in a sequence that recurs often in the book. They have begun to work in a shop with great hopes, with a sense of new possibilities. But now, as previously with other new experiences that offered the same sense, the possibilities are going just a bit sour. The work exhausts them and leaves them hungry. Later, the situation will get worse: they will find out that they are being exploited and cheated; they will leave the shop to go on strike; and the strike, another provider of utopian possibilities, will also go sour. But there will be no pogroms, they will not be beaten up or shot by strikebreakers, they will not go to jail; they will make some money, even though it is less than they deserve. This shifting, realistic sequence of hope and disappointment is the context for Brokhe's linguistic soliloquy.

We learn first that Brokhe hates the English word "supper" (heard by Yiddish ears as rhyming with "shopper" rather than "upper") the way an observant Jew hates pork. This puts Brokhe in a bad light, for two reasons. First, the intensity of her dislike is out of proportion to its object; "supper" doesn't carry an ideology, and nothing in the word has a charge anything like the charge that pork carries for Jews. Second, Brokhe's intense dislike is juxtaposed to one of Motl's favorite and most reasonable formulae – that is, *do heyst es x.*, "here it's called x." He is simply describing what happens, and that makes Brokhe and her linguistic conservatism seem willful.

The argument over "vinde" is more complicated. For one thing, though the word itself doesn't carry much of a charge, it became, as Benjamin Harshav notes, the object of considerable controversy:

A notorious case was **VINDE**, adopted in America from the English "window" instead of the German-stock **FENTSTER**. **VINDE** became a symbol of barbarism to the purists but there is no objective reason why the European Yiddish *vinde* for "lift" (which came to Yiddish from Russian) should be more legitimate than its homonym derived from the English "window." (65)

So Brokhe isn't the only person upset by this particular word. More important, though, is that, as noted previously, Brokhe's objection to *vinde* is

---

[51] For this complicated passage, and other translations in this chapter, a complicated typography is used. Yiddish words that I have chosen to retain in the English translation are printed in bold. English words used in the Yiddish original are printed in italics. Necessary explanations of both sorts of word are given in brackets.

witty rather than spiteful. She puns on *vinde* ("window") and *vind* ("wind"), adroitly transforming the familiar Yiddish phrase *vind un vey* ("wind and woe," something like "alas and alack") into a punning rejection of the English-based neologism. So if she's a linguistic purist, she's a purist who takes a lot of pleasure in the creative manipulation of the language, and that makes her position more interesting. Nor is she the sort of purist Harshav is taking aim at – not a writer, not in the ideologically charged sense a Yiddishist; just a skeptic about linguistic innovation who cares about language and uses it well.

This makes her more interesting to Motl, who shifts his position in relation to her. He notes that "today" she can't bear *stahkings*, implying perhaps that her position is shifting, perhaps that she's just capricious. But then his own position and mode of analysis change. *Stahkings* is not just the way they say it here – it's something mysterious, maybe something absurd: "you'll never guess that *stahkings* are socks." The same for *dishez* – Motl puts an open question to his presumably European reader, rather than offering the neutral notation that "here it's called x." And in answering the question, he starts moving towards Brokhe's viewpoint. "It seems that **posude**, Brokhe says, is a lot prettier." This is a more reasonable position – a legitimate esthetic preference rather than an untenable religious one, and one that Motl, by the syntax of the sentence, is less distant from.

He's still less distant from the next verbal judgment; in fact, Brokhe has at least nominally disappeared from it: "Or what can be simpler than a **lefl**? Wrong. They won't buy it [*loynt zey nit*]. With them it turns out that a **lefl** is a *spun*." It's Motl, now, who takes up the cause of ordinary Eastern European Yiddish words, and who finds the words of Americans peculiar and arbitrary. He also suggests that American motivations regarding words are commercial. Americans, he says, don't like *lefl* because *es loynt zey nit* – literally, "it doesn't pay them." Accordingly, he concludes the passage by explicitly associating himself with Brokhe, with her skepticism about America and American English, and also with her verbal ability: "It's not for nothing that Brokhe says her **vertl** (she has her own **vertlekh**)."[52] It is one thing to quote proverbs. Brokhe does this a lot, and when she does

---

[52] Why exactly does Brokhe's remark qualify as a *vertl?* In a personal communication, Dovid Braun suggested two parallels for Brokhe's remark: *odem a mentsh, un katshke drey zikh/ ruk zikh* ("Adam: a man; Duck: turn about"); and *purim iz nit keyn yontev, kadokhes iz nit keyn krenk* ("Purim is no holiday, and cholera no disease"). The point in both is that the truth of the first statement, and the formal parallel between the first statement and the last, lead one to expect the last statement to be true; but it isn't, and that's the comedy. America is a country, but English may or may not be a language. (Purim is a holiday in some senses of the word, but not in the legal one; it entails no work restrictions, and is not mentioned in the Hebrew Bible.)

it she's usually dramatizing both the conservatism and the taste for pungent language that Sholem Aleichem associates with proverb-quoters – for example, Menakhem-Mendl's wife Sheyne-Sheyndl. It's another thing to invent proverbs. Quoting proverbs presents people as conservative. Inventing proverbs makes such conservatism almost innovative.

MOTL

But not so innovative that we can take Brokhe as a model for dealing generously and openly with America. For that, the only plausible model – pun unintended but inevitable and suggestive – is Motl.

The adult participants in the disputes, whether over etymologies or over neologisms, always take the same roles. They are frozen in their predictable attitudes. Motl is an improviser. He moves from role to role, and looks to be in the process of developing a sensible synthesis – not an echo, and not silence. We can see that even in the passage just discussed. The shifting attitudes towards Brokhe, the revelation of her as being both benightedly conservative and poetically innovative, are Motl's attitudes and revelation; it is his pragmatic movement from particular judgment to particular judgment that the passage is dramatizing.

Motl in America retains his sharp *Sprachgefühl*. He hears and exactly reproduces some of the words spoken by the Italians he meets on Ellis Island (208–9), and the hampered pronunciations of a good-hearted woman who consistently speaks as if she had a stuffed-up nose (271). He is fascinated by, and brilliantly reproduces, the quasi-linguistic sounds of the machines of New York (216). He zestfully notes competing Yiddish pronunciations of the English-derived word *foyrnitsher* (274).

In America, Motl has a wider linguistic field to play in. Consider his role in the debates over etymology. His overall position is a reasonable compromise. He stands with Pinye on America and on ethics. On etymologies, however, he stands with Elye. He is an enthusiast for America, as Pinye is, but an inquisitive and critical one; he wants to know what and how things mean, rather than applauding them on faith. And he's a much better etymologist than Elye. He's more ingenious, but also more attentive to linguistic probabilities. He derives *bos* ("boss") from *balebos* – literally "master of the house," but defined in Weinreich's dictionary as "proprietor, owner; host; boss, master; landlord" (245). What could be more probable? Certainly not the true etymology (from Dutch *baas*)! Elsewhere Motl wants to understand the word *vatsh* ("watch," i.e., the noun denoting a timepiece). He notes about the object that it is small, indeed that its smallness is among its defining traits. He thinks, reasonably enough, that on this basis the word should be a diminutive, and asks why it isn't *vatshl* (244). (The final /l/ in Yiddish marks a diminutive.) He wants to understand the word *titsher* ("teacher"). He has, of course, no access to the Middle English root of the modern English word. But in working out a false etymology for it he makes a brilliant and plausible pun. *Titshen* in Yiddish means to poke or prod. Teachers in Jewish schools were notorious for what we might call physically abusing their students. Motl, presuming the same is true of American teachers, derives *titsher* from *titshen*: a teacher is a prodder! (255) Unlike Elye's etymologies, this makes perfect sense, accounts for the whole word, and illuminates a whole culture.[53]

Motl is also a gifted and undogmatic translator. Most of the time, we see him translating individual words, often introducing them, as noted, with the reasonable and unpolemical formula, *do heyst es* ("here it's called . . ."). That formula makes him seem quick and knowledgeable, but passive. In other passages we see him dealing with sentences, and dealing with them imaginatively and idiomatically. In the fourth section of "The Gang at Work," for example, Motl tells us about his friend Sam, who works for a box-maker. The box-maker promises to teach the friend about the business, and says to him, *Du zay nor a gud boy, vest du zayn olrayt* (228; "just be a good boy and you'll be all right"). Motl says, "in our language that means, 'be a *mentsh* and you'll eat in the sukkah'" (228). Is a *mentsh* a "good boy"? Not exactly. To be a *mentsh* is something all Jews aspire to be – decent, humane, kind. It's a bigger term than "good boy," representing a higher and more normative goal. But there's something audacious and apt in Motl's rendering the one term with the other, some sort of linguistic resistance to the commercial values implicit in the original phrase. The second part of the translation reflects a similar process. We know already that *olrayt* is a quasi-commercial term. (One possible translation of the original is, "be a good boy and you'll end up on easy street.") To eat in the sukkah is something different, referring as it does to the fulfillment of a religious obligation as well as to a moment of leisure and plenitude. It would be going too far to claim that this brief, improvised translation of Motl's makes a bridge between American virtues and Jewish ones. But

---

[53] Consider also in this connection Motl's brief, wonderful reflections on the difference between the Yiddish *gaz* ("gas") and the English "gas" (transcribed in Yiddish as *gez*): "Here they don't say *gaz*, but '*gez*.' That is – as far as stinking is concerned, it stinks just the way *gaz* does with us, but you can't say *gaz*. You have to say *gez*. Exactly the reverse. And if at home it was called *gez*, here they'd probably say *gaz*" (245). Motl makes both a linguist's point and a satirist's point on the fact of variation for variation's sake.

that's certainly the direction it's going in – which, in the context of his usual straightforward and deferential translations, again makes Motl a figure of remarkable cultural flexibility.

VENTRILOQUISM

Many of these themes and characters are set in counterpoint in a wonderful scene towards the end of the book, where Motl and his family go to the movies to see Charlie Chaplin. They are accompanied by a new character – new, at any rate, in the American scenes, and certainly having a new meaning in the American context. His name too is Motl – Big Motl, to distinguish him from Motl the narrator. Motl and his friend Mendl run into Big Motl in the street; they talk; they agree to go the movies; Elye and Pinye join them for the expedition; at the movies, Big Motl, who is a ventriloquist, plays a ventriloquist's joke on Motl's brother Elye, calling him an idiot in a voice that seems to come from the cellar and the ceiling; and Elye decides he'll never go to see Charlie Chaplin again.

Big Motl is small Motl's possible future. He has been in America longer than Motl and his family have, knows more facts about it, is more of an enthusiast for it. (He is not like Pinye, though; he doesn't have a theory about America. He's just becoming American, quickly and adeptly.) His Yiddish is more Americanized than small Motl's is. His salary is higher, too. Small Motl and his friend Mendl together make $1 a week, sometimes a dollar and a quarter; Big Motl makes $3 – 60 cents more than the narrator of "I: As Echo," though minus the free laundry.

Big Motl is also small Motl's guru, linguistically as well as in other ways. We can see this even in small Motl's first statements to him; these are fuller of American terms than are most of his statements, as if to say, "see – I can be an American too!" He says, "we *deliver* . . . *newspapers*. We carry papers to our *customers*, before we go to *school*. And when we leave *school*, we help with *attending* the *bizness*. We have a *stand* on the *corner* and we **makhn a lebn**" (287–88). And Big Motl recognizes what small Motl is doing, saying, "Hey, you already speak great English" (288). But not great enough – and certainly not with as many American terms as Big Motl's speech has. Furthermore, Motl still has his Old World name, as does his friend Mendl. Big Motl does away with both of these names: Motl becomes Max, and Mendl becomes Mike. This may not seem portentous, and the conversation about the name-change isn't charged with meaning. But Motl always refers to his friends and his family by their name and epithet, seldom using pronouns; and after 250 pages of *mayn khaver mendl* ("my friend Mendl"), *mayn khaver mayk* ("my friend Mike") is an earthquake.

Big Motl is also associated with Charlie Chaplin. It's Big Motl who proposes going to see Chaplin's movies, it's Big Motl who does a virtuosic Chaplin imitation at the theater, and it's because of being insulted by Big Motl that Elye (though he doesn't actually know that Big Motl is doing the insulting) won't go to see Chaplin again.

The association with Chaplin matters. Sholem Aleichem was an admirer of American movies, and was eager to have some of his stories filmed. Moreover, he seems to have wanted them filmed in a Chaplinesque style. His son-in-law Benjamin Waife-Goldberg recalls how Sholem Aleichem discussed the subject:

We both roared repeatedly as he improvised the action [of one of the European scenes in *Motl*] on the silent screen. He laughed fully, freely, heartily. I have never seen him laugh so much and so boisterously. I have never laughed so much on one occasion in my life. If a stranger saw us then he would think we were touched in the head. Two men sitting and bursting into laughter, like two kids at a Charlie Chaplin movie.[54]

Sholem Aleichem wrote warmly and perceptively of Chaplin:

Chaplin has the ability to fill many hearts with joy, particularly children's hearts; without children's laughter the world couldn't exist. Charlie's image fascinated me. Everything about him is grandiose: the small moustache, the excessively large, worn-out shoes, the wide, ragged trousers, the tight frock-coat, the tattered derby, the crooked cane, the bizarre walk. This image in itself is a genuine work of art. No one has ever created anything of the like, neither with pen, nor with brush.[55]

The great Yiddish poet Perets Markish wrote that "in the character of his comic elements, Sholem Aleichem is close to Charlie Chaplin. In essence, Sholem Aleichem's little man, just like Charlie, takes the road of his misfortunes."[56] Being associated with Chaplin gives Big Motl a lot of prestige; for Sholem Aleichem, Chaplin was a great and authentically American artist.

---

[54] Marie Waife-Goldberg, *My Father, Sholom Aleichem* (New York: Simon & Schuster, 1968), p. 292.

[55] I owe this citation to Esther Vaysman, who identifies its source as follows: "this quote comes from the journal *Tsaytshrift* 14 (Paris, 1956), 147–50. I found it in a collection of essays entitled *Sholom Aleikhem: Pisatel' i Chelovek* ("Sholom Aleichem: the Writer and the Man"; Moscow: Sovetskiĭ pisatel', 1984), compiled and edited by M. S. Belen'kii."

[56] My thanks again to Esther Vaysman for the Markish citation, which also comes from Belen'kii, *Sholom Aleikhem*.

For further, fascinating remarks on the topic, both by Esther Vaysman and by Louis Fridhandler, see the archived issues of the Yiddishist mailing list *Mendele*, vols. 9.016 and 9.020, at http://shakti.cc.trincoll.edu/~mendele/toc09.htm. I'm grateful to both correspondents for so generously helping me figure out what one great artist meant to another. A fascinating essay might be written on the subject; such an essay could investigate whether Chaplin's partly Jewish ancestry

Big Motl is no more respectful of stuffy dignity than Chaplin was, and his chief activity in this scene is poking fun at Motl's brother Elye. He does this by means of ventriloquism. A comic version of the ghost of Hamlet's father, he projects his voice first down into the cellar, then up into the ceiling. And what his ventriloquized voice says to Elye is the one word, "idiot" (a Yiddish word as well as an English one, and having the same meaning in both languages).

It is irresistible to see his mocking ventriloquism as a figure of how the miraculous bilingualism of immigrant children would present itself to a dogmatic and stiff adult. To the older immigrants, the younger ones must seem to have some magical gift for doubled speech, displaced speech. Speaking English, that is, is *like* ventriloquism. This is, moreover, ventriloquism where the second voice appears to come, not from a puppet, but from the ground or the air. It is more anarchic and less contained than making a puppet talk – not so much an echo, we might say. And what that ventriloquized voice says, again and again, is, "you are an idiot."

Elye's questions are poignant: "Why doesn't he answer hello? Have you gotten so big in America that it's already beneath your dignity to say a Yiddish word?" (289)[57] The answer is yes; Big Motl has in fact gotten so big, and Elye's humiliation is real. But here, as elsewhere in Sholem Aleichem's vision of America, that real humiliation isn't the end of the story, or even the heart of it. That is partly because, as Sholem Aleichem knows but Elye doesn't, having dignity does not necessarily mean speaking Yiddish. In an earlier scene, asked what it means to speak "vi a mentsh" (267), like a *mentsh*, Elye says, "a mentsh redt oyf yidish" ("a *mentsh* speaks Yiddish").[58] Elye has made, and continues to make here, a too rigid association between a language and a mode of behavior; his humiliation is partly the result of this, and partly the result of a related inability to laugh at himself or to appreciate the satiric genius of a Chaplin or a *boykhreder*. Motl and Mendl, we hear repeatedly, can hardly contain their laughter.

There is something more than laughter here, something spooky and magical in the ghostlike mobility of Big Motl's ventriloquized voice from beneath the cellar to above the ceiling, and in the way that the ordinary

plays any role in this relationship, either as regards Chaplin's art or as regards Sholem Aleichem's response to it, and also the importance of Chaplin's being a performer in silent (though captioned) comedy.

57 What I am translating as "hello" here is, ironically enough, *sholem aleichem*, the author's pen-name; its literal sense is "peace be with you," its idiomatic sense is that of a friendly greeting after an absence.

58 The continuation of the scene is wonderful: "the *boss* asks him another question: 'and if I speak English, does that make me a monster?'" Elye answers, "could be."

word gradually becomes an incantation – at first, Big Motl just says *idiot*, in two syllables then in three, saying finally to Elye, *bekoz dos zent ir aleyn take der i-di-ot!* . . ." (292; "*because* you yourself are in fact the i-di-ot"). The ventriloquism – that is, the bilingualism – of immigrant children inflicts pain on immigrant adults. (The adults must sometimes regard their children as language traitors.) But that same ventriloquism, that same bilingualism, is also a source of wild laughter, rich invention, and dizzying success.

TWO CONCLUDING REFLECTIONS

(1) *Motl* is a great language novel because Sholem Aleichem had a fine ear, linguistic curiosity, inventiveness, irreducible talent. But other causes were in play as well, matters less of talent than of temperament and artistic choice.

One might expect the great dramatization of the encounter between English and Yiddish to turn up in a work of realistic fiction. In practice, though, realistic fiction does a surprisingly bad job in this area. Many of the great language fictions belong rather to the romance (Cooper's *The Last of the Mohicans*), the sensational novel (Mercier's *L'Habitation Saint-Ybars*, but also Eugène Sue's *Les Mystères de Paris* and George Du Maurier's *Trilby*), the modernist novel (Roth's *Call It Sleep*, but also Joyce's *Ulysses*), and the novel of magical realism (Patrick Chamoiseau's *Texaco* and Salman Rushdie's *Midnight's Children*). In practice, the conventions of realistic fiction seem to get in the way of the difficult, exacting, momentum-slowing task of representing the multilingual world. So Sholem Aleichem, who didn't write well in realistic genres, who preferred and was much better off in the monologue, the sketch, the children's story, the traveler's tale, the letter, was the beneficiary of his own limitations here. However we define *Motl*'s genre – the satirical sketch, the children's story, the picaresque novel – it posed fewer obstacles than the realistic novel would have done to the author's interest in complex linguistic representation.

Motl was also the beneficiary of its author's comic temperament, even more so perhaps than his European fictions were. A great American Yiddish language story almost has to be comic. Not because there were no grim aspects to the encounter between English and Yiddish, of course. The United States has a way of making languages disappear. As Kenji Hakuta writes, "at the rate of change observed in other nations, it would take 350 years for the average nation to experience the same amount of [language] loss as that witnessed in just one generation in the United States."[59] Certainly that trend is related to some of the less benign aspects of the American response to immigrant and autochthonous cultures. The melting pot is a crucible, in which distinctive cultural traits are burned away. Hillel Halkin puts the situation very well:

> If Motl – who once told us in Kasrilevke, in one of his few expressions of visceral Jewishness, of his hatred for pigs – has not already eaten his first New York ham sandwich, can we doubt that this is only a matter of time? . . . Internally, there is nothing we can detect in him – no inelasticity of self, no allegiance to his father's memory – to keep him within the Jewish fold . . . Motl is the happy ending of the eastern European Jewish tragedy, the rise after which there is no longer any fall. But he is also the end of Sholem Aleichem's world, his face lifted to the kiss that will kill it benignly at the same time that it is being murdered brutally in Europe.[60]

But nothing in the Jewish experience of American immigration is comparable to the European pogroms that preceded it or the European slaughter that followed it. Motl himself doesn't understand what "pogrom" means, and to make sense of America he doesn't have to. Cynthia Ozick's grudging remark, that America "is a good diaspora, as diasporas go," is on the mark.[61] The great story of that diaspora must therefore be a comic one – not ignorantly optimistic, but cheerful in tone, and animated by imaginative excitement. That it should fall to the greatest Jewish comic artist to write that story is almost inevitable.[62]

Finally, Sholem Aleichem chose a narrator of the right age. Motl himself tells us why: he says, "America is a country that was just made for the sake of children" (224). He means most immediately that in America there are people on the street who keep your older brother from hitting you, and that school is free and compulsory rather than forbidden. But he is also getting at a deeper truth: not just that America is a land made for children, but also that it is not a land made for adults, that is, immigrant adults. Sholem Aleichem knew that. It is probably why, as Khone Shmeruk puts it, "the gates of 'the blessed land' had to stay shut to his two great *adult* characters."[63] Shmeruk is thinking of Sholem Aleichem as an altruistic

---

[59] Kenji Hakuta, *Mirror of Language: The Debate on Bilingualism* (New York: Basic Books, 1986), pp. 166–67.

[60] Halkin, "Translator's Introduction," pp. xxv–xxvi.

[61] Cynthia Ozick, "Towards a New Yiddish," in *Art and Ardor* (New York: Knopf, 1983), p. 170.

[62] Seth Wolitz has persuasively suggested that *Motl*'s master narrative is the Passover Haggadah. If that is true, then America cannot be Egypt and slavery, but must be the wilderness or even Canaan. Neither the wilderness nor Canaan is paradise, but they are not Egypt either, and no American Pharaoh is commanding the slaughter of Jewish children.

[63] Shmeruk, "*Sholem Aleichem un amerike*," p. 65 (Shmeruk's emphasis). The two adult characters in question are Tevye the Dairyman and Menakhem-Mendl.

artist, unwilling to expose his characters to the degradation of American immigrant experience. We might also think of him, though, as a more self-centered, Joycean artist, simply wanting to describe a charged scene through the consciousnesses capable of best registering it – as Joyce himself had done in "The Sisters" and at the beginning of *Portrait of the Artist as a Young Man*; as Mark Twain had done in *Huck Finn*. Shmeruk's formulation is perhaps richer than he knew: "among the emigrants, the future belongs only to the young, to those who have come at an age when they can free themselves from the old and take in the new words" (74). America is a land for children. That means, we presume, a land where children can live well. But it also means a land that only children – among immigrants, at any rate – can understand well. The greatest Jewish American language fiction in English, Henry Roth's *Call It Sleep*, reveals its world through the vision of the child David Schearl. The greatest Jewish American language fiction in Yiddish, Sholem Aleichem's *Motl*, reveals its world through the vision of the child Motl. If we believe that artists become great partly through understanding the deep meanings of truisms, then we might claim that a part of Sholem Aleichem's greatness lay in understanding just what is meant when we say that children can assimilate languages in ways that adults cannot.

(2) It is both heartbreaking and fascinating to imagine how American Yiddish literature might have dealt with English in the generations after Sholem Aleichem. Heartbreaking because imagining that future is all we can do; and because that future's never being realized was the result, not only of what happens to immigrant languages in America, but also of the effect on all Yiddish writers everywhere of the mass murder of European Jews – Yiddish-speaking European Jews numerous among them. Fascinating because before the effects of the Shoah began to be fully felt, enough innovative work had been done to suggest the promise of what in the end did not happen.

Aaron Tsaytlin's "A Monolog in pleynem yidish" is, in a grimly punning way, a dead end: the English-saturated Yiddish of the Holocaust survivor can't lead anywhere; the English is there only because Yiddish is dying:

> O, Warsaw . . .
> I am, you say, a little bit dead myself?
> *well*, I'll tell you, **lantsman**;
> you are – *between us* – a little bit right.
> *Because* today, every Jew is a little bit dead,
> a corpse, not sleeping nights.
> They say: "Maidanek . . . all burned . . ."

Really,
I can't understand, I can't.
Honestly *plain* burned?[64]

Lamed Shapiro's 1931 novella *Nuyorkish*, on the other hand, suggests
how Yiddish in America might have become as cosmopolitan a language
as English itself, as able to depict English as English was to depict Yiddish.
Consider this characteristic passage, a dialogue between Jewish Manny and
Gentile Jenny, whom Manny wants to call "Dolores":

> She looked at him uncertainly.
> "I'm an American girl."
> "Sure," he said reassuringly, "a real American girl. But say it yourself: Do-lo-
> res. Now that's a name with a ring to it. You know what? I'm going to call you
> 'Dolores'!"
> She was suddenly pleased and stretched her hand across the table and put it over
> his.
> "*Olrayt!*[65] Dolores, if that's what you want. Ha ha ha! Dolores! . . . but what
> should I call you?'
> In tone, they had gone over to *du* or the informal "you" in Yiddish, although
> modern English does not have particular words corresponding to the formal "*ir*"
> or informal "*du.*"[66]

Manny and Jenny are, Shapiro tells us, speaking English. They are the
principal characters in the story, and they are speaking English all the time.
Shapiro is not, then, describing a language encounter in the world; the
encounter takes place between the language of the narrator and the language
of the characters. Shapiro is using Yiddish to represent English in somewhat
the same way as Roth is using English to represent Yiddish (or Hemingway
English to represent Spanish); not as ambitiously, but as thoughtfully and
exactly. How does one render a change in "tone" in English, conveyed by
intonation or tempo? By means of a resource Yiddish has but English does
not – that is, the distinction between the formal pronouns and the familiar,
a distinction that Shapiro uses skillfully and expressively.

The most ambitious project of this sort is Sholem Ash's 1946 *East River*,[67]
maybe the last great American Yiddish work aiming to represent American

---

[64] Aaron Tsaytlin, *Gezamlte lider* (New York: Matones, 1947), vol. I, p. 91.

[65] In transliterated English in Shapiro's text.

[66] Lamed Shapiro, *Nuyorkish un ander zakhn* ("Nuyorkish and other matters") (New York: Farlag
Aleyn, 1931), pp. 13–14. For a translation of the story see Lamed Shapiro, "New Yorkish," trans.
Lawrence Rosenwald, in *The Cross and Other Jewish Stories*, edited, with an introduction by, Leah
Garrett (New Haven: Yale University Press, 2007), pp. 198–212.

[67] The title is significant. Yiddish has *taykh* for "river" and *mizrekh* for "east," but Ash uses neither,
choosing rather to transliterate the English name of the body of water into Yiddish – anglicizing
and stretching Yiddish from the outset, we might say.

life – and, most challengingly, American Christian life. A central plot-line of that sprawling New York novel, which reaches from pigeon-flying to Franklin Delano Roosevelt, is the story of a mixed marriage. Jewish Irving Davidowsky marries Catholic Mary McCarthy, has a child with her and leaves her; Mary, a serious Catholic and at the same time deeply fond of Irving's father Meyer Wolf, raises her son Nathan (Nat) in a mix of Christian and Jewish values, texts, and practices. At one point she goes, not implausibly, to confession, and Ash has to figure out how to describe that process in a language not having a large vocabulary for talking about Christianity. He describes the absolution Mary seeks from the unseen priests by the Hebrew term *slikhe umekhile*, "penitential prayer and pardon," audaciously and inventively evoking a Jewish prayer, the *avinu malkeinu* repeatedly recited during the Days of Awe, to describe a Christian ritual.[68] Later, when Meyer Wolf hands Nat a piece of bread, he asks him why he's not reciting the blessing, and Mary and Nat recite not the Hebrew blessing over bread, but the Lord's prayer – which Ash must also figure out how to translate (447). Meyer Wolf's response is surprisingly open-minded: "What he understands, he likes, and he thinks that it is after all like a Jewish prayer . . . He hears the child say, 'our father in heaven' – it is after all like, and yet unlike, what we say: *avinu shebashomayim*."

Ash's interest in Christianity had made him notorious; *The Nazarene*, the first of his three christological novels, published in English in 1939 but not in Yiddish until 1943, "involved him," as Sol Liptzin tells us, "in unending controversies with Jews who felt betrayed in their hour of utmost need by his apparent apostasy."[69] But *East River* was something different – not a christological novel, simply an ambitious attempt to represent Jewish life in New York in its entirety, and thus in its relations with everything in its vicinity. Ash was pushing Yiddish to extend to the whole territory of American life, even those areas most remote from it. A strange enterprise, in some ways; we expect immigrant writers in immigrant languages to represent the experiences of immigrants, not to write the Great American Novel. But a language used for literature in America that does not seek to cover the whole territory is provincial. Ash on a larger scale was doing what Shapiro was doing in *Nuyorkish*, transforming an immigrant language into a national one. A promising and necessary development, and a great novel; but for the reasons stated, not a new beginning but the end of a line.

---

[68] *1st River* (New York: Laub, 1946), p. 330. Page numbers for subsequent quotations from this work will be given in the text. See on this passage, and on some other aspects of Ash's novel, my "Four Theses on Translating Yiddish in the 21st Century," *Pakn Treger* 38 (Winter 2002), pp. 14–20.

[69] Sol Liptzin, *A History of Yiddish* (Middle Village: Jonathan David, 1985), p. 153.

CHAPTER 4

"New language fun," or, on translating multilingual American texts

> Don Luis told me that one could not translate the bilingual text, because all one could do was to translate from one language to another all over again. I disagreed gently, because I was interested in how the work would turn out.
>
> – Rolando Hinojosa

In a broad sense, translation is the central topic of this book. In a narrower sense it has so far been in the background, and needs to be brought forward and considered explicitly. First and most practically, English is the dominant (though not the official) language of multilingual America; non-anglophone works of American literature that vividly represent language encounters will have to be translated into English if they are to matter to most American readers and students of American literature, and how they are translated will affect how they are read. Second, asking how to translate such works, in general and in particular into English, opens up some interesting questions. Translation theory has not dealt extensively with the translation of multilingual texts, nor very rigorously.[1] They seem an anomaly, a small cluster on the margins; in fact they are surprisingly abundant, almost constituting a center of their own. Third, for these works

---

[1] Some studies: Leo Tak-hung Chan, "Translating Bilinguality: Theorizing Translation in the Post-Babelian Era," *The Translator* 8:1 (2002), pp. 49–72; Carrol F. Coates, "Problems of 'Translating' Bi-/Multilingual Literary Texts: The Haitian French of Jacques Stephen Alexis," in Marilyn Gaddis Rose (ed.), *Beyond the Western Tradition*, Translation Perspectives XI (Binghamton: State University of New York at Binghamton, 2000); Dirk Delabastita, "A Great Feast of Languages: Shakespeare's Multilingual Comedy in *King Henry V* and the Translator," *The Translator* 8:2 (2002), pp. 303–40; Abdelouahed Mabrour, "La bi-langue ou l'(en)jeu de l'écriture bilingue chez Abdelkebir Khatibi," *Linguistica antverpiensia* 2 (2003), pp. 105–14; Samia Mehrez, "Translation and the Postcolonial Experience: The Francophone North African Text," in Lawrence Venuti (ed.), *Rethinking Translation* (London and New York: Routledge, 1992), pp. 229–47; and Kathy Mezei, "Bilingualism and Translation in/of Michèle Lalonde's *Speak White*," *The Translator* 4:2 (1998), pp. 229–47. All the studies adduce interesting examples and raise interesting theoretical questions, but only Chan's and Delabastita's make a real start at answering them.

My thanks to Mona Baker for generous bibliographical help in this area.

as for many others, the question of how to translate becomes a lens of analysis, showing us things about the works that we could not otherwise see. Finally, being translated is part of the life of every important literary work. *Traduttore traditore*, translators betray. But that does not make translation any less necessary – for readers, but also for the life and growth of the works themselves, regardless of how inextricably rooted they seem or are in a particular place and moment. Reflecting on the translation of multilingual language fictions is a necessary part of taking them seriously as literature.

The present chapter consists of some orienting reflections, five case studies, and a brief conclusion. In comparison with the chapters preceding it, it is more technical, more tentative, and more personal. More technical, because any rigorous account of translation has to be technical if it is not to be sloppy. More tentative, because it deals with a field in which there are few successful models and fewer tenable theories. More personal, because as a practicing translator, in particular as a translator of two of the texts considered in the case studies, I need to be personal in order not to be disingenuous.

REFLECTIONS

Many influential ideas about translation are based on two linked assumptions: that the source text is written in a single language, and that it does not thematize that fact. Those assumptions are often legitimate. Homer's epics, for example, are written in Greek. But Homer does not start the *Iliad* by asking his Muse to sing in that language; he simply asks her to sing. The book of Genesis tells us, *vayomer elohim yehi or*, "and God said, let there be light" – that God said something, not that God said it in Hebrew.

Clearly some texts are multilingual and do thematize that fact. Not all of them, though, raise the questions I want to investigate here. Consider *Lolita* or *Finnegans Wake*. These are multilingual texts of a particular kind: playful, sometimes sublimely playful, and what matters in them is not so much the specific languages that are being played with as the play itself. Translators of them are free to play with whatever languages they and their real or ideal readers can use. Umberto Eco expresses this distinction in different terms when he writes that whereas in Joyce's other work "Dublin is the center," in *Finnegans Wake* "Dublin is only its pretext; its center is elsewhere, in language" – which allows Eco to argue, paradoxically but justly, that by the very fact of being theoretically untranslatable, *Finnegans Wake* is also, of all texts, the easiest to translate, since it allows a maximum of inventive liberty and does not impose obligations of fidelity that are in any way fixed and calculable.[2]

There is another class of multilingual texts, however, or more precisely another mode in which a text can be multilingual, in which "obligations of fidelity" are indeed "fixed and calculable," and meaning shifts to the specific languages being used and the historical and political relations among them. That is the mode of multilingual writing this book is concerned with.

A wonderful passage in Rabelais's *Pantagruel* illustrates the difference between the two modes by moving from one to the other. Pantagruel meets a young student and asks him where he's from; the student answers, "de l'alme, inclyte, et célèbre académie que l'on vocite Lutèce" ("from the alme, inclyte and celebrate Academie, which is vocitated *Lutetia*"). The student continues speaking this hyperlatinized academic jargon till Pantagruel grabs him by the throat and says, more or less, "if you keep on slaughtering Latin in this way, I'm going to slaughter *you*." At this point the student speaks his own language, that is, Limousin: "Vée dicou! gentilastre. Ho, Sainct Marsault, adjouda-my! Hau, hau, laissas à quau, au nom de Dious, et ne me touquas grou" ("haw, *gwid* Maaster, haw, Laord, *my halp and St.* Marshaw, haw, *I'm worried*: Haw, *my thropple, the bean of my cragg is bruck!* Haw, *for* gauads *seck, lawt my lean*, Mawster; *waw, waw, waw*"). Pantagruel relents, saying, "now you're speaking naturally."[3]

In writing the student's jargon, Rabelais is playing with language the way Nabokov does, and translating that jargon means finding or devising a similarly playful and learned diction in the target language. That diction needs to be grotesquely bookish; but it does not need to be Latinate, nor to be in the same historical relation to the ordinary speech of the target language that Latinate diction is in with regard to French – that is, a diction based on a linguistic ancestor of that ordinary speech. If Rabelais were being translated into Yiddish, for example, the student's diction would probably come from Yeshiva Aramaic or contemporary academic German, neither of which is an ancestor of Yiddish.

[2] Umberto Eco, "Introduction" to *Anna Livia Plurabelle di James Joyce*, ed. Rosa Maria Bollettieri Bosinelli (Turin: Einaudi, 1996), p. xi (my translation). My thanks to Alide Cagidemetrio for calling this essay to my attention.

[3] François Rabelais, *Pantagruel* (Paris: Gallimard, Le Livre de Poche, 1964), pp. 95–108; the 1653 English translation I quote is Thomas Urquhart's, from *Gargantua and Pantagruel*, 3 vols. (London: Oxford University Press, Oxford World's Classics, 1934), vol. I, pp. 190–92. See also Michel Butor, "Le parler populaire et les langues anciennes," in *Cahiers Renaud Barrault* 67 (September 1968), pp. 83–98.

When the student speaks Limousin, though, Rabelais is representing his "natural" speech, his mother tongue, and marking him, in comparison to the Île-de-France French of the narrative, as the speaker of a related but distinct and politically subordinated language. Here translators will need to find, not a particular register in the target language, but a second particular language, outside the target language but in an equivalent historical and political relation to it, which may plausibly be the student's native language also. There may not *be* such a language, of course; but finding one is still the goal.[4]

Sometimes translators of multilingual texts have to deal with a more specific challenge, namely, when a secondary language of the source text is also the principal language of the target text – for example, to take a text already considered, when Sholem Aleichem's *Motl the Cantor's Son* is rendered into English. Dealing with that challenge may seem unimportant; any such text can be rendered into any of the world's written languages, and the challenge in question only comes up with one of them. In practice, though, it is often the case that the language into which we want to translate a multilingual text is one of the languages it represents. We are more likely to want to translate immigrant-language American immigrant fiction into English than into any other language, because American anglophone readers have more reason to read American non-anglophone fiction than do the reading publics of Europe. An Algerian writer dramatizing in Arabic or Berber the relations between either of those languages and French is more likely to find a French public than an American or German one. The problem is more pressing than it might seem.

Nor is it easy to solve. In the source text, English is marked and heterophone. In the target text, English is the one unmarked and non-heterophone language, not alien but domestic. English in the source text necessarily means something. English in the target text need not mean anything; it is the medium, not the message, and unless painstakingly made thematic, it will be read as neutral.

Between the broader challenge and the narrower one, it might seem that multilingual texts of the sort under discussion here cannot be translated. In fact, though, impossibility of one sort or another is the ground

---

[4] These points may seem obvious, but one indication that they are not is a Rabelais translation by Burton Raffel (*Gargantua and Pantagruel* [New York: Norton, 1990]), in which, when the Limousin student finally speaks "naturally," he speaks almost exactly the same language as Pantagruel himself.

of every translation and of all translational renown. Franz Rosenzweig wrote:

Translating means serving two masters. It follows that no one can do it. But it follows also that it is, like everything that no one can do in theory, everyone's task in practice. Everyone must translate, and everyone does.[5]

As in general, so with the translation of multilingual texts: the apparent impossibility is sometimes an obstacle, sometimes the necessity that inspires invention. The following, wildly diverse case studies document both the former outcome and the latter.

CASE STUDIES

Alfred Mercier, L'Habitation Saint-Ybars[6]

The obvious question here is how to translate the Creole utterances. The book has too many of them for them to be treated as special effects; they have to be treated systematically. But how?

Answering that question is hard enough that it's understandable why, in such cases, translators finesse the problem. Some do what I myself have done in the earlier discussion of the novel: retain the Creole passages of the original untranslated in the English text, then provide English translations of them in footnotes. I might also have put English translations of these passages directly into the text, marked the passages by bolding or italicizing them, then indicated in an initial note to the reader that italicized or bolded passages in the translation correspond to Creole passages in the original.

Those are good approaches for scholars, in that they preserve and clearly present the salient features of the original text. They are not such good approaches for readers; they imply a translator's confession of failure. The translator who makes use of them is saying to the reader, "I can't translate the multilingualism of this text; all I can do is give you a map of it."

The more ambitious alternative is to translate the Creole utterances into a language that is neither Creole nor English, and which has a relation to English similar to the relation Creole has to French. If successful, this will offer readers that direct experience of the interlinguistic drama of Mercier's

---

[5] Franz Rosenzweig, "Scripture and Luther," in Martin Buber and Franz Rosenzweig, *Scripture and Translation*, trans. Lawrence Rosenwald with Everett Fox (Bloomington: Indiana University Press, 1994), p. 47.

[6] The reader who is skipping around in this book, and has come to this chapter without reading all of what precedes it, will find an extended presentation of Mercier's novel above, pp. 53–64.

novel which the scholarly approach denies them. But there are severe constraints on what that third language can be. Two are evident: it must be as closely related to English as Creole is to French, and speakers of it and of English must reasonably find one another's languages as unintelligible as speakers of Creole and French do in Mercier's novel.[7] These two constraints are just manageable, and an adventurous translator could find a language to meet them – say, the extreme Edinburgh Scots that gets subtitled in the film of *Trainspotting*. But there is a third constraint: in novels like Mercier's, languages are bound to places and histories. The characters on the Saint-Ybars plantation speak Louisiana French and Louisiana Creole because, on real plantations like that fictional plantation, those were the languages people spoke. Its historical and geographical plausibility is a distinguishing strength of the novel, and should be a distinguishing strength of any translation of it.[8]

The problem is that the constraints push in different directions. If we want to maintain plausibility, then the best solution would be to translate the Creole passages into African-American English as spoken in Louisiana. But that English was not unintelligible to speakers of Standard Louisiana English; to make it seem so, we would have to caricature it, to present it in an extremely distorted orthography.[9] Nothing could be farther from Mercier's exact transcription of Creole in the novel, or his account of the language in his essay on it.

If, on the other hand, we want to maintain the relatedness and reciprocal unintelligibility of the two languages, then probably the best solution is to translate the Creole passages into an English-based creole: Gullah, or a creole from the Caribbean. But those languages were not spoken in Louisiana; introducing them into a translation of Mercier's novel is at odds with the novel's sense of place.

---

[7] More precisely: the Creole passages in *L'Habitation Saint-Ybars* make clear that one cannot understand Creole just by being a native speaker of French. It is less clear whether Mercier thinks that one can understand Standard French just by being a native speaker of Creole.

[8] I should note here, as a kind of thought experiment, that none of these constraints would matter very much if one were translating this novel into Chinese. In Chinese, geographical and historical plausibility would be impossible, so geographical and historical *im*plausibility wouldn't be anything to worry about. If people are presented speaking Chinese on a nineteenth-century Louisiana Creole plantation, we know that it's a fiction; we know there's no Louisiana variety of Chinese, so the characters don't have to speak it. In English, such plausibility is at least imaginable, and such implausibility is something we could experience as disrupting our reading of the text – suppose, for example, that the Creole-speaking characters of Mercier's novel were made to speak Brooklynese!
   Ordinarily we focus on the advantages of translating between closely related languages; here, though, the close relation between the two languages is part of the problem.

[9] On the problems with such an approach, see above, pp. 65–66.

I myself would argue for stressing relatedness and unintelligibility, and sacrificing (or at any rate stretching) geographical and historical plausibility. Other translators would argue the opposite. In either case a further problem arises, practical but also theoretical: to translate into a language one needs to know it. Ordinarily that is a truism. Here it is a formidable challenge. It is one thing to argue that the Creole passages of Mercier's novel should be rendered in a strongly marked or caricatured Louisiana variety of African-American English, or in Gullah, or in Jamaican Creole, and another thing to have mastered the languages one's argument requires one to deploy. I would want to translate the Creole passages into basilectal Gullah; but not knowing that language well enough to write in it, I would need to learn it. Seeking to retain the original text's multilingualism in the translation might demand that the translator be, or become, a multilingual writer. Or it might demand a new model of collaborative translation. Collaborative translation in the West has most often involved a division of labor between philologist and poet, the former providing raw material, the latter the finished product. That has been a productive strategy, whatever critiques might be offered of it as a model.[10] Dealing with multilingual texts might require developing a new and less hierarchical model, a collaboration not between possessors of different gifts but between speakers of different languages.

English in Yiddish into English

The challenges involved in trying to translate Mercier's novel do not include that of translating into English what is already in English in the source text. That other challenge is central to the four case studies that follow.

Of these, the first concerns a small group of Yiddish texts considered in Chapter 3. These have the advantage, for the critic, of having been translated more than once and in more than one way – for example, to begin with an extreme example, the way made use of by the late Ted Gorelick in his translation of Sholem Aleichem's "A Tale with a Greenhorn":

You was saying how America was a lend of business? Never mine! Det's how it's suppose to be. But a fella getting merry wid a goil for business? Det, you'll poddon me, is mean and doity. Now, I ain't preaching no morality here, but I am telling you it's a fect; when nine-end-ninety procent of grinnhorns in dis country is getting merry for business, it is making me med! End if I am meeting op with such a kind

---

[10] See my own critique in "Buber and Rosenzweig's Challenge to Translation Theory," introduction to Buber and Rosenzweig, *Scripture and Translation* (Bloomington: Indiana University Press, 1994).

of grinnhorn, believe me he don't get off dry. You live it to me! Wanna hear a good one? Listen![11]

This is both virtuosic and disastrous. It would play well on stage, it's the result of focused hard work, but it's a travesty. Mr. Baraban's petty, effective malevolence is linked to his linguistic proficiency, his deployment of English phrases (whether in real relation to American habits or as a fan-dance), his knowledge of the American scene. His English reflects his wicked cosmopolitanism. In Gorelick's version of it, Mr. Baraban's speech reflects his ignorance. He speaks a very limited English and pronounces it badly. He cannot be a language traitor, because he barely has a language.

Hillel Halkin's strategies for dealing with *Motl the Cantor's Son* are almost as unsatisfying, but for different reasons. Halkin is a great translator, one of the best now dealing with Yiddish. His strategies fail here not through willfulness or narcissism, but because the task is hard and because he is playing the game with unnecessarily restrictive rules.

In Sholem Aleichem's Yiddish text, English words are presented in Yiddish letters, which represent their sounds as immigrant speakers of Yiddish would have heard them, rather than their standard English spelling – for example, *foyrnitsher* for "furniture." In Halkin's translation, these same English words[12] are differentiated from other English words by being spelled as a phonetic transcription into English of Sholem Aleichem's phonetic transcription into Yiddish. An example:

All things come to an end. We arrived at our stahp and climbed down to the strit . . . . We stood there in the strit with all our bundles. We had to go on foot the rest of the way. The Americans call that vawkink. We vawked.[13]

This works in some ways. We know – and without footnotes, which is an important advantage – that there exists a class of words new to Motl and his family, which he knows according to their sound rather than to their spelling, but which he is going to use anyway, bold experimenter with

---

[11] Sholem Aleichem, "A Business with a Greenhorn," in *Nineteen to the Dozen: Monologues and Bits and Bobs of other Things*, trans. Ted Gorelick, ed. Ken Frieden (Syracuse: Syracuse University Press, 1998), p. 158.

[12] More precisely: not quite the same English words. Sometimes, and to his credit, Halkin makes different choices than does Sholem Aleichem about which words will work best as foci of Motl's dealings with English.

[13] Sholem Aleichem, *The Letters of Menakhem-Mendl & Sheyne-Sheyndl and Motl, the Cantor's Son*, translated, with an introduction by, Hillel Halkin (New Haven: Yale University Press, 2002), p. 266.

new languages that he is. We know, or rather if patient we can learn, what those words mean. ("Strit" is easy, "vawkink" harder.) The phonetically transcribed words in the translation affect the rhythm of our reading much as do the phonetically transcribed words in the original.

In other ways this strategy works less well. The original has two different spelling systems for dealing, however imperfectly, with words in two different languages. The translation has two different spelling systems for dealing with words in the same language. One system is standard, one is more or less phonetic. Usually writers use phonetic spelling to indicate individual and non-standard pronunciations, so usually that is what we read such spellings as conveying. Here, though, phonetic spelling is doing something else, so to read it we have to go against our first habits. There are other problems also. For one thing, sometimes the phonetic transcription bewilderingly indicates standard pronunciation, for example, "kitshn" for "kitchen" or "rumz" for "rooms." For another, it makes no sense as regards pronunciation that Motl should drop the final /r/ of "stritkah" and sound it in "fire" or "water" (two words that are not presented in phonetic transcription). Finally, the boundaries between what is spelled standardly and what is spelled phonetically are arbitrary. In the original, Motl uses the English word "subway" (spelled *sobvey*) because the subway is a new thing, an American thing. But walking is neither new nor American; so why "vawkink" for "walking" rather than, say, "klaymbd" for "climbed"?

The overall effect is different too. In Sholem Aleichem's text, Motl's adroit deployment of English words in Yiddish marks him as quick-witted, open-minded, curious. He becomes the Yiddish reader's guide to this new culture. In the translation, he is most of the time a speaker of Standard and standardly spelled English. His apparent inability to deploy a good number of relatively common English words marks him for the English reader as slow, ignorant, bumbling.

Is there a better approach? Maybe – but only if Halkin were to rid himself of his severest constraint, namely, not to let Motl be what Motl most dazzlingly is, namely, bilingual. The one language that Halkin almost never admits into his translation is Yiddish. But that constraint is unnecessary; the unexplained presentation of Yiddish in a text intended for anglophone readers can work wonderfully. Consider this passage from the beginning of Cynthia Ozick's "Envy":

In judging [Jewish American writers, the Yiddish poet Edelshtein] dug for his deepest vituperation – they were, he said, "*Amerikaner-geboren.*" Spawned in America, pogroms a rumor, *mamaloshen* a stranger, history a vacuum . . . A few were blue-eyed, like the *cheder yinglach* of his youth. Schoolboys.[14]

Halkin might get a better result by allowing Motl as much Yiddish as Ozick allows Edelshtein, or a bit more.[15]

Jeannette Lander, A Summer in the Week of Itke K.

Jeannette Lander's 1971 German novel, *Ein Sommer in der Woche der Itke K.*, is an extraordinary work and an extraordinary challenge for the translator – as I myself found when preparing a translation of it, some six years ago.[16]

Lander was born in 1931, in New York, to Yiddish-speaking Polish Jews, but grew up in the Black quarter of Atlanta, where her parents lived and kept a store. She spoke Yiddish with her parents at home, English with her Black neighbors and friends on the street, who were also her parents' friends and customers; her two native languages were Yiddish and African-American English. She went to Sarah Lawrence, won prizes as a creative writer in English, did some writing in Yiddish. Later she met and married a German, moved to Germany, started learning the language (five words a day, every day). At the age of twenty-eight she went to the Free University of Berlin, and took her doctorate there in 1966. In conversations with German friends, she kept noticing how little they understood about America, and resolved to educate them by writing an American novel in German. She published *Itke K.* in 1971.

Like Lander herself, the novel's Itke Kovsky is the daughter of Yiddish-speaking Polish Jews, her family like Lander's lives in the Black quarter of Atlanta, and the year of Itke's summer is 1942, which makes fourteen-year-old Itke just three years older than the narrator would have been. The book

---

[14] Cynthia Ozick, "Envy; or, Yiddish in America," in *The Pagan Rabbi* (New York: Schocken, 1976), p. 41. Usually Ozick provides an English equivalent for the Yiddish words and phrases – *cheder yinglach* is glossed by "schoolboys," *Amerikaner-geboren* is glossed, more freely, by "spawned in America." *Mamaloshen* ("mother tongue," but also simply a name in Yiddish for Yiddish) is unglossed. Using such a strategy means that readers ignorant of Yiddish will get most of the meaning of the Yiddish words; they will not, however, *know* that they are getting it.

[15] Or as much Hebrew as Halkin allows Tevye the Dairyman; see Sholem Aleichem, *Tevye the Dairyman and The Railroad Stories*, translated, with an introduction by, Hillel Halkin (New York: Schocken, 1987).

[16] For the result, see "A Summer in the Week of Itke K.," *Antioch Review* 58:2 (Spring 2000), pp. 134–62. Page numbers for subsequent quotations from this work will be given in the text.

On Lander see also Esther Dischereit, "Über Jeannette Lander," in *Übungen, jüdisch zu sein* (Frankfurt am Main: Suhrkamp, 1999); Jeannette Clausen's translation of the first chapter of Lander's novel, "One Summer in the Week of Itke K.," and Marjanne Goozé and Martin Kagel, "'I am not a part of this. I can laugh at it. But I know it.' A Conversation with Jeannette Lander," the latter two both in *Women in German Yearbook* 15 (2000), pp. 1–16, 17–31.

pulls off an astonishing juggling act. Itke's narrative voice speaks German –
high, inventive, self-conscious, beautiful. Her parents speak Yiddish, not
just tags and epithets but real talk, varied and flexible, in all their conversations with each other and their children, and often in conversations with
their Black neighbors and customers. The Black characters speak German
with occasional bits of English, but a German different from Itke's, equally
rich, but shaped to imitate some of the lexical and syntactical patterns of
Black English.

Two challenges for the translator, then, the Yiddish and the German
representing Black English. Yiddish first:

When it was Sunday morning, and Tateh was still sleeping in the big double bed,
not having gotten up at six, not in the store at seven, not waiting on the early
customers at 7:01, who left for work at 7:08 (for work in the Whites' houses, the
Whites' businesses, the Whites' offices) – that one Sunday morning in the week,
we sisters ran down the front stairs, got the fat Sunday paper that was wedged
beneath the door, and ran up the front stairs again to Tateh in the big double bed.
　　Sunday morning.
　　Laikeleh, Heikeleh, Mameh, Tateh, Itkeleh-me-myself, all in the same big double
bed on Sunday morning.
　　"I get the comics first." – "No, this time I get the comics first – you got the comics
first last time." "But I want to get the comics first too. You two always get them,
and I never get them!" Throwing of cushions, covers, black-and-white pages –
where are the comics? No comics! Comics nowhere! Tateh had them under his
bottom.
　　Sultan of the Comics Tateh, cross-legged on the lavish pile of cushions, covers,
quilts, lifted a commanding hand and read from the brightly colored page:
　　"'Di shtraln veln zey farnikhtn!' Azoy zogt der Phantom. 'Ikh hob a shtralnshis-
gever, velkhe es vet zey ale farnikhtn!' 'Neyn, neyn!' Azoy zogt dos meydele mit
di kirtse rekele: 'Neyn! Groyse, shtarke Phantom, farnikht zey ale nisht. Ikh hob
eynen lib!' Ober der Phantom hert nisht, vos zi zogt, dos meydele mit di kirtse
rekele. Der Phantom gikt gornisht amol oyf ire sheyne beyndelakh. Un er shist a
groyse shtral aroys, un es makht: Bum!"[17]
　　Little sister Laikeleh screamed.
　　"Max! Far vos dershreksti di kinderlakh?!"[18]
　　Mamma held Laikeleh in her arms. Laikeleh Who Gets the Comics.[19]

---

[17] "'The rays will destroy them!' says the Phantom. 'I have a raygun that will destroy them all!' 'No,
no!' says the girl with the short skirt, 'no! O great and powerful Phantom, do not destroy them all.
I love one of them!' But the Phantom does not hear what she says, the girl with the short skirt. The
Phantom doesn't even look at her pretty legs. And he shoots a big ray-blast, and it goes, Boom!"
[18] "Max! Why are you frightening the children?"
[19] Jeannette Lander, *Ein Sommer in der Woche der Itke K.* (Frankfurt am Main: Insel, 1971), p. 39; my
translation, but not the one I published, for reasons explained below, p. 133.

There is a close linguistic relation between German and Yiddish. For a German reader, the Kovskys' Yiddish speech as Lander has transcribed it[20] is largely intelligible, and the fact that German-speaking characters in the novel can understand it is plausible. The linguistic relation between English and Yiddish is more distant. For English readers ignorant of Yiddish, the Kovskys' Yiddish speech will be largely unintelligible, and the fact of its being understood by the other characters will seem less plausible. Retaining the Yiddish in an English translation, changing only the system for transcribing it, as is done in the passage quoted above, means altering the relations between text and reader and straining the plausibility of the relations between character and character. (Footnoted translations help with the first problem but not the second.) On the other hand, an English translation that retains the Yiddish comes closer than the German original does to presenting the real languages of the world that Lander is describing. English and Yiddish, that is, were the languages actually spoken in Lander's childhood, in the historical and biographical world of which this novel is a depiction; German was not.

I hold three views here. As a zealot, I want to retain the Yiddish, even at the cost of the footnotes; doing that positions the reader closer to the world the book is set in, offers the reader something of the book's multilingualism, defies the constraining conventions that hamper multilingual writing.[21] As a practical advocate of Lander's book, though, when in 2000 I was trying to publish a translation of the novel's second chapter, I replaced the Yiddish with English, because I wanted above all to get the chapter published and because the editor, no doubt for good reasons, wanted it that way. The pressures driving translators to such solutions are hard to resist.

As a critic, looking for some way out of the box that translating multilingual texts seems to put us into, I keep thinking of a letter Lander wrote me:

I would leave it entirely up to you to retain the Yiddish or not. I tried, immediately following a sentence in Yiddish, always to repeat it in some other way in German. I'm sure you can find a fitting solution for English, even to having the Kovskys speak English with a Polish-Yiddish accent, and interspersed with Yiddish words the Blacks pick up. That could be funny in itself or lead to new language fun. It would make the mutual understanding more plausible. But having them speak Yiddish has merits as well.

---

[20] I have changed her transcription into one more helpful for readers of English.

[21] Christian Lagarde, in *Des écritures "bilingues": sociolinguistique et littérature* (Paris: L'Harmattan, 2001), quotes Juan Marsé, author of *El amante bilingüe*, on these difficulties: "as for mixing the two languages, as in the ending of *El amante bilingüe* – it's only possible for half a page. You can't write a whole novel that way; they'd throw it at your face" (20; my translation).

I did not, as is clear, adopt Lander's suggestion, for reasons connected with my critique of Gorelick's rendering of "A Tale with a Greenhorn." My reasons still seem valid to me. But as time goes by, and as I reread, and find wanting, the solutions I came up with, I wonder more and more about what "new language fun" might mean, about what a productive goal it might be even if based on imperfect arguments.

The other challenge is the Black characters' German – as in this haunting passage at the end of the second chapter, in which Itke, left alone by her parents and suddenly frightened by solitude and darkness, invites her Black neighbor Mrs. Stevens into her house for companionship:

Mrs. Stevens shook her white-wool-colored head wellwishingly, wellwisely, wide-wittingly, well and truly willingly, willweakeningly, wellwelcomely in the dwelling-place of the Whites.

"Y'all sure do have it nice here," said Mrs. Stevens softly. Itke Lord and Master nodded benevolently.

"I ain't never yet been up here."

Itke Mild in Might murmured, "ah."

"Y'all sure do have pretty things."

Cherrywood pride.

"Mr. Jägel and Mrs. Jägel, they used to live here, huh?"

"Mmm hmmm."

"I see Mrs. Jägel 'round here sometimes. She don't never look at me. If she sees me come 'long, she look the other way, as far away as she can, and then she runs further 'long, as if I ain't never bought nothing from her for nigh on twenty years, and never paid her none of my rent from that day to this. You know? And I ain't got nothing against Mrs. Jägel. Mrs. Jägel, she always been nice to me. It wasn't none of her fault. But she don't come no closer to me than a hare to a hound. So I can't tell her she ain't never done me no wrong and all. Wasn't none of her fault."

"Why? Does she think she did something wrong to you?"

"Oh, Miss Itke, I can't rightly say. I am just an ole black woman and can't rightly say, how whitefolks think. Oh, that was so - o - o - o long ago . . ." (143–44)

Mrs. Stevens's speech in German has some features modeled on Black English, which read oddly and unidiomatically for native speakers of that language. These include the Black English system of negative concord, what is sometimes called a double negative; German words and phrases calqued on Black English words and phrases – for example, *rechnen* for "reckon," *lang* for "'long," *Honigkind* for "honeychild," *nahe an* for "nigh on"; truncation of final and initial syllables and consonants; and turns of syntax that are strange in German but idiomatic in Black English – for example, *es war nicht keine von ihrer Schuld*, which is strikingly odd in

German, but translate it back word for word into English and it becomes, "it wasn't [or, better, "warn't"] none of her fault," which is fine and familiar.

In some ways, it might be finer even than the original, more original than the original – which sounds paradoxical but is only common sense. Suppose one is translating into English a book in French that quotes, in French translation, some phrase originally in English, from an Emerson essay or a Martin Luther King speech or a Janis Joplin song or a McDonald's commercial. The translator will want not to translate the French version of the phrase back into English, but to find and use the English phrase itself. A translator of Lander's novel into English is in a similar situation. The Black characters' German is a translation into German of a set of phrases that Lander heard or imagined in English. If we simply translate that German back into English, what we get is something like the dialogue in the passage quoted above: a partial Black English, marked by some but not all the characteristic features of that dialect. Ideally the translator would go further, would have the Black characters speak a Black English as alive as Zora Neale Hurston's. Had Lander sought to retain all the salient features of Black English in German, she might have made the book unreadable or the dialect seem degraded. For the translator into English, though, these concerns do not apply, and Black English can and should be entirely itself.

Here, as with Mercier's novel, though, one would have to be, or become, competent in the languages and dialects one was translating into, and here, as with Mercier's novel, we might have to develop a new model of collaborative translation or translational training. But the reward would be in proportion: a restoration of parts of the German novel to their original anglophone state.[22]

Ana Lydia Vega, "Pollito: Chicken"

Vírgenes y mártires, the 1981 book in which Vega's dazzling story appears, is usually catalogued not in PS but in PQ, as Hispanic rather than American literature.[23] (Lander's books are catalogued in PT, with Goethe.) There is a logic to that: the text is mostly in Spanish, and Vega's place of origin and

---

[22] Lander's comment: "I think it's a good idea to work with someone, who knows Black dialect peculiar to the South in the forties. Much of the melody no longer exists today, as a gain in status is a loss in color. We all become pale ponderers of that lost, without grasping what it was, we had. No return, of course."

[23] Reed Way Dasenbrook points out that in the *MLA Bibliography*, "Chicano literature, whether written in English, Spanish, or both, is considered American literature, though Puerto Rican literature is given a section of its own in *Foreign Literature* (volume 2) as part of Spanish-American literature" ("English Department Geography: Interpreting the *MLA Bibliography*," in Maria-Regina Kecht

residence is Puerto Rico rather than any of the fifty states. But there is a greater logic to considering the story an American work, part of American literature. Puerto Rico is not a foreign country but a commonwealth or unincorporated territory of the United States. Its inhabitants are American citizens. The themes of Vega's story are as American as apple pie: immigration, assimilation to an American norm, ambivalence about such assimilation, seeking an identity somewhere between the mainland and the homeland. What sensible definition of American literature would exclude such a work by such an author?[24]

The story recounts "el surprise return de Suzie Bermiúdez[25] a su native land tras diez años de luchas incesantes" ("the *surprise return* of Suzie Bermiúdez to her *native land* after ten years of uninterrupted struggle").[26] Suzie Bermiúdez is of Puerto Rican origin, hates that fact about herself, lives in New York, and works as a secretary in a Black housing project (the Blacks, says the narrator-as-Suzie Bermiúdez, "were no better than New York Puerto Ricans but at least were other than New York Puerto Ricans" [75]). One day Suzie sees a "breathtaking" poster in a travel agency, is dazzled by it, and resolves to take her savings and go to Puerto Rico for a vacation. She arrives, looks about, thinks scornfully about Puerto Ricans (above all those seeking Puerto Rican independence), looks in vain for an "all-American" husband, and ends up having an affair with the Puerto Rican bartender at her hotel – who reports, in the story's conclusion, that what Suzie Bermiúdez cries out at the moment of her orgasm is, "¡*VIVA PUELTO RICO LIBREEEEEEEEEEEEEEEE!*" (79; "Long live free Puerto Rico," the /l/ in "puelto" reflecting Puerto Rican pronunciation).

"Pollito: Chicken" is bilingual in two ways. First in its dialogue; when Vega judges that the characters should be speaking English, English is what they speak, and the same for Spanish. Second in its narrative, which is roller-coasterishly bilingual, filled with adroit, surprising, suggestive codeswitchings: "Pensó con cierto amusement en lo que hubiese sido de ella si a Mother no se le ocurre la brilliant idea de emigrar" (76; "she thought with a certain *amusement* about what would have become of her if *Mother* hadn't had the *brilliant idea* of emigrating").

[ed.], *Pedagogy Is Politics: Literary Theory and Critical Teaching* [Urbana: University of Illinois Press, 1992], p. 203).

[24] For extended reflections on this point, see below, pp. 146–59.

[25] My colleague Nancy Hall acutely suggests that the non-standard spelling "Bermiúdez" (the standard spelling has no "i") reflects an Americanized pronunciation of the name.

[26] Carmen Lugo Filippi and Ana Lydia Vega, *Vírgenes y mártires* (Rio Piedras, Puerto Rico: Editorial Antillana, 1981), p. 75. Page numbers for subsequent quotations from this work will be given in the text. All translations from the work are my own.

The first sort of bilingualism is no great problem, because there's not much dialogue to deal with. The second sort is the real challenge. The two languages of the narrative have different functions.[27] The structure of the sentences, their syntax, is Spanish; English is used chiefly to relexify individual words and phrases, for the plums in the Spanish pudding: nouns, adjectives, and adverbs. Some English words have to do with travel, and with American institutions and products. Some of them express judgments of value. Some but not all of those judgments seem to belong to Suzie Bermiúdez. Some seem to belong to someone slyer and more sophisticated, not Suzie but plausibly Vega herself, cosmopolitan, trilingual professor of French and Comparative Literature at the University of Puerto Rico with a doctorate from the University of Aix-Marseilles. It's Suzie who is impressed by the "breathtaking poster" depicting "beautiful people holding hands." It's probably Vega, though, who describes Suzie as being inexorably pressed by the bartender's eyes towards a "sudoroso, maloliente y alborotoso ["sweaty, stinking, swarming"] streetcar named desire" (78), or refers to "los skyscrapers inalcanzables de un intra-uterine orgasm" ("the unattainable *skyscrapers* of an *intra-uterine orgasm*").

The English phrases that reflect Suzie's judgments are manageable. Most of them have a prefabricated feel to them, as if they were in quotation marks, and if one put a selection of them into actual quotation marks – single quotation marks, perhaps, to differentiate them from actual dialogue – one could produce something like their effect in the Spanish original:

All of which puts us into position to recount Suzie Bermiúdez' 'surprise return' to her 'native land' after ten years of incessant struggle.

What decided her was the 'breathtaking' Fomento poster she saw at the travel agency in the lobby of her building. The 'breathtaking' poster in question showed a pair of 'beautiful people holding hands.'

Dealing with the more sophisticated English phrases is harder, because in being more closely linked to the author, they are also more closely linked to the politically significant structural relationship in the story between English and Spanish. The narrator's Spanish (as distinct from the quoted, orthographically non-standard Spanish of the Puerto Rican characters) is the neutral medium, the framework, the context in which English can become the object of analysis; we are led, as we read, to ask what it means that

---

[27] See on this Lagarde, *Des écritures "bilingues,"* pp. 191–208. I owe much to Lagarde's fine analysis; but he seems not to want to see the shifting character of the narrative voice or the English terms, instead finding everywhere that "the dominant imposes its viewpoint on the dominated, by means of its language" (200).

the phrase "beautiful people holding hands" comes into Suzie Bermiúdez's mind when she sees the "poster," what mixture of cliché and longing that phrase expresses, what degree of assimilation to anglophone American commercial norms. We are not so much led to examine the Spanish; in "Lo que la decidió fue el breathtaking poster de Fomento que vio en la travel agency" ("what decided her was the *breathtaking* Fomento *poster* she saw in the *travel agency*"), "lo que la decidió" ("what decided her") does not call attention to itself. The narrator's Spanish is not the object of analysis but its means.

Vega's structure stands the chief convention of local color fiction on its head, and with it the power structure that it reflects. In Puerto Rico and in the Puerto Rican community of New York, English is the language of social advancement, the prestige language, functionally what linguists call a *langue véhiculaire*, the language used for communicating between one local group and another. Spanish in that situation is what linguists call a *langue vernaculaire*, a vernacular, local and native.[28] Usually the vehicular language gets to comment knowingly on the vernacular, to display the latter's idioms as curios. Here the reverse is true: Spanish is the commentator, English the object of commentary. Translating the story into English means losing the political meaning of the non-anglophone place from which the narrator can speak.

Is there a mode of translation that would retain these political meanings? Not by ordinary means, maybe not by any means at all, but two strategies are at least imaginable. First, one might retain some Spanish as part of the structure, the grammar, though less than in the original. That would produce something like this:

Lo que la decidió was the 'breathtaking' Fomento poster in the travel agency in her building lobby. The 'breathtaking' poster in question *representaba una pareja* of 'beautiful people holding hands' . . .

Such a strategy keeps the two languages more or less in the same relations, but it has problems. Functionally it is not a translation at all, since the bits inaccessible to a reader ignorant of Spanish are the bits that describe the actions going on and the relations among the actors and objects. It is also mechanical and unlifelike; what author or speaker, Puerto Rican or American, cosmopolitan or parochial, would actually improvise such a language?

---

[28] Elsewhere, of course, Spanish is the vehicular language, in relation to, say, Quechua or Nahuatl. Its being the vernacular language in Puerto Rico and Puerto Rican New York has to do with its situation in those places, not with its linguistic nature or long history.

A second strategy involves some rewriting – "new language fun," to borrow Lander's phrase. It is riskier but more promising, because it might produce living language. Like the first strategy, its goal is to keep the Spanish in its role as a vehicular language, but it seeks to reach that goal by other means – not by using Spanish for the syntactic skeleton of sentences, but by presenting it as a language of prestige, mystery, philosophical density, literary allusion. The original has an untranslated French-language epigraph by Albert Memmi: "*Un homme à cheval sur deux cultures est rarement bien assis*" (75; "A man riding horseback on two cultures tends not to be comfortably seated"). In a rewritten version, that epigraph would be replaced by some equally challenging and equally untranslated maxim in Spanish. The quick allusion to Tennessee Williams might be replaced by one to Calderón. The original: "Y Suzie Bermiúdez sintió que la empujaban fatalmente, a la hora del más febril rush, hacia un sudoroso, maloliente y alborotoso streetcar named desire" (78; "and Suzie Bermiúdez felt that she was being inexorably pushed, at this most fevered of all *rush* hours, towards a sweaty, stinking, swarming *streetcar named desire*"). A possible translation: "And suddenly Suzie Bermiúdez felt that she was being driven on by some *hipogrifo violento* ["violent hippogriff"] hunted inexorably down to the *confuso laberinto* ["bewildering labyrinth"] of her untamable heart," where the interpolated Spanish phrases are drawn from the celebrated opening speech of Calderón's *La vida es sueño*. Ideally the translator would thicken the translated text with allusions to the Spanish literature of Puerto Rico and the New World. If the allusions were challenging and dense enough, the effect would be to keep Spanish from being local color, and situate it as a central *langue véhiculaire* of the translated and adapted story. Maybe Vega would hate such an approach, maybe it would fail, but it holds out more promise than the alternatives do.

Rolando Hinojosa, Dear Rafe/Mi querido Rafa

Few authors have written bilingual novels; few translators have translated such novels; fewer still are the authors of bilingual novels who have made their own translations of them. The Chicano writer Rolando Hinojosa may in fact be the only author in this last category, with a 1985 English translation (*Dear Rafe*) of his dazzlingly bilingual but predominantly Spanish 1981 original (*Mi querido Rafa*). The translation is brilliant, suggestive, and disappointing; as with Halkin, the problem is not talent but self-imposed limitation.

Hinojosa was born in 1929, to an Anglo mother and a Mexican father, in Mercedes, Texas; he grew up bilingual, attended both American and Mexican schools, served in the Korean War, began writing at the age of fifteen but had to wait until 1972 for his first paid publication. A good chunk of his work belongs to the *Klail City Death Trip* series, a sequence of linked texts (novels, mysteries, books of poetry) all focusing on the characters and history (local and long-range) of Hinojosa's invented territory, Belken County with its county seat Klail City, somewhere near the border between Texas and Mexico. The linked texts and invented territory have reminded some readers of Faulkner; Hinojosa makes that comparison himself.

Mi querido Rafa centers around a cluster of questions: what is the story with Jehú Malacara, former chief loan officer at the Klail City First National Bank? Has he left his job or not? If so, has he resigned or been fired? If he was fired, was the cause his affairs with married women or his land deals? Where is he now and what is he doing? Or, more succinctly: "as for Jehú, there's no telling where he is, and hence this story."[29]

The novel begins with a series of letters from Jehú to his friend Rafa Buenrostro, recuperating in a hospital from the aftereffects of a wound sustained during the Korean War. The letters are presented by one Galindo, also in the hospital, dying, with some nine months to live. Galindo is intrigued by the letters and puzzled by them, and to figure out what has actually happened with Jehú he interviews everyone connected to, or with an opinion about, the central story; these interviews make up the second part of the book. Unlike the letters, the interviews are annotated, Galindo appearing repeatedly to preface, annotate, and conclude them. The brief third part of the book presents Galindo's final assessments of the evidence.

The bilingualism of *Mi querido Rafa* is presented by Galindo as resulting not from caprice but from fidelity:

¿Sería mucho pedir que no se sorprendieran cuando les Anglos Texanos hablen inglés? Es su idioma natural y casero; se sabe que unos hablan español y cuando así suceda, el español saldrá por delante. Si se hablan ambos idiomas así saldrán también. También es natural que la raza del Valle hable más en español. Ahora, si la raza sale en inglés, así se reportará. (Hay que ser fidedigno, hay que ser etc.) (MQR 142)

---

[29] From *Dear Rafe*, in Rolando Hinojosa, *Dear Rafe/Mi querido Rafa* (Houston: Arte Público Press, 1985), with an introduction by Manuel Martín-Rodríguez, p. 3. The book contains both original and translation; page numbers for subsequent quotations from both original (marked MQR) and translation (marked DR) will be given in the text. My own translations are given in square brackets.

[Would it be too much to ask that readers not be surprised when Texas Anglos speak English? It's their natural language, their home language; it's known that some of them speak Spanish too, and when that happens, Spanish will come forward. If they speak both languages, those languages will appear as well. It's also natural for Valley Mexicanos to speak more in Spanish. And if *la raza* speaks in English, that's the way it will be reported. (One has to be trustworthy, one has to be etc.)]

This simple, noble claim turns out to mean two different things. The first is that some of the interviews in the second part of the book, those with Anglos who mostly speak English, are in English. The second is that Jehú's own letters to Rafa are filled with code-switching. This too results from Hinojosa's (or Galindo's) stubborn realism, given the histories and capacities of the two correspondents. A small sample:

Item: Lo de Ira parece que va en serio: la hermana de Noddy Perkins vino al banco tres veces hoy mismo, and where there's smoke, pero por ahora no sé nada.(More on her in a minute.) (MQR 146)

[Item: The thing about Ira's deal seems to be serious; Noddy Perkins' sister came to the bank three times today, *and where there's smoke,* but for now I don't know anything. *(More on her in a minute.)*]

The novel is thus bilingual in two ways, representing both the linguistic spectrum of the community and the language play of the individual characters.

In 1985, in spite of all dissuasion and hazard, Hinojosa published a translation of this most translationally challenging of his works, transforming *Mi querido Rafa* into *Dear Rafe*. Manuel Martín-Rodríguez calls Hinojosa's translation a "transreading," a "transculturation," undertaken so that the work "may be accommodated to the needs of the new readers";[30] he notes Hinojosa's omission from the translation of a possibly confusing passage about *la raza papelera*[31] in Jehú's seventh letter to Rafa, and his addition of explanations regarding kinship relations and mesquite trees. Angie López, working out further details of what a "transculturation" might be, notes

---

[30] Manuel Martín-Rodríguez, "Introduction" to Hinojosa, *Dear Rafe/ Mi querido Rafa*, pp. x–xi.
[31] Literally "wastebasket race," i.e., a people that could be thrown in the garbage. Presumably the confusion in question has to do with the complex tone of the passage, in which the speaker both indicts his own people and ironizes the indictment: "We seem like monkeys, man, we can be comfortable anywhere, climb any tree. Some might call it adaptability, but there's got to be another word for it" (MQR 160; my translation).
My thanks to my colleague Nancy Hall for her help with this passage.

how Hinojosa's translation gives preciser indications of time than does the original, and preciser information about historical events anglophone readers are likely to be ignorant of.[32]

None of the criticism gets at the two most interesting aspects of the translation: its exhilarating inventiveness and its strict unilingualism. This extended passage is a good example of both:

Wherever that may happen to be, diría yo, pero quién soy yo para andar rompiendo ilusiones. A estas alturas tú bien sabrás que lo que Ira quería era dejármelo saber and that was it. Adelante: lo último que querría serían consejos y yo para eso tampoco sirvo. Estaba Ira que no cabía en sí y debieras haberlo visto cuando decía County Commissioner, Place Four; lo único que pensé era que qué serían los motivos de Noddy (y de la demás bolillada, although they're one and the same), ya que teniendo casi toda la tierra – AND ALL THAT MONEY, SON – allí tendría que haber gato encerrado. (If all this were true, of course.) Por ahora todo esto me tiene sin cuidado; para acabar, Ira se fue derechito a su casa a ver a su mujer para darle el notición. (MQR 145)

[*Wherever that may happen to be*, I'd say, but who am I to go around shattering illusions. At this point you'll know perfectly well that what Ira wanted was to let me know *and that was it*. Onward, then: the last thing he'd want would be advice, and I'm not so useful for that either. It was Ira who was all full of himself, and you ought to have seen him when he said "*County Commissioner, Place Four*"; and the only thing I thought was that whatever Noddy's motives were (and the motives of the other Anglos, *although they're one and the same*), since he owns almost all the land – *AND ALL THAT MONEY, SON* – he'd have to smell a rat there. (*If all this were true, of course.*) For now, all this isn't bothering me; and to finish, Ira went straight back to his house to see his wife and give her the news.]

Wherever that may happen to lead, say I. But who am I to go around breaking hearts and illusions? By now, you're prob. way ahead of me here since the only thing Ira was interested in was to let me know the Good News, and that was it.

Forward! Haaarch! The last thing he'd want from me would be some advice, and I'm not good at that either. There we were, two lonely people in a treeless parking lot, at 6 m., with 97 degrees F staring us in the face, and Ira saying: "Jay, Jay, don't you see? County Commissioner Place Four, the *fat* one, Jay." (Yes, he calls me *Jay*.) About all I could think of was to wonder what Noddy, the Ranch, the Bank, etc. were up to this time; I mean, they already own most of the land 'in these here parts' and they have ALL THAT MONEY, SON; so it's prob. something else in that woodpile aside from the wood, right? I finally shook his hand, or the other way round, and then he went straight home to give his wife the second surprise of her life. (DR 7)

[32] Angie López, "Transfer Strategies in Rolando Hinojosa's Self-translation of *Mi querido Rafa*," in Rosa Morillas Sánchez and Manuel Villar Raso (eds.), *Literatura chicana: reflexiones y ensayos críticos* (Granada: Editorial Comares, 2000).

Most sentences of the original are not only translated but also altered. Some of the alterations can be explained as Martín-Rodríguez and López explain them, as means of "transculturing" the text. But many cannot, and in them something else seems to be going on, some more general compensatory thickening of the verbal texture. "Illusions" is amplified into the zeugmatic "hearts and illusions"; "what Ira wanted was to let me know" amplified and sharpened into "the only thing Ira was interested in was to let me know the Good News"; *"adelante"* into "Forward! Haarch!"; and "smelling a rat" into "prob. something else in that woodpile aside from the wood."[33] There are additions from scratch, too – for example, "two lonely people in a treeless parking lot," or the suggestive added detail about how Ira drastically anglicizes Jehú's name, the mock folksiness of "in these here parts," the new raunchy ending to the paragraph, the aggressive colloquialism of "prob."

I call such thickening "compensatory" because, as noted, what Hinojosa's translation also does is to get rid of the original's complex bilingualism. In the original, English is switched into for filler and cliché, but also for Jehú's skepticism ("if all this were true, of course"). English is also used for the central, challenging claim of the passage, "ALL THAT MONEY, SON," the claim that money is at the heart of the political negotiations and interpersonal pirouettings. Maybe that is because, in fictions of this sort, English is associated with money, the vernacular with its absence. Maybe it is because Jehú likes the sound of the phrase, its rich sentence sound, or likes distancing himself from avarice by speaking of it in his second language. Whatever is going on in the code-switchings, though, whatever patterns of meaning are being revealed by them, the translation does not retain them, and that is a big loss.

Hinojosa's translation, with its brilliance and its systematic elimination of the original's bilingualism, implies an argument in two parts. First, the audience for the original work is presumed to be cosmopolitan and curious, engaged by the challenge of a realistically, rigorously bilingual novel; the audience of the "translation," on the other hand, is presumed *not* to be any of those things.[34] Then, imagining such an audience, Hinojosa capitulates to it. Friedrich Schleiermacher famously divided translations into two

---

[33] Not all readers will know the idiom Hinojosa is referring to here, i.e., "nigger in the woodpile," meaning something more than is actually seen, and possibly referring to the practice of concealing escaped slaves in woodpiles. Why Hinojosa would want to evoke a racist idiom in an antiracist book is not clear to me.

[34] Klaus Zilles, *Rolando Hinojosa: A Reader's Guide* (Albuquerque: University of New Mexico Press, 2001), states that "Hinojosa himself spoke out adamantly against the idea of mixed-code narration" (36). That seems to me a slight but significant misreading of a quite interesting passage in an Hinojosa

sorts: those that leave the reader in peace and move the text, and those that leave the text in peace and move the reader. Clearly Hinojosa has chosen to do the former.

That seems to me an error, partly because translations that move the reader and leave the text in peace are in the long run more durable and alive, partly because Hinojosa is short-changing his actual audience. No doubt a good many American anglophone readers could not or would not read a translation into English that was to any significant degree bilingual. But Hinojosa's books (Spanish and English alike) are published by Arte Público Press, a self-styled "David to New York publishing industry Goliaths . . . the oldest and most accomplished publisher of contemporary and recovered literature by U.S. Hispanic authors."[35] That fact suggests that Hinojosa is willing to limit himself to a relatively small, self-selecting audience, a literary audience. Such an audience can have demands made on it, is in fact eager to have demands made on it. There is more room for play here than Hinojosa is allowing himself, more patience with bewilderment, more appetite for meeting challenges, more willingness to be transformed by an author's demands.

Hinojosa is pointing the way towards a mode of translating bilingual texts but not arriving at it. Pointing the way, because the general freedom he allows himself as translator is the first essential, the freedom to adapt, add, subtract, rewrite, rethink, thicken, simplify, complicate the original. Not getting there, because the one sort of freedom he doesn't allow himself is the one that most needs to be in play here, polyglot freedom. By all means change the ratio, make English predominant, Spanish secondary. Work out how to do that, have every putatively bilingual character speak mostly English, the narrator included. But no one needs to speak *only* English, any more than characters need to speak only English in *Call It Sleep* or *Moby-Dick* or *Dictée*. Characters whose identity is indissoluble from the fact that they speak chiefly Spanish in the bilingual world of Klail City and Belken County need to speak some Spanish even in the translation – and why

interview. Miguel Riera asks Hinojosa, "and these experiments mixing both languages, for whom are they intended?" Hinojosa replies: "there is no novel written in Spanglish; some stories, and above all poetry. Some are very bad, but some authors are famously good. I tell my students that if they insist on mixing the two idioms, then they themselves are going to be reducing their audience. They're making themselves untranslatable, and neither Anglos nor Chicanos will understand them. So if that's what they choose, fine, but they shouldn't complain that they're not being read! Mixing idioms doesn't usually get you anywhere, though I admit that there are some very fine poems" (Miguel Riera, "El otro sur: Entrevista con Rolando Hinojosa," *Quimera* 70/71 [1987], p. 115; my translation).
35 www.arte.uh.edu/artepublico/about/index.aspx

shouldn't they? To translate such a work adequately, we need to expect – to demand, to believe – more of the reader.

CONCLUSION

No grand synthesis is possible here; to end, then, a small packet of observations, recommendations and predictions. (1) Translating multilingual fictions may require translators to be, or become, multilingual writers, or to work with speakers of languages they themselves do not know. (2) American anglophone readers of literature have a broader tolerance, a livelier curiosity, and a deeper fund of energy for dealing with heterophone material in their reading than is often presumed. Translators can and should write for those readers, should allow themselves as broad a language range as authors do. Publishers and editors should have those readers in mind when they make decisions about what to publish and promote. (3) The best translations of multilingual language fictions will probably be the most inventive, the freest in their relation to the letter of the original, the most animated by "new language fun." (4) It is in part accident that the most challenging examples considered in this chapter are the most recent ones. But only in part, because despite attacks on bilingual education, on multilingual ballots, on translating "The Star-Spangled Banner" into Spanish, on illegal non-anglophone immigrants, the United States is becoming still more richly multilingual than it has been in the past. H. L. Mencken's *The American Language*, published in 1937, listed 28 non-English languages spoken in the United States; the 2000 Census lists 350, and indicates that in the 1990s, the number of persons living in the United States who speak a language other than English at home increased by 47 percent. Some distinguished non-anglophone language fiction is going to get written to depict this aspect of American life, and it will be broadly, exhilaratingly useful to be able to translate it.

CHAPTER 5

Towards a history of multilingual American literature

> Given the multilingualism of so many national literatures, including American literature . . . one can no longer assume that the categories of national literature and literature in a given language are at all compatible.
>
> – Reed Way Dasenbrook

> It's been forty-one years that I've lived between your borders, America, and have carried within me the fruits of your freedom consecrated and blessed by the sacrificial blood of Lincoln and the hymns of Walt Whitman.
>
> – from the Yiddish of H. Leivick, trans. Richard Fein

For non-anglophone language fictions to matter they need to be widely read, and to be widely read they need to be translated – hence the previous chapter. But once translated, once widely read, they need to be made part of the large narratives we construct of our literary history. To make that happen, we have to figure out how to write the single history of a literature created in multiple languages.

The present chapter is meant to aid in that task. It states the reasons for undertaking it, assesses what some of the comprehensive histories of American literature have done in this area, sketches one alternative approach, and concludes with an image of utopian hope.

WHY?

A comprehensive history of American literature needs to take account of American literature written in languages other than English. There are two chief reasons: that so much wonderful American work has been created in those other languages, and that taking account of that work will solve some important methodological problems.

We are only starting to see what's there, to have a cloudy sense of how rich the material is, but we can at least name some of what needs to be included. To begin with, some of the language fictions discussed previously in this book: Mercier's *L'Habitation Saint-Ybars* and *Johnelle*, the stories of Abraham Cahan and Moshe Nadir and Sholem Aleichem, Jeannette Lander's *Ein Sommer in der Woche der Itke K.*, Ana Lydia Vega's "Pollito: Chicken," the *Klail City Death Trip* series of Rolando Hinojosa. Then the astonishingly rich and diverse imaginative works created in what Roger Williams rightly called "the languages of America," that is, the languages of Native Americans: the Navajo Night Chant, the Iroquois Ritual of Condolence, the Dena'ina stories of Raven and the Kalapuya stories of Coyote and the Ojibwe stories of Nanabush, the Lenape epic called *The Walam Olum or the Red Score of the Lenape*. After them, in chronological order, with much omitted that has been shown to be of value: Omar Ibn Said's Arabic slave narrative; Ludwig von Reizenstein's wild *roman-feuilleton*, *Die Geheimniße von New-Orleans* ("The Mysteries of New Orleans"); Mozart's librettist Lorenzo Da Ponte's "Poet's Lament" and the American sections of his memoirs; Reinhold Solger's *Anton in Amerika*; Ole Rölvaag's *Giants in the Earth* and Dorothea Dahl's *Kopper-Kjelen* (*The Copper Kettle*); the *corridos* of the Southwest, notably the "Ballad of Gregorio Cortez"; Joseph Opatoshu's *From the New York Ghetto*; Moyshe-Leyb Halpern's *In New York* and Anna Margolin's *Poems*; Adorno's *American Dreams*, published in the German-language American newspaper *Aufbau*; the plays of Luis Valdez and Dolores Prida; and of course whatever is being written right now for the underfunded newspapers and publishing houses and theaters and cabarets of newer immigrant groups to the United States.

It cannot be right not take account of such work. It is too distinguished, and too closely connected with other strands of American writing. "I think of your grass, Whitman," wrote the American Yiddish poet B. Alkvit-Blum, "and hear the stir of the great/ stone forest Manhattan."[1] How can that not be part of American literary history?

Taking account of such work would not only enrich the story; it would also make it more coherent. The story we tell now is about American literature in English. That is a problematic subject; the reason, as Reed Way Dasenbrook argues, is that it depends on conflating two approaches to literary history:

There are at least two ways of mapping literature. We can map it according to language, the language in which the work of literature is written, or we can map it according to nationality, the national literature of which the work seems to be

---

[1] Richard Fein (trans.), not yet published, used by permission.

a member. Neither approach is without its problems or problematic examples . . . The mistake we have fallen into is to try to use both simultaneously.[2]

Literature written in English is a coherent subject. American literature in all its languages is a coherent subject. American literature written in English is not.

Most critics who have considered this problem have rejected the choice to map by nationality. Dasenbrook himself uses his convincing analysis to argue for "a conscious move away from organizing our institutions around national and nationalistic categories . . . [and] a recommitment to the full world of the English language today" (208). Others who have made similar critiques draw different conclusions. William Spengemann, for example, argues for replacing the category of "early American literature in English" with that of "the literature of British America," defined as "literature written in English before 1765 by persons who spent some time in the New World";[3] he thus moves from a body of work defined by its relation to a country not in existence when it was written to one more organically corresponding to a domain of historical experience. Wai Chee Dimock draws a more radical conclusion, arguing thoughtfully against national literary history, but also against literary history mapped by language.[4]

All success to those seeking to imagine transnational literary history, whether in one language or many. But to reject national literary history altogether – to say, with Dimock, that "Emerson is *American* only in caricature" (770) – is a mistake. Emerson is American only in caricature only if "American" means "American and nothing else"; Emerson is American if not only American, and the American Emerson is important. Nations remain important even in this age of globalization; histories of national literatures remain important even in the context of what Dimock calls "deep time." These histories need to be polyglot, of course. French literature includes works in Breton and Occitan, German literature works in Turkish. But once made polyglot, these histories become coherent and pertinent.

[2] Reed Way Dasenbrook, "English Department Geography: Interpreting the *MLA Bibliography*," in Maria-Regina Kecht (ed.), *Pedagogy Is Politics: Literary Theory and Critical Teaching* (Urbana: University of Illinois Press, 1992), p. 206. Page numbers for subsequent quotations from this work will be given in the text.
[3] William Spengemann, "Discovering the Literature of British America," *Early American Literature* 18 (1983), p. 8.
[4] Wai Chee Dimock, "Deep Time: American Literature and World History," *American Literary History* 13:4 (2001), pp. 755–75. Page numbers for subsequent quotations from this work will be given in the text. See also Gavin Jones, "Language Nation," *American Literary History* 13:4 (2001), pp. 776–88, and Jonathan Arac, "Global and Babel: Two Perspectives on Language in American Literature," *ESQ* 50:1–3 (2004), pp. 95–119. My thanks to Jonathan Arac for sending me his essay.

To turn from generalizations to examples: putting Emerson together with Carlyle, or with Hafiz (whom he read chiefly in German!), reveals things that are concealed by situating him in his national tradition. But putting Emerson together with Frederick Douglass reveals things too, among them American literature's central engagement with slavery and freedom – all the more so when we set both Emerson and Douglass in relation to the non-anglophone American writers equally occupied with that subject, among them Ottilie Assining in German and Mercier in French. Mercier himself no doubt needs to be linked with his French model Alexandre Dumas, but also and more importantly with his anglophone contemporary George Washington Cable – two Louisiana writers animated by passionate curiosity about the multicultural place they lived in.

Give up, then, the incoherent subject of national literature in a single language. Look around for more coherent subjects: literature in a single language regardless of nation, Goethean *Weltliteratur*. But bear in mind the continuing importance of nations and national literatures; leave room for the study of a nation's literature in all the languages in which it has been written; and – to touch on the training of scholars as well as the topics of scholarly writing – let the study of comparative literature include comparisons within multilingual national literatures as well as between them.

PRECEDENTS

No comprehensive history of American literature successfully integrates non-anglophone American literatures into its narrative. But most of them offer accounts of those literatures, and it will be useful to define both the limitations of these accounts and their occasional successes.

The first limitation is of scale: not enough space, nowhere near enough space, sometimes no space at all. The 1917 *Cambridge History of American Literature* (henceforth *Old Cambridge*) has sixty pages out of fourteen hundred, twenty-four for Native American literatures, thirty-six for all other non-anglophone literatures, one sentence for Mercier's *L'Habitation Saint-Ybars*, no sentence at all for Sholem Aleichem's *Motl*.[5] The small scale is at least partly deliberate, given the editors' falsifiable assertion that among the languages spoken in the United States "only German, French, and Yiddish may be said to show something like a special literature of their own"

---

[5] William Peterfield Trent *et al.* (eds.), *The Cambridge History of American Literature*, 3 vols. (New York: Macmillan and Cambridge: Cambridge University Press, 1943, first published 1917). Page numbers for subsequent quotations from this work will be given in the text.

(vol. III, 572). Even so, *Old Cambridge* is more accommodating than Robert
Spiller's 1948 *Literary History of the United States* (henceforth *LHUS*), which
devotes only twenty-seven of its fourteen hundred pages to non-anglophone
literatures: nine for "The Indian Heritage" and eighteen for "The Mingling
of Tongues" – the latter covering German, Pennsylvania Dutch, French,
Spanish, Italian, Scandinavian, and Yiddish, with the wider range of literatures meaning that less gets said about any one literature in particular.[6]
Not a sentence about Mercier's novel, nor about Sholem Aleichem's. Both
writers also go unmentioned in Emory Elliott's 1988 *Columbia Literary
History of the United States* (henceforth *Columbia*), which runs to twelve
hundred pages; eleven of those pages go to N. Scott Momaday's "The Native
Voice," twenty-one to Werner Sollors's "Immigrants and Other Americans"
(the latter devoted for the most part to the non-anglophone press, rather
than to the major works of non-anglophone literature that Sollors has done
so much to excavate and describe), and half a dozen to a part of Raymond
Paredes's chapter on Mexican American literature.[7]

The second limitation is structural: in all three histories, the principal
strategy for presenting these literatures involves sequestering them. All three
histories have a chapter on Native American literature and a chapter, or
group of mini-chapters, on American literatures in European languages.
Better to have those chapters than not; but sequestering the material in
those chapters makes it hard to integrate it into the large story. To have
chapters on Yiddish literature and German literature that include remarks
about drama, and then to have a general chapter on drama that says nothing
about drama in languages other than English, means that a major literary
genre is being silently identified with the practice of that genre in a particular
language.[8]

When significant connections are suggested between anglophone and
non-anglophone literatures, they are almost always suggested by the scholars discussing the latter. In *Old Cambridge*, for example, Edward Fortier
very briefly compares Charles Testut's *Le Vieux Salomon* and *Uncle Tom's
Cabin*. Carl Van Doren, however, the author of the chapter where the latter novel is treated at greatest length, has nothing to say about the former.
Louise Austin's visionary, maddening chapter on Native American literatures in *Old Cambridge* suggests a good many such connections. Austin

[6] Robert Spiller *et al.* (eds.), *Literary History of the United States*, 3 vols. (New York: Macmillan, 1948).
   Page numbers for subsequent quotations from this work will be given in the text.
[7] Emory Elliott (ed.), *Columbia Literary History of the United States* (New York: Columbia University
   Press, 1988). Page numbers for subsequent quotations from this work will be given in the text.
[8] Ruby Cohn's chapter on drama in *Columbia* does talk about Chicano drama, but only for a paragraph.

lumps all Native Americans together, and her abrupt transitions and vatic pronouncements must have perplexed the history's respectable editors. But she makes a case for telling the story of Native American literature as an integral part of American literature generally: "the earlier . . . we leave off thinking of our own aboriginal literary sources as the product of an alien and conquered people, and begin to think of them as the inevitable outgrowth of the American environment, the more readily we shall come into full use of it" (vol. III, 633–34). She links American and Native American literatures with respect to oratory, democracy, and landscape. She makes connections between Native American storytelling and the work of Joel Chandler Harris, between Native American meter and the work of Longfellow.

Nowhere else in the history, though, are those suggestions picked up; like the chapter itself, the connections it makes are sequestered and lie sterile. N. Scott Momaday's essay in *Columbia* makes the same big claims that Austin's does: "the American Indian oral tradition . . . is so deeply rooted in the landscape of the New World that it cannot be denied . . . It is the very integrity of American literature" (14–15). As in *Old Cambridge*, though, that claim never gets worked out.

The American Yiddish poet Jacob Glatshteyn, author of a great poem on Sacco and Vanzetti and essays on Poe and Dreiser and Maryanne Moore and Richard Wright, was asked by Irving Howe what it meant to be the poet of an abandoned culture. His answer: "It means that I have to be aware of Auden but Auden need never have heard of me."[9] A version of that asymmetry is hardwired into the structure of most of the large American literary histories.

New Cambridge

The major literary history of our time is Sacvan Bercovitch's *Cambridge History of American Literature* (henceforth *New Cambridge*), eight sizable volumes of innovative and authoritative scholarship.[10] In one respect *New Cambridge* is a significant improvement: the ghettoes are gone. No scholar has been asked to write only on Native American poetry, or only on the non-anglophone literatures created in European or Asian languages. With a few exceptions, moreover – for example, Barbara Packer's wonderfully fresh account of the Transcendentalists – the topics of individual scholars'

[9] Irving Howe, *World of Our Fathers* (New York: Simon & Schuster, 1976), p. 452.

[10] Sacvan Bercovitch (general ed.), *The Cambridge History of American Literature*, 8 vols. (Cambridge and New York: Cambridge University Press, 1994–96). Page numbers for subsequent quotations from this work will be given in the text.

contributions are capacious enough to include any accounts of non-anglophone writing the scholars may choose to offer.

That being the case, it is striking how few accounts are to be found. Volume III, on prose between 1860 and 1920, has almost nothing on non-anglophone work – for example, no mention of Mercier's work or Testut's in Susan Mizruchi's brilliant chapter, "Remembering Civil War."[11] Volume IV, on poetry between 1800 and 1910, is similar, dealing neither with Cable's translations of Creole songs nor with the distinguished trans-lations of Native American songs and poems included in John Hollander's great anthology of nineteenth-century poetry.[12] So are volume V, on poetry and criticism between 1900 and 1950, and volume VIII, on poetry and criti-cism between 1940 and 1995.[13] Volume VII has five pages on hispanophone writing in Cyrus Patell's "Legacies of the Sixties," and a few remarks on Nobel laureate Isaac Bashevis Singer in Morris Dickstein's "Fiction and Society, 1940–1970."[14] Somehow, that is, despite a structure open to non-anglophone material, very little non-anglophone material actually appears – proportionally less, in fact, than in the earlier histories with their struc-tural impediments and intellectual parochialism. Having an open structure, though important, is not enough.

We can see something of how that openness might be made use of by looking at the history's three large accounts of non-anglophone material: Myra Jehlen's discussion of exploration narratives; Eric Sundquist's discus-sion of Native American literature; and Werner Sollors's discussion of some distinguished non-anglophone fictions in his account of "Ethnic Mod-ernism."

Jehlen's "The Literature of Colonization" is the simplest to describe and assess. It is multilingual but not proclaimed or theorized as such. Without

---

[11] The exception is two pages of Richard Brodhead's chapter, "The American Literary Field, 1860–1890," on non-anglophone drama. Of this Brodhead writes, "Chinese, Polish, Yiddish, and other theaters are not usually mentioned in histories of American literature. But if 'literature' is understood to include all word-based imaginative expression and 'American' the whole people of the United States, such theaters must form an integral part of that history" (vol. III, 33). Indeed; but presumably forming "an integral part" would mean occupying more than two pages in eight volumes.

[12] John Hollander (ed.), *American Poetry: The Nineteenth Century* (New York: The Library of America, 1993). The section of "American Indian Poetry" (the phrase appears on the cover of volume II) runs to nearly a hundred pages.

[13] Robert Von Hallberg's account of American poetry in volume VIII has a section on translation, which includes a brief account of *Alcheringa*, the journal founded in 1970 by Jerome Rothenberg and Dennis Tedlock "to encourage poets to participate actively in the translation of tribal/oral poetry" (vol. VIII, 171); but Von Hallberg does not treat the translation of Native American poetry in an American journal as different in kind from the translation of poetry from elsewhere.

[14] The relatively scanty coverage of non-anglophone material in this volume is reflected in some oddities in the chronological list of works considered: the Spanish works considered are listed in the year of their English translation, and the Singer works, all of them translations, as if they were originals.

fanfare, though with wide learning and intelligence, Jehlen considers writings by Columbus, Jean de Léry, Bernal Díaz del Castillo, and Álvar Núñez Cabeza de Vaca, as well as anglophone works by Thomas Harriot, John Smith, and Roger Williams, and draws her sense of the European colonial enterprise from all these texts together.

Of all the accounts of discovery narratives in the comprehensive histories, Jehlen's is by far the best, the most probing and philosophical. But its practical multilingualism is simply common sense. How did the Europeans who were to become Americans respond to, represent, make sense of, control by interpreting, the "New World"? No one answering that question can legitimately answer it only with respect to the works of William Bradford and John Winthrop, while excluding from consideration those of Cortés and Samuel Champlain. Not treating the topic with respect to all the relevant literatures, anglophone and non-anglophone alike, would be uncomplicatedly silly.[15]

Sundquist has the hardest task, because integrating Native American literature into literary history raises two important theoretical problems. First, how can we integrate an oral literature, what some critics these days call an "oraliture," into a chronologically ordered history, given that, as Jehlen notes in her contribution, "an unwritten culture is not readily identified with a precise period" (vol. I, 40)? Second, how can we treat as literature a mode of art that is as much musical, theatrical, religious, and therapeutic as it is literary?[16]

Sundquist does not deal adequately with the second problem. But neither does Christopher Bigsby's account of American drama, which treats theater pieces chiefly as literary texts rather than performances. In both cases that

---

[15] In the course of his considerably less ambitious account of discovery narratives in *Columbia*, one of the few exceptions in the three earlier histories to the principle of sequestration, Wayne Franklin makes the point perfectly: "The first classics of American literature were written for, if not always in, Europe. And most were written not in English but in Spanish and French" (18).

[16] A third theoretical problem, again noted by Jehlen, is this: how can we integrate into a history, which must be based on an idea of meaningful change over time, a body of work produced by people who saw not change but continuity, not lines but cycles?

The first two problems are significant. This one, though, is bogus. The fact that a people or peoples imagine time cyclically and stress continuity over change does not mean that those peoples and their works do not have a history, any more than the fact that a people or peoples imagine time linearly and stress change over continuity means that those peoples do not have unchanging or slowly changing cycles and continuities. However difficult to date, however expressive of a sense of deep continuity, the Navajo Nightway has a history, changes over time, comes into recognizable form rather than having always been in that form; see James Faris, *The Nightway: A History and a History of Documentation of a Navajo Ceremonial* (Albuquerque: University of New Mexico Press, 1990).

is a limitation, in neither case a crippling or theoretically important one, because it is easy enough to imagine how the limitation could be dealt with.

Sundquist does deal adequately with the first problem, the problem of chronology, in an imperfect way but one that makes sense, namely, by associating works of Native American poetry and storytelling with the moment of their being written down or translated. An imperfect solution, because that moment is determined more by European needs than by Native American ones; the reason that a Nahuatl account of the Spanish conquest got written down and published, and that all the other stories and myths and songs created by the native peoples of "New Spain" did not, was the Spanish sense, not the Aztec one, that the story of the conquest was important and the other material less so. Nor does the Navajo Nightway have an essential link in Navajo minds to the moment at the end of the nineteenth century when Washington Matthews studied and translated it.

But there may be no better solution. It is at the point of being written down that any work becomes literary in the etymological sense. Centering analysis around the moment of a work's being written down associates the work with a date. It is also at the moment of being written down, and then still more at the moment of being translated (in practice the two moments are often the same), that the work can enter more vividly into relations with works of American literature – anglophone literature but also, to the extent that English is an American lingua franca, American literature in all other languages than the one the work was produced in. An example of the process at its richest: Native American legends were translated into English by Henry Rowe Schoolcraft, George Catlin, and John Heckewelder; their translations were the source for Longfellow's *Hiawatha*; in 1910, Yehoash made a celebrated translation of Hiawatha into Yiddish.

So Sundquist's account is defensible in theory. How well does it work in practice? Sundquist is a great scholar. His account of the material is perceptive and learned. He rightly situates the material in a context outside itself; the chapter in which his account appears is called "The Frontier and American Indians," and also considers a wide variety of writing about the frontier and about Native Americans, including translations of Native American works into English.

But this particular contextualizing of Native American literary creation almost perpetuates its isolation, because the context chosen has no organic relation to the material. Native American work is made in relation to Native American cultures; it is not only and not principally created in response to European American exploration narratives or European American ethnography, and a large asymmetry is created by implying that it is. Treating

Native American work under the heading "The Frontier and American Indians" is an argument, an implicit and partially misleading categorization.

Sundquist is too good a critic not to know this, and many of his individual observations break the distorting frame he has created. At one point, for example, he makes the fine observation that "the kinetic figures of [the Navajo song of the Black Bear] are drawn at once from the human and from the inanimate world; repetition and catalogue (in some respects not unlike that of Whitman's poetry) create a ceremonial voice and motion for the surrogate tribal singer who takes on the bear's role in performance" (vol. II, 202). Fine analyses might arise from that observation – of how American poets, Native American poets included, see the relations between the human and the "inanimate"[17] world, or of how American poets, Native American poets included, make use of those fundamental poetic figures of repetition and catalogue. But the structure keeps the analyses from being written.

In the end, Sundquist's observations are almost as isolated in their chapter as Louise Austin's are in hers. If Jehlen's work reminds us that some clearly important topics are open to, indeed almost demand, a multilingual account, Sundquist's work reminds us that the right topic can be hard to find.

Sollors's "Ethnic Modernism" treats non-anglophone writing in two ways. In a chapter called "American Languages," his strategy is to push against the boundaries he has been assigned. He knows too much about the long history of non-anglophone writing, and too much about the neglect of that history, not to give some account of it in his contribution, but has too fine a sense of form not to know that such an account does not belong in the place where he puts it; as he writes, "the present section on prose literature of the first half of the twentieth century is not the place to review the long multilingual history in all genres of American literature" (vol. VI, 430). True enough; but the other imperative, to tell the story, leads him to break the frame of his own section and sketch "the long multilingual history" in question, from Omar Ibn Said's 1831 Arabic slave narrative to the work of the Portuguese writer José Rodrigues Miguélis, who died in Manhattan in 1980. The announced out-of-placeness of Sollors's excellent sketch sharpens our sense of the problem.

In a later chapter of his account, Sollors offers a thoughtful model for solving that problem. The chapter is called "'All the Past We Leave Behind'?

---

[17] "Inanimate" might betray an unconscious bias towards a European American perspective, since Native American poets tend not to see the non-human world as without an anima.

Ole E. Rölvaag and the Immigrant Trilogy"; it is, to my knowledge, the only extended critical analysis of a single non-anglophone work in any comprehensive history of American literature, and the account of such work that most generously links it to the American literary traditions with which it is conversing. Sollors situates Rölvaag both in the context of Norwegian writing in America and in the context of immigrant writing generally. He links Rölvaag to Whitman and Carl Sandburg and Du Bois and Cather and Maxine Hong Kingston, to the tradition of the historical novel, to other American work dealing with Native Americans and with the railroad. He examines the process by which the trilogy was translated into English. Exemplary on all counts – or rather on all counts but one, namely, that such an account should not be unique in an eight-volume history, but ordinary, supplemented by enough additional accounts that the reader will develop a consistent consciousness of the presence and influence of American writers working in languages other than English, of the vibrantly, turbulently multilingual American literary scene.

The moral of *New Cambridge* is both depressing and encouraging. What is keeping us at the present moment from writing a satisfying literary history of American multilingual literature is not the conceptual difficulties of the task, not the narrative structures we create, but prosier factors: ordinary ignorance, the way that Americanists are trained, and the failure up to this point of those making the case for non-anglophone American literatures to make it persuasively and forcefully enough, to translate and explicate and teach enough of the works, to explore enough of the connections between the apparently sundered literatures. Large tasks and a depressingly long list of them, which could surely be lengthened. But not impossible tasks, and requiring for their accomplishment only patience and diligence.

BIOGRAPHY, LITERARY HISTORY, AND MULTILINGUALISM

Some contributions to *New Cambridge* are organized around writers rather than topics. Christopher Bigsby's account of drama, for example, has chapters on Tennessee Williams, Arthur Miller, Edward Albee, Sam Shepard, and David Mamet, along with a brief introduction and a kitchen-sink chapter called "Changing America." Andrew DuBois and Frank Lentricchia organize their account of "Modernist Lyric in the Culture of Capital" largely as a series of chapters on individual poets: Frost, Stevens, Eliot, Pound. Irene Ramalho Santos organizes "Poetry in the Machine Age" in the same way: Stein, Williams, H. D., Moore, Crane, and Hughes. All compelling figures, all presented in a wide variety of significant contexts, but not the context of their non-anglophone colleagues in drama or poetry – for example, the dramatist and activist Luis Valdez (he gets two paragraphs in Bigsby's account), or the American Yiddish poets Anna Margolin, Moyshe-Leyb Halpern, and Jacob Glatshteyn, who were as concerned as Eliot and Stein were with modernism, capital, and the machine age. Empirically, focusing on individuals – writing biography rather than history, as Emerson recommended – seems to get in the way of representing the multilingual literary world.

One reason for this is that foregrounding a set of individuals invites us to focus on what links them, where their lives touch, the circle that bounds them all. An account that foregrounds Williams and Miller but not Valdez, Frost and Stevens but not Margolin, has an appealing coherence to it. The foregrounded authors have common concerns, have read one another's work, have read the same work by earlier poets or playwrights, are responding to similar crises. Introducing someone outside their circle complicates, almost violates, the order and orderliness of the story.

It also makes new stories possible. The challenge of expanding the circle, of disrupting an earlier story to construct a new one, is one that American literary history has met repeatedly. The story of nineteenth-century American poetry, for example, was surely easier to tell when it included only male poets who read one another. When Emily Dickinson became important, telling the story got harder. None of the other major poets had read her, nor had she herself read the greatest of them, Whitman; she famously wrote to Thomas Higginson, "I never read his Book – but was told that he was disgraceful –"[18] How could one tell a story that included them both?

Today that question is bewildering, so accustomed have we gotten to telling the story in that way. We are familiar with the strategies by which, as it turned out, the two great poets could be linked: the concerns they had in common about the nature of the soul, how expansive or contractive it is; about the relation between public space and private, inner life and outer, between grimmer and more optimistic religions, Calvinists and Quakers; about the possibilities for innovation in poetic form – we can hardly remember when those strategies had to be invented, or why.

Integrating the great non-anglophone works and writers into the story would in some cases be more difficult than integrating Dickinson proved to be. She was at least *able* to read Whitman, and aware of his presence. In the multilingual American literary scene, great writers went to their graves

---

[18] Nina Baym *et al.* (eds.), *The Norton Anthology of American Literature*, fourth edition (New York: Norton, 1994), vol. I, p. 2480.

never having read a word of one another's work, and for that matter not knowing of one another's existence. How can we tell a single story about lives that never touch?

In some cases, though, it would be easier. Glatshteyn and Halpern and Margolin were all considerably less sequestered from the world of Frost and Stein and H. D. than Dickinson ever was from Whitman's. (They also had probably all read more Whitman than Dickinson ever did, given the fascination Whitman had for many Yiddish poets.) Like the anglophone poets, they wrote about New York, tense relations between women and men, Sacco and Vanzetti and lynchings, nights spent on city streets, strikes and bosses and revolutions. Glatshteyn at least was an omnivorous reader and wide-ranging critic; read and wrote about Poe and Dreiser and Richard Wright and Maryanne Moore; read and wrote also about some of what Moore and Wright and Dreiser (and Eliot and Pound) were reading and reading about, Joyce and translations of Chinese poetry and the Spanish Civil War; read Avrom Tabatshnik's essays about modernism, if not Eliot's. In this context, Glatshteyn's remark, that being the poet of an abandoned culture meant that he had to read Auden but that Auden need never have heard of him, has a more productive resonance. Because it was Glatshteyn who was reading Auden and Moore and not the reverse, it is Glatshteyn through whom the lines of connection run. From Moore's viewpoint, from Auden's, those lines were invisible. From Glatshteyn's, they are alive and important, and by centering on him we can get a larger view of the still closely knit story.[19]

How can a writer-centered model of literary history take account of non-anglophone writers? Not simply by picking out a writer or two, by way of tokenism, even by way of representativeness, but by picking out writers who were part of the liveliest literary discourse, even if other participants in that discourse had no idea they were there.

CONCLUSION

From one door comes the sound of Lithuanian Yiddish, from another Polish Yiddish; in one hallway a man and a woman are conversing in the Yiddish of Volhinia and, in another, a woman is cursing in the Yiddish of Galicia . . . More

---

[19] Edmund Wilson's magnificent anthology, *The Shock of Recognition: The Development of Literature in the United States Recorded by the Men Who Made It* (Garden City: Doubleday, Doran and Co., 1943), offers a welcome precedent here; it gives us a larger view of the story by focusing on those who recognized others even when the recognizers seems marginal in relation to the recognized, e.g., Poe as a reader of Hawthorne, John Jay Chapman and James Russell Lowell as readers of Emerson, and, crossing both national and linguistic boundaries, Mallarmé as a reader of Poe.

often Americanized Yiddish is heard, and very frequently Yiddishized English, seasoned with the coarse language of the streets, and not infrequently the noble diction of Shakespeare and Byron and, sometimes, even the beautiful literary Russian of Turgenev.[20]

I quoted that passage from Leon Kobrin's "The Tenement House" in Chapter 3 as an image of my own utopian vision. I quote it here as an image of what our literary history might be: a house where the sounds of different languages are all audible, maybe even intrusively audible, as near to one another as a hallway is to a door, as one apartment is to another, as a house is to a street. There is a messiness to Kobrin's vignette; some of the speech is cursing, some of it is coarse. There would be a messiness to a multilingual literary history, too, as we figured out how to put it together, a messiness resulting from the problem of ordering the diverse voices, a further messiness from the sheer number of those voices, with 350 languages other than English now being spoken in homes in the United States.

But there are no conceptual obstacles to writing such a history. Its subject is more coherent than is exclusively anglophone American literary history. The polyphony and structural openness of *New Cambridge* are big steps forward. The wide-ranging curiosity of some non-anglophone writers makes them figures through whom connections can be seen. Distinguished works of non-anglophone American literature have been excavated, are being translated, can be read. Construction work on the multilingual house of American literary history is at least under way.

[20] Leon Kobrin, "The Tenement House," in Henry Goodman (ed. and trans.), *The New Country: Stories from the Yiddish about Life in America* (New York: YKUF, 1961), p. 31.

Bibliography

Aarsleff, Hans, *From Locke to Saussure* (Minneapolis: University of Minnesota Press, 1982).

Allen, Dennis W., "'By All the Truth of Signs': James Fenimore Cooper's *The Last of the Mohicans*," *Studies in American Fiction* 9:2 (1981), pp. 159–79.

Antin, Mary, *The Promised Land* (New York: Penguin, 1997).

Anzaldúa, Gloria, *Borderlands/ La Frontera: The New Mestiza* (San Francisco: Spinsters/Aunt Lute, 1987).

Appiah, Kwame Anthony, *The Ethics of Identity* (Princeton: Princeton University Press, 2005).

Arac, Jonathan, "Babel and Vernacular in a Postcolonial Empire of Immigrants: Howells and the Languages of American Fiction," *Boundary 2* 34:2 (Summer 2007), pp. 1–20.

"Global and Babel: Two Perspectives on Language in American Literature," *ESQ* 50:1–3 (2004), pp. 95–119.

Arends, Jacques, Pieter Muysken, and Norval Smith (eds.), *Pidgins and Creoles: An Introduction* (Amsterdam and Philadelphia: John Benjamins, 1995).

Ash, Sholem, *Der amerikaner*, recorded by Chaim Ostrowsky on *Jewish Classical Literature* (New York: Folkways Records, 1960).

Ist River (New York: Laub, 1946).

Axtell, James, "Babel of Tongues: Communicating with the Indians in Eastern North America," in Edward Gray and Norman Fiering (eds.), *The Language Encounter in the Americas 1492–1800* (New York: Berghahn, 2000).

Baym, Nina *et al.* (eds.), *The Norton Anthology of American Literature*, fourth edition (New York: Norton, 1994).

Belen'kii, M. S. (ed.), *Sholom Aleikhem: Pisatel' i Chelovek* (Moscow: Sovetski pisatel', 1948).

Benveniste, Émile, "L'antonyme et le pronom en français moderne," in *Problèmes de linguistique générale*, 2 vols. (Paris: Gallimard, 1974), vol. II.

"De la subjectivité dans le langage," in *Problèmes de linguistique générale*, 2 vols. (Paris: Gallimard, 1966), vol. I.

"La nature des pronoms," in *Problèmes de linguistique générale*, 2 vols. (Paris: Gallimard, 1966), vol. I.

Bercovitch, Sacvan (general ed.), *The Cambridge History of American Literature*, 8 vols. (Cambridge and New York: Cambridge University Press, 1994–96).

Bernabé, Jean, Patrick Chamoiseau, and Raphaël Confiant, *Éloge de la créolité* (Paris: Gallimard, 1993).

Blakemore, Steven, "Strange Tongues: Cooper's Fiction of Language in *The Last of the Mohicans*," *Early American Literature* 19 (1984), pp. 21–41.

Boyer, Henri (ed.), *Plurilinguisme: "contact" ou "conflit" de langues?* (Paris: L'Harmattan, 1997).

Brunet, François, "'Linguisters on the prairie': formes et enjeux littéraires de la polémique herméneutique dans *The Prairie*," *Revue française d'études américaines* 37 (July 1988), pp. 238–66.

Butor, Michel, "Le parler populaire et les langues anciennes," *Cahiers Renaud Barrault* 67 (September 1968), pp. 83–98.

Cable, George W., "Creole Slave Songs," in Arlin Turner (ed.), *Creoles and Cajuns* (Garden City: Doubleday, 1959).

"The Dance in Place Congo," in Arlin Turner (ed.), *Creoles and Cajuns* (Garden City: Doubleday, 1959).

"The Freedman's Case in Equity," in Arlin Turner (ed.), *The Negro Question: A Selection of Writings on Civil Rights in the South by George W. Cable* (New York: Norton, 1958).

The Grandissimes (New York: Hill and Wang, 1957).

The Negro Question, ed. Arlin Turner (New York: Norton, 1958).

Cage, John, "Indeterminacy," in *Silence: Lectures and Writings* (Middletown: Wesleyan University Press, 1961).

Cahan, Abraham, *Bleter fun mayn lebn*, 5 vols. (New York: Forward Association, 1926).

The Education of Abraham Cahan, trans. Leon Stein, Abraham Conan, and Lynn Davison (Philadelphia: Jewish Publication Society of America, 1969).

The Imported Bridegroom and Other Stories of the New York Ghetto (Boston and New York: Houghton Mifflin, 1898).

Yekl: A Tale of the New York Ghetto (New York: D. Appleton and Co., 1896).

Yekl and the Imported Bridegroom, and Other Stories of Yiddish New York (New York: Dover, 1970).

Calvet, Louis-Jean, *Linguistique et colonialisme: petit traité de glottophagie* (Paris: Payot, 1974).

Canetti, Elias, *Die gerettete Zunge: Geschichte einer Jugend* (Frankfurt am Main: Fischer, 1984).

Carkeet, David, "The Dialects in *Huckleberry Finn*," *American Literature* 51 (1979), pp. 315–32.

Carr, Helen, *Inventing the American Primitive: Politics, Gender and the Reception of Native American Literature, 1790–1936* (Cork: Cork University Press, 1996).

Cass, Lewis, "Structure of Indian Languages," *North American Review* 26 (April 1828), pp. 357–403.

Chan, Leo Tak-hung, "Translating Bilinguality: Theorizing Translation in the Post-Babelian Era," *The Translator* 8:1 (2002), pp. 49–72.

Cheyfitz, Eric, *The Poetics of Imperialism: Translation and Colonization from* The Tempest *to* Tarzan (New York: Oxford University Press, 1991).

"Literally White, Figuratively Red: The Frontier of Translation in *The Pioneers*," in Robert Clark (ed.), *James Fenimore Cooper: New Critical Essays* (London: Vision and Barnes & Noble, 1985).

Child, Lydia Maria, *Hobomok and Other Writings on Indians*, ed. Cardyn L. Karcher (New Brunswick: Rutgers University Press, 1986).

Chopin, Kate, *The Awakening and Selected Stories* (New York: Penguin, 1984).

Clausen, Jeannette, "One Summer in the Week of Itke K.," *Women in German Yearbook* 15 (2000), pp. 1–16.

Coates, Carrol F., "Problems of 'Translating' Bi-/Multilingual Literary Texts: The Haitian French of Jacques Stephen Alexis," in Marilyn Gaddis Rose (ed.), *Beyond the Western Tradition*, Translation Perspectives XI (Binghamton: State University of New York at Binghamton, 2000).

Cooper, James Fenimore, *The Last of the Mohicans* (New York: Penguin, 1986).

Crawford, James (ed.), *Language Loyalties: A Source Book on the Official English Controversy* (Chicago: University of Chicago Press, 1992).

Crystal, David, *Cambridge Encyclopedia of Language* (Cambridge: Cambridge University Press, 1997).

Dasenbrook, Reed Way, "English Department Geography: Interpreting the *MLA Bibliography*," in Maria-Regina Kecht (ed.), *Pedagogy Is Politics: Literary Theory and Critical Teaching* (Urbana: University of Illinois Press, 1992).

DeGraff, Michel, "Against Creole Exceptionalism," *Language* 79:2 (2003), pp. 391–410.

Delabastita, Dirk. "A Great Feast of Languages: Shakespeare's Multilingual Comedy in *King Henry V* and the Translator," *The Translator* 8:2 (2002), pp. 303–40.

Dickens, Charles, *Martin Chuzzlewit* (New York: Penguin, 1986).

Dillard, J. L., *Black English* (New York: Vintage, 1973).

Dimock, Wai Chee, "Deep Time: American Literature and World History," *American Literary History* 13:4 (2001), pp. 755–75.

Through Other Continents: American Literature Across Deep Time (Princeton: Princeton University Press, 2006).

Dischereit, Esther, "Über Jeannette Lander," in *Übungen, jüdisch zu sein* (Frankfurt am Main: Suhrkamp, 1999).

Doyle, Arthur Conan, *Works* (New York: Walter J. Black, n.d.).

Drechsel, Emmanuel, "'Ha, Now Me Stomany That': A Summary of Pidginization and Creolization of North American Indian Languages," *International Journal of the Sociology of Language* 7 (1976), pp. 63–68.

Dunn, Oliver and James E. Kelley, Jr. (eds. and trans.), *The* Diario *of Christopher Columbus's First Voyage to America, 1492–1493, Abstracted by Fray Bartolomé de las Casas* (Norman: University of Oklahoma Press, 1989).

Eco, Umberto, "Introduction," in *Anna Livia Plurabelle di James Joyce*, ed. Rosa Maria Bollettieri Bosinelli (Turin: Einaudi, 1996).

Ekström, Kjell, *George Washington Cable* (Lund: Carl Blom, 1950).

Elliott, Emory (ed.), *Columbia Literary History of the United States* (New York: Columbia University Press, 1988).

Equiano, Olaudah, "The Life of Olaudah Equiano, or Gustavus Vassa, the African, Written by Himself," in Arna Bontemps (ed.), *Great Slave Narratives* (Boston: Beacon Press, 1969).

Evans, William, "French-English Literary Dialect in *The Grandissimes*," *American Speech* 46:3–4 (1971), pp. 210–22.

Ezrahi, Sidra, *Booking Passage* (Berkeley: University of California Press, 2000).

Fanon, Frantz, *Les damnés de la terre* (Paris: Gallimard, 1991, first published 1961).

Faris, James, *The Nightway: A History and a History of Documentation of a Navajo Ceremonial* (Albuquerque: University of New Mexico Press, 1990).

Fassin, Eric, "Théorie du langage et idéologie dans *La Prairie* de James Fenimore Cooper," *Revue française d'études américaines* 37 (July 1988), pp. 267–82.

Filippi, Carmen Lugo and Ana Lydia Vega, *Vírgenes y mártires* (Rio Piedras, Puerto Rico: Editorial Antillana, 1981).

Fishman, Joshua A., *Yiddish in America*, Indiana University Research Center in Anthropology, Folklore, and Linguistics, publication 36, *International Journal of American Linguistics* 31:2(2) (Bloomington: Indiana University Press, 1965).

Fortier, Alcée, "The French Language in Louisiana and the Negro-French Dialect," *Transactions of the Modern Language Association of America* 2 (1884–85), pp. 96–111.

Gates, Henry Louis, "Dis and Dat: Dialect and the Descent," in *Figures in Black: Words, Signs, and the "Racial" Self* (New York: Oxford University Press, 1987).

Gilman, Sander, *Jewish Self-Hatred: Anti-Semitism and the Hidden Language of the Jews* (Baltimore: Johns Hopkins University Press, 1986).

Gilroy, Paul, *Black Atlantic: Modernity and Double Consciousness* (Cambridge, MA: Harvard University Press, 1993).

Glantz, Margo, "Doña Marina and Captain Malinche," in Doris Sommer (ed.), *Bilingual Games: Some Literary Investigations* (New York: Palgrave Macmillan, 2003).

Goodman, Henry (ed. and trans.), *The New Country: Stories from the Yiddish about Life in America* (New York: YKUF, 1961).

Goozé, Marjanne and Martin Kagel, "'I am not a part of this. I can laugh at it. But I know it. A Conversation with Jeannette Lander," *Women in German Yearbook* 15 (2000), pp. 17–31.

Gray, Edward, "The Making of Logan, the Mingo Orator," in Edward Gray and Norman Fiering (eds.), *The Language Encounter in the Americas 1492–1800* (New York: Berghahn, 2000).

and Norman Fiering (eds.), *The Language Encounter in the Americas 1492–1800* (New York: Berghahn, 2000).

Greenway, John, *Literature among the Primitives* (Hatboro, PA: Folklore Associates, 1964).

Hakuta, Kenji, *Mirror of Language: The Debate on Bilingualism* (New York: Basic Books, 1986).

Halkin, Hillel, "Translator's Introduction," in Sholem Aleichem, *The Letters of Menakhem-Mendl & Sheyne-Sheyndl and Motl, the Cantor's Son* (New Haven: Yale University Press, 2002).

Hall, Gwendolyn Midlo, *Africans in Colonial Louisiana* (Baton Rouge: Louisiana State University Press, 1992).

Harkavy, Alexander, *Yiddish-English-Hebrew Dictionary*, introduced by David Katz (New York: Hebrew Publishing Company, 1928, repr. New York: Schocken, 1988).

Harrison, James, "The Creole Patois of Louisiana," *American Journal of Philology* 3 (1882), pp. 285–96.

"Negro English," in J. L. Dillard (ed.), *Perspectives on Black English* (The Hague: Mouton, 1975).

Harshav, Benjamin, *The Meaning of Yiddish* (Berkeley: University of California Press, 1990).

Hazaël-Massieux, Marie-Christine, *Écrire en créole: oralité et écriture aux Antilles* (Paris: L'Harmattan, 1994).

Hearn, Lafcadio, "The City of the South," in *Occidental Gleanings*, 2 vols. (Freeport: Books for Libraries, 1967, repr. of original 1925 edition), vol. I.

"Los Criollos," in *Occidental Gleanings*, 2 vols. (Freeport: Books for Libraries, 1967, repr. of original 1925 edition), vol. I.

"A Sketch of the Creole Patois," in *The American Miscellany* (New York: Dodd, Mead, and Co., 1924).

Heckewelder, John, *History, Manners, and Customs of the Indian Nations Who Once Inhabited Pennsylvania and the Neighbouring States* (Philadelphia: Historical Society of Pennsylvania, 1876, repr. 1990).

Hellman, Lillian, *The Little Foxes. Six Plays by Lillian Hellman* (New York: Vintage, 1979).

Hinojosa, Rolando, *Dear Rafe/ Mi querido Rafa* (Houston: Arte Público Press, 1985).

Hollander, John (ed.), *American Poetry: The Nineteenth Century*, 2 vols. (New York: The Library of America, 1993).

Howe, Irving, *World of Our Fathers* (New York: Simon & Schuster, 1976).

Hymes, Dell, "Some North Pacific Coast Poems: A Problem in Anthropological Philology," in *'In vain I tried to tell you': Essays in Native American Ethnopoetics* (Philadelphia: University of Pennsylvania Press, 1981).

Jacobson, Dan, *The Beginners* (London: House of Stratus, 2001).

James, Henry, "Preface to *Daisy Miller*," in *The Art of the Novel: Critical Prefaces*, ed. R. P. Blackmur (New York: Scribner's, 1934).

Jefferson, Thomas, *Notes on the State of Virginia* (New York: Penguin, 1999).

Jones, Gavin, "Language Nation," *American Literary History* 13:4 (2001), pp. 776–88.

Strange Talk: The Politics of Dialect Literature in Gilded Age America (Berkeley: University of California Press, 1999).

Kachuk, Rhoda S., "Sholom Aleichem's Humor in English Translation," *YIVO Annual of Jewish Social Science* 11 (1956–57), pp. 39–81.

Karttunen, Frances, *Between Worlds* (New Brunswick: Rutgers University Press, 1994).

Kobrin, Leon, "A Common Language," in Max Rosenfeld (ed. and trans.), *Pushcarts and Dreamers* (Philadelphia: Sholom Aleichem Club Press, 1967).

Krupat, Arnold, "On the Translation of Native American Song and Story: A Theorized History," in Brian Swann (ed.), *On the Translation of Native American Literatures* (Washington, DC: Smithsonian Institution Press, 1992).

Kushner, Tony, *Homebody/ Kabul* (New York: Theatre Communications Group, 2002).

Lagarde, Christian, *Des écritures "bilingues": sociolinguistique et littérature* (Paris: L'Harmattan, 2001).

Lander, Jeannette, *Ein Sommer in der Woche der Itke K.* (Frankfurt am Main: Insel, 1971).

Lang, George, "Islands, Enclaves, Continua: Toward a Comparative History of Caribbean Creole Literatures," in A. James Arnold (ed.), *A History of Literature in the Caribbean*, 3 vols. (Amsterdam: John Benjamins, 1997), vol. III.

Link, Caroline, *Jenseits der Stille* (Berlin: Aufbau, 1997).

Liptzin, Sol, *A History of Yiddish* (Middle Village: Jonathan David, 1985).

López, Angie, "Transfer Strategies in Rolando Hinojosa's Self-translation of *Mi querido Rafa*," in Rosa Morillas Sánchez and Manuel Villar Raso (eds.), *Literatura chicana: reflexiones y ensayos críticos* (Granada: Editorial Comares, 2000).

Mabrour, Abdelouahed, "La bi-langue ou l'(en)jeu de l'écriture bilingue chez Abdelkebir Khatibi," *Linguistica antverpiensia* 2 (2003), pp. 105–14.

Maddox, Lucy, *Removals: Nineteenth-Century American Literature and the Politics of Indian Affairs* (New York: Oxford University Press, 1991).

Marshall, Margaret M., "The Origin and Development of Louisiana Creole French," in Albert Valdman (ed.), *French and Creole in Louisiana* (New York: Plenum Press, 1997).

Martín-Rodríguez, Manuel, "Introduction," in Rolando Hinojosa, *Dear Rafe/ Mi querido Rafa* (Houston: Arte Público Press, 1985).

Mehrez, Samia, "Translation and the Postcolonial Experience: The Francophone North African Text," in Lawrence Venuti (ed.), *Rethinking Translation* (London and New York: Routledge, 1992).

Mencken, H. L., *The American Language* (New York: Knopf, 1937).

Mercier, Alfred, "Étude sur la langue créole en Louisiane," *Comptes-rendus de l'Athénée Louisianais* 4 (1880), pp. 378–81.

  L'Habitation Saint-Ybars, ou, Maîtres et esclaves en Louisiane (Récit social), ed. Réginald Hamel (Montreal: Guérin, 1989).

  Johnelle (New Orleans: Eugène Antoine, 1891).

Mezei, Kathy, "Bilingualism and Translation in/of Michèle Lalonde's *Speak White*," *The Translator* 4:2 (1998), pp. 229–47.

Miron, Dan, "Bouncing Back: Destruction and Recovery in Sholem Aleichem's *Motl Peyse dem khazns*," *YIVO Annual of Jewish Social Science* 17 (1978), pp. 119–84.

Murray, Laura, "Vocabularies of Native American Languages: A Historical and Literary Investigation of an Elusive Genre," *American Quarterly* 53:4 (2001), pp. 590–623.

Nabokov, Peter, *Native American Testimony: A Chronicle of Indian-White Relations from Prophecy to the Present* (New York: Penguin, 1991).

Nadir, Moyshe, "Ikh – als viderkol," in *Zeks bikher* (New York: Yidisher Farlag far Literatur un Visnshaft, 1928).

Neumann, J. H., "Notes on American Yiddish," *Journal of English and German Philology* 37 (1938), pp. 403–21.

Neumann-Holzschuh, Ingrid (ed.), *Textes anciens en créole louisianais* (Hamburg: Helmut Buske, 1987).

Newman, Andrew, "Sublime Translation in the Novels of James Fenimore Cooper and Walter Scott," *Nineteenth-Century Literature* 59:1 (2004), pp. 1–26.

Niger, Shmuel, "Lomir zey kashern," *Yidishe shprakh* 1 (1941), pp. 21–24.

Orwell, George, "The Art of Donald McGill," in *A Collection of Essays* (San Diego: Harcourt Brace & Company, 1981).

Overland, Orm, "From Melting Pot to Copper Kettles," in Werner Sollors (ed.), *Multilingual America: Transnationalism, Ethnicity, and the Languages of American Literature* (New York: New York University Press, 1998).

Ozick, Cynthia, "Envy; or, Yiddish in America," in *The Pagan Rabbi* (New York: Schocken, 1976), pp. 39–100.

"Towards a New Yiddish," in *Art and Ardor* (New York: Knopf, 1983).

Page, Norman, *Speech in the English Novel* (Atlantic Highland: Humanities Press, 1988).

Paz, Octavio, *The Labyrinth of Solitude*, trans. Lysander Kemp (New York: Grove, 1962).

Prida, Dolores, *Coser y cantar*, in *Beautiful Señoritas and Other Plays* (Houston: Arte Público Press, 1991).

Rabelais, François, *Pantagruel* (Paris: Gallimard, Le Livre de Poche, 1964).

Gargantua and Pantagruel, trans. Burton Raffel (New York: Norton, 1990).

Gargantua and Pantagruel, trans. Thomas Urquhart (London: Oxford University Press, Oxford World's Classics, 1934).

Reinecke, George, "Alfred Mercier, French Novelist of New Orleans," *Southern Quarterly* 20:2 (Winter 1982), pp. 145–76.

Reyzn, Avrom, *Gezamlte shriftn*, 14 vols. (New York: Frayhayt Publishing Association, 1928), vol. XIV: *Tsvishn grenetsn: ertseylungen*.

Ricks, Christopher, "Literature and the Matter of Fact," in *Essays in Appreciation* (New York: Clarendon Press, 1996).

Riera, Miguel, "El otro sur: entrevista con Rolando Hinojosa," *Quimera* 70/71 (1987), pp. 112–17.

Robertson, Gloria Nobles, "The Diaries of Dr. Alfred Mercier: 1879–1893" (master's thesis, Louisiana State University, 1947).

Rogin, Michael, *Fathers and Children: Andrew Jackson and the Subjugation of the American Indian* (New Brunswick: Transaction, 1991).

Rosenfeld, Max (ed. and trans.), *New Yorkish and other American Yiddish Stories* (Philadelphia: Sholom Aleichem Club Press, 1995).

Pushcarts and Dreamers (Philadelphia: Sholom Aleichem Club Press, 1967).

Rosenwald, Lawrence, "Anglophone Literature and Multilingual America," in Werner Sollors (ed.), *Multilingual America: Transnationalism, Ethnicity, and the Languages of American Literature* (New York: New York University Press, 1998).

"A Summer in the Week of Itke K.," *Antioch Review* 58:2 (Spring 2000), pp. 134–62.

"Buber and Rosenzweig's Challenge to Translation Theory," introduction to Martin Buber and Franz Rosenzweig, *Scripture and Translation*, trans. Lawrence Rosenwald with Everett Fox (Bloomington: Indiana University Press, 1994).

"Four Theses on Translating Yiddish in the 21st Century," *Pakn Treger* 38 (Winter 2002), pp. 14–20.

"Language Traitors, Translation, and *Die Emigranten*," in Winfried Fluck and Werner Sollors (eds.), *German? American? Literature? New Directions in German-American Studies* (New York: Peter Lang, 2002).

"*The Last of the Mohicans* and the Languages of America," *College English* 60:1 (January 1998), pp. 9–30.

"Sur quelques aspects de la traduction de textes créoles louisianais du xixème siècle," *Études créoles* 25:2 (2002), pp. 153–71.

Rosenzweig, Franz, "Scripture and Luther," in Martin Buber and Franz Rosenzweig, *Scripture and Translation*, trans. Lawrence Rosenwald with Everett Fox (Bloomington: Indiana University Press, 1994).

Roskies, David, *A Bridge of Longing: The Lost Art of Yiddish Storytelling* (Cambridge, MA: Harvard University Press, 1996).

Roth, Henry, *Call It Sleep* (New York: Noonday Press, 1991).

Sampson, Geoffrey, *Writing Systems* (Stanford: Stanford University Press, 1985).

Schoolcraft, Henry Rowe, *Oneota, or Characteristics of the Red Race of America* (New York: Wiley and Putnam, 1845).

Schreyer, Rüdiger, "Deaf Mutes, Feral Children and Savages: Of Analogical Evidence in Eighteenth Century Theoretical History of Language," in Günther Blaicher and Brigitte Glaser (eds.), *Anglistentag 1993 Eichstätt* (Tübingen: Niemeyer, 1994).

Sebald, W. G., *Austerlitz* (Frankfurt am Main: Fischer, 2003).

Sedgwick, Catharine Maria, *Hope Leslie; Or, Early Times in the Massachusetts*, ed. Mary Kelley (New Brunswick: Rutgers University Press, 1987).

Seyersted, Per, *Kate Chopin: A Critical Biography* (Baton Rouge: Louisiana State University Press, 1969).

Shapiro, Lamed, *Nuyorkish un andere zakhn* (New York: Farlag Aleyn, 1931).

"New Yorkish," trans. Lawrence Rosenwald, in *The Cross and Other Jewish Stories*, edited, with an introduction by, Leah Garrett (New Haven: Yale University Press, 2007).

Sheehan, Bernard W., *Seeds of Extinction: Jeffersonian Philanthropy and the American Indian* (Chapel Hill: University of North Carolina Press for the Institute of Early American History and Culture at Williamsburg, Virginia, 1973).

Shell, Marc (ed.), *American Babel: Literatures of the United States from Abnaki to Zuni* (Cambridge, MA: Harvard University Press, 2002).

"Babel in America: Or, The Politics of Language Diversity in the United States," *Critical Inquiry* 20:1 (Autumn 1993), pp. 103–27.

and Werner Sollors (eds.), *The Multilingual Anthology of American Literature* (New York: New York University Press, 2000).

Shmeruk, Khone, "Sholem Aleichem un amerike," *Di Goldene keyt* 121 (1987), pp. 56–77.

Shoemaker, Nancy, *A Strange Likeness: Becoming Red and White in Eighteenth-Century North America* (New York: Oxford University Press, 2004).

Sholem Aleichem, *Adventures of Mottel the Cantor's Son*, trans. Tamara Kahana (New York: Henry Schuman, 1953).

"A Business with a Greenhorn," in *Nineteen to the Dozen: Monologues and Bits and Bobs of Other Things*, trans. Ted Gorelick, ed. Ken Frieden (Syracuse: Syracuse University Press, 1998).

The Letters of Menakhem-Mendl & Sheyne-Sheyndl and Motl, the Cantor's Son, translated, with an introduction by, Hillel Halkin (New Haven: Yale University Press, 2002).

"A Mayse mit a grinhorn," in *Ale Verk fun Sholem-Aleichem*, 28 vols. (New York: Sholem Aleichem Folks-Fond, 1921), vol. XXI.

Motl Peyse dem khazns, ed. Khone Shmeruk (Jerusalem: The Magnes Press, 1997).

Tevye the Dairyman and The Railroad Stories, translated, with an introduction by, Hillel Halkin (New York: Schocken, 1987).

Silverstein, Michael, "Dynamics of Linguistic Contact," in Ives Goddard (ed.), *Handbook of North American Indians* 17: *Languages* (Washington, DC: Smithsonian Institution, 1996), pp. 117–36.

"Encountering Language and the Languages of Encounter," *Journal of Linguistic Anthropology* 6 (1996), pp. 126–44.

Simon, Sherry, *Le trafic des langues: traduction et culture dans la littérature québécoise* (Montreal: Boréal, 1994).

Simpson, David, *The Politics of American English, 1776–1850* (New York: Oxford University Press, 1986).

Singer, Isaac Bashevis, "Problemen fun der yidisher proze in Amerike," *Svive* 2 (March–April 1943), pp. 2–13.

"Problems of Yiddish Prose in America," trans. Robert Wolf, *Prooftexts* 9 (1989), pp. 5–12.

Sollors, Werner (ed.), *Multilingual America: Transnationalism, Ethnicity, and the Languages of American Literature* (New York: New York University Press, 1998).

Sommer, Doris, *Bilingual Aesthetics: A New Sentimental Education* (Durham, NC: Duke University Press, 2004).

Spengemann, William, "Discovering the Literature of British America," *Early American Literature* 18 (1983), pp. 3–16.

Spiller, Robert, Willard Thorp, Thomas H. Johnson, Henry Seidel Canby, and Richard M. Ludwing (eds.), *Literary History of the United States*, 3 vols. (New York: Macmillan, 1948).

Steinmetz, Sol, *Yiddish and English: A Century of Yiddish in America* (Birmingham: University of Alabama Press, 1986).

Sternberg, Meir, *Hebrews between Cultures: Group Portraits and National Literature* (Bloomington: Indiana University Press, 1998).

"Point of View and the Indirections of Direct Speech," *Language and Style* 15 (1982), pp. 67–117.

"Polylingualism as Reality and Translation as Mimesis," *Poetics Today* 2:4 (1981), pp. 221–39.

"Proteus in Quotation-Land: Mimesis and the Forms of Reported Discourse," *Poetics Today* 3:2 (1982), pp. 107–56.

Taubenfeld, Aviva, "'Only an L': Linguistic Borders and the Immigrant Author in Abraham Cahan's *Yekl* and *Yankel der Yankee*," in Werner Sollors (ed.), *Multilingual America: Transnationalism, Ethnicity, and the Languages of American Literature* (New York: New York University Press, 1998).

Tedlock, Dennis, *The Spoken Word and the Work of Interpretation* (Philadelphia: University of Pennsylvania Press, 1983).

Tetel Andresen, Julie, *Linguistics in America 1769–1924: A Critical History* (London and New York: Routledge, 1990).

Tinker, Edward Larocque, *Les écrits de langue française en Louisiane* (Paris: Honoré Champion, 1932).

"Gombo: The Creole Dialect of Louisiana, with a Bibliography," *Proceedings of the American Antiquarian Society* 44 (April 1935), pp. 101–42.

Tocqueville, Alexis de, *Democracy in America*, trans. Henry Reeve, rev. Francis Bowen, ed. Phillips Bradley, 2 vols. (New York: Vintage, 1990, copyright Knopf, 1945).

Toth, Emily, *Kate Chopin* (New York: William Morrow, 1990).

Tregle, Jr., Joseph G., "Creoles and Americans," in Arnold R. Hirsch and Joseph Logsdon (eds.), *Creole New Orleans* (Baton Rouge: Louisiana State University Press, 1992).

Trent, William Peterfield, John Erskine, Stuart P. Sherman, and Carl van Doran (eds.), *The Cambridge History of American Literature*, 3 vols. (New York: Macmillan, Cambridge: Cambridge University Press, 1943, first published 1917).

Tsaytlin, Aaron, *Gezamlte lider* (New York: Matones, 1947).

Turner, Arlin (ed.), *Critical Essays on George W. Cable* (Boston: G. K. Hall, 1980).
  George W. Cable: A Biography (Durham, NC: Duke University Press, 1956).
Twain, Mark, *The Adventures of Huckleberry Finn*, ed. Sculley Bradley, Richmond Croom Beatty, and E. Hudson Long (New York: Norton, 1977).
Valdman, Albert, "La diglossie français-créole dans l'univers plantocratique," in Gabriel Manessy and Paul Wald (eds.), *Plurilinguisme: normes, situations, stratégies* (Paris: L'Harmattan, 1979).
  and Thomas A. Klinger, Margaret M. Marshall, and Kevin J. Rottet (eds.), *Dictionary of Louisiana Creole* (Bloomington: Indiana University Press, 1998).
Viatte, Auguste, *Histoire littéraire de l'Amérique française des origines à 1950* (Quebec: Presses Universitaires Laval, 1954).
Waife-Goldberg, Marie, *My Father, Sholom Aleichem* (New York: Simon & Schuster, 1968).
Walcott, Derek, *Omeros* (New York: Farrar Straus and Giroux, 1990).
Walker, Willard B., "Native Writing Systems," in Ives Goddard (ed.), *Handbook of North American Indians* 17: *Languages* (Washington, DC: Smithsonian Institution, 1996), pp. 158–84.
Weinreich, Max, *History of the Yiddish Language*, trans. Shlomo Noble, assisted by Joshua A. Fishman (Chicago: University of Chicago Press, 1980).
  "Vegn englishe elementn in unzer kulturshprakh," *Yidishe shprakh* 1 (1941), pp. 33–46.
Weinreich, Uriel, *Languages in Contact* (The Hague: Mouton, 1970).
Wilson, Edmund (ed.), *The Shock of Recognition: The Development of Literature in the United States Recorded by the Men Who Made It* (Garden City: Doubleday, Doran and Co., 1943).
Wirth-Nesher, Hana, *Call It English: The Languages of Jewish American Literature* (Princeton: Princeton University Press, 2006).
  (ed.), *New Essays on* Call It Sleep (Cambridge and New York: Cambridge University Press, 1996).
Wishnia, Kenneth, "'A Different Kind of Hell': Orality, Multilingualism, and American Yiddish in the Translation of Sholem Aleichem's *Mister Boym in Klozet*," *AJS Review* 20:2 (1993), pp. 333–58.
Wogan, Peter, "Perceptions of European Literacy in Early Contact Situations," *Ethnohistory* 41 (1994), pp. 407–29.
Wolfe, George L., "Notes on American Yiddish," *American Mercury* 29 (August 1933), pp. 473–79.
Yezierska, Anzia, *Red Ribbon on a White Horse* (New York: Persea, 1987).
Zeisberger, David, *Zeisberger's Indian Dictionary: English, German, Iroquois – the Onondaga and Algonquin – the Delaware* (Cambridge, MA: John Wilson & Son University Press, 1887).
Zilles, Klaus, *Rolando Hinojosa: A Reader's Guide* (Albuquerque: University of New Mexico Press, 2001).

Index [1]

[1] In a good many cases, authors are discussed exclusively or almost exclusively in relation to a single work. In such cases, there is no separate index entry for that work, and the only references to specific works under that author's name are to works other than the principal one. The cases in question are: James Fenimore Cooper and *The Last of the Mohicans*; Alfred Mercier and *L'Habitation Saint-Ybars*; George Washington Cable and *The Grandissimes*; Sholem Aleichem and *Motl the Cantor's Son*; Jeannette Lander and *A Summer in the Week of Itke K.*; Ana Lydia Vega and "Pollito: Chicken"; and Rolando Hinojosa and *Mi querido Rafa/ Dear Rafe*.